Capitalists, Workers, and Fiscal Policy

Capitalists, Workers, and Fiscal Policy

A Classical Model of Growth and Distribution

Thomas R. Michl

Harvard University Press
Cambridge, Massachusetts
London, England
2009

Library of Congress Cataloging-in-Publication Data

Michl, Thomas R.
Capitalists, workers, and fiscal policy : a classical model of growth and distribution / Thomas R. Michl.
p. cm.
Includes bibliographical references and index.
ISBN-13: 978-0-674-03167-8 (cloth : alk. paper)
1. Economic development. 2. Fiscal policy. 3. Income distribution. I. Title.
HD75.M53 2008
330.1—dc22
2008019197

Contents

Part II. Long-run Models of Fiscal Policy

Figures

Tables

Preface

This book gathers together three main strands of the research project that I have pursued for the last decade. Rather than simply assembling a series of journal publications, some effort has been made to present the three strands as one more or less coherent whole.

I owe a tremendous debt of gratitude to Duncan K. Foley, with whom I have had the privilege of collaborating on some of these issues. His unrelenting methodological pluralism has left an indelible mark on my thinking about political economy. Work with Christophre Georges showed me how to incorporate the government budget constraint into the growth model, which made it possible to make some progress on characterizing the political economy of debt. Michael Aronson has been a source of encouragement and wisdom without which this project would never have gotten off the ground. Many students, particularly Robert Cathcart, have contributed valuable comments on early versions of this work. And for their helpful comments and criticism I would also like to thank the anonymous referees arranged by Harvard University Press. I retain full responsibility, of course, for any and all errors that remain, and for the views and opinions expressed in this book.

Adalmir Marquetti deserves thanks for creating the Extended Penn World Tables that were indispensable for some of the empirical results here. Along with a large community of macroeconomists, I owe a huge debt to Robert Summers and Alan Heston for having created the Penn World Tables in the first place. I am grateful to Douglas Gollin and Refet Gürkaynak for sharing their unpublished data sheets with me, and to Henning Bohn, Wojciech Kopczuk, and Emmanuel Saez for sharing their data publicly on their websites. The Colgate University Research Council provided helpful publication support.

Main Symbols

$\mathcal{A}$	Locally defined parameter
$\mathcal{B}$	Locally defined parameter
$\mathcal{C}$	Locally defined parameter
$\mathcal{D}$	Locally defined parameter
$\mathcal{L}$	Lagrangian
A	Circulating capital
B	Government debt
C	Capitalist consumption
H	Current-value Hamiltonian
I	Net investment
J	Jacobian
J_i	Jacobian modified to implement Cramer's Rule
K	Aggregate capital stock
K^i	Capital stock of capitalists ($i = c$), workers ($i = w$), or government ($i = G$)
L	Labor force
N	Employment
P	Potential profit
R	Maximal rate of profit
S	Saving
T	Lump sum tax revenues
V	Indirect utility of individual worker
W	Capitalist gross wealth, $K^c + B$
W_N	Capitalist net wealth, $K^c + (1 - \Omega)B$
X	Output
$\dot{Z}$	Time derivative, dZ/dt
a	Inflation sensitivity of monetary authority, Chapter 2; target deficit-capital ratio, Chapters 5–6
b	Demand sensitivity of inflation, Chapter 2; public pension benefit, Chapters 7–9

c	Consolidating parameter, Chapter 2; consumption per worker, Chapter 9
$c^{w,r}$	Worker consumption during working years (w) or retirement (r)
d	Propensity to invest in fixed capital
d_0	Investment parameter
d_1	Interest sensitivity of investment
d_2	Demand sensitivity of investment
e	Employment rate, N/L
f	Government saving per worker, K^G_{+1}/N
$\bar{f}$	Maximal funding level consistent with two-class structure
g	Growth rate of capitalist capital stock
g_K	Growth rate of aggregate capital stock
g_Z	Growth rate of variable, Z
h	Individual worker's lifetime wealth
i	Real interest rate
i_n	Inflation-neutral rate of interest
k	Capital-labor ratio, K/N
m	Internal rate of return (money's worth) of public pension
n	Natural rate of labor force growth
n^*	Workers' optimal rate of growth
p	Inflation rate
$\bar{p}$	Target inflation rate
r	Net rate of profit
r^e	Expected profit rate
r_n	Normal rate of profit
s	Saving propensity out of profit
s^w	Worker individual saving
t	Time subscript (often implicit); or index, $Z(t)$, in continuous time
u	Capacity utilization
v	Gross rate of profit, $r + \delta$
w	Real wage
$\bar{w}$	Conventional real wage
x	Labor productivity, X/N
y	Net output per worker, $x - \delta k$
z	Difference equation $z(\cdot)$, locally defined
$\mathbf{A}$	Matrix for endogenous growth model
$\mathbf{B}$	Transformed matrix for endogenous growth model

$\mathbf{C}$	Matrix for exogenous growth models
$\mathbf{k}$	Vector of total capital and workers' capital, (K, K^w)
$\tilde{\mathbf{k}}$	Vector of capitalist and workers' capital wealth, (K^c, K^w)
α	Viability threshold parameter
β	Capitalist discount factor
$\beta_{c,w}$	Discount factor, capitalists (c) or workers (w)
$\bar{\beta}_w$	Maximum worker discount factor consistent with two-class solution
β'	Consolidating parameter, $\beta_c - \Omega\beta_c + \Omega$
χ	Rate of capital-saving technical change
Δ	Discriminant
ΔZ	First difference, Chapter 2; test minus control, Chapters 7–8
δ	Depreciation rate
ϵ	Funding premium
γ	Rate of labor-saving technical change
κ	Capital-labor force ratio, K/L
λ_i	Eigenvalues
μ	Shadow price (Lagrangian multiplier or co-state variable)
Ω	Capitalist share of taxes
ω	Switch point wage rate
ϕ	Workers' share of capital wealth, K^w/K
$\tilde{\phi}$	Distribution of wealth consistent with capitalist saving
$\hat{\phi}$	Distribution of wealth consistent with workers' saving
ϕ^G	Government share of capital wealth, K^G/K
π	Profit share
ψ	Consolidating term, exogenous growth model
ρ	Capital productivity, X/K
σ	Debt-capital ratio, B/K
ς	Switch point rate of profit
τ	Individual worker's tax
τ^c	Tax on capitalist
θ	Primary fiscal surplus (normalized), T/K
*	Steady state value of a variable
ˇ	Best-practice technical coefficient

Capitalists, Workers, and Fiscal Policy

— I —

From the Short Run to the Long

— 1 —

Introduction

Toward a Classical Growth Model

> First came the astronomers observing the motions of the heavenly bodies and collecting data. Secondly came the mathematicians inventing mathematical notation to describe the motions and fit the data. Thirdly came the technicians making mechanical models to simulate those mathematical constructions. Fourthly came generations of students who learned their astronomy from these machines. Fifthly came scientists whose imagination had been so blinkered by generations of such learning that they actually believed that this was how the heavens worked. Sixthly came the authorities who insisted upon the received dogma. And so the human race was fooled into accepting the Ptolemaic System for a thousand years.
>
> Christopher Zeeman, quoted in Stewart (1989)

When I was an undergraduate in 1972, a student request led to the arrival on campus of a young visiting professor hired to teach us about Marxian economics. His first lecture, full of references to Ricardo's Corn model, captured my imagination. The idea that we could learn something useful from a thought experiment about an economy that produced an output that was itself the key ingredient in its own production process was intriguing. Little did I realize that decades later I would still be learning from the same model, in the company of literally thousands of macroeconomists around the world who use the one-commodity fiction to construct a wide variety of growth models.

Simplified models of reality play an important role in the development of science. Astronomers have benefited from a whole series of mechanical models of the solar system, and one can still admire their orreries and armillaries in museums of natural history. No one would confuse an astronomer's orrery with a real planetary system, but these devices have helped fix ideas, for better or worse, and fired the scientific imaginations of practitioners. More than mere teaching tools, Evans (1998, 79) tells us that these mechanical models were even "aids in the discovery of the world." Manipulation of numerical examples and formal models led to the discovery of many of the results addressed in this book. These economic models are designed for the purpose of working out the logical relationships between economic categories under highly abstract and stylized conditions. They should not be treated as literal models of real economies; rather, they model an underlying theory of the capitalist economy. To the extent that the theory is correct, these models can inform us about the behavior of real economies, but only if they are used carefully, with humility and good judgment. Like all such models, they suppress certain important features of the world in order to showcase others.[1]

The models in this book draw heavily on the classical tradition in economic theory that begins with the early economists, Smith, Ricardo, and Malthus in particular, extends through Marx (who was both a critic and a contributor to the tradition), and arrives in the twenty-first century on the shoulders of Joan Robinson, Michal Kalecki, Nicholas Kaldor, and Luigi Pasinetti, among others. The mainstream of the profession has more or less written these figures out of the canon that students are expected to master, and their names have vanished like images of Trotsky from a Stalinist photograph. In recognition of the resulting lacuna, this chapter devotes a few pages to introducing the reader to the heterodox tradition. Injecting this tradition back into the conversation of economics should have a salutary effect. There was more real controversy in the main journals in the 1960s and 1970s than there is today; to use one of Marx's unforgettable expressions, "splendid tournaments" were held, such as the Cambridge Controversies. It is hard to see what advantage today's academic monoculture can offer, since intellectual diversity and debate are widely recognized by experts on methodology (e.g., Popper or Lakatos) as the foundation for scientific progress.

The book investigates a family of classical models of capital accumulation and draws out their implications for fiscal policies, in particular public debt and public pension programs. This objective, modest as it is, requires at least some explanation directed toward rival schools of economic thought. Chapter 2 presents an argument for situating the problem in a long-run growth setting that suppresses considerations of aggregate or effective de-

1. "A model which took account of all the variegation of reality would be of no more use than a map at the scale of one to one" (Robinson 1962, 33).

mand, a modeling decision that may be questioned by Keynesian economists but regarded as self-evident by neoclassical readers. Chapters 10 and 11 present some analytical and empirical results that motivate the extensive use of fixed-coefficient technology, a modeling decision that may be questioned by neoclassical economists but accepted without concern by Keynesians. These two discussions are arranged like bookends flanking the theoretical core of classical long-run models, and the three main parts of the book are semi-autonomous.

Basing research on economic models that rely on specific functional forms always raises the question of generality. Yet there is a tradition of pursuing this kind of work; neoclassical growth models erected on constant elasticity of substitution (CES) or Cobb-Douglas foundations are numerous, for example. The specific models that occupy the core of this book in Chapters 3 through 8 serve as the cleat upon which we endeavor to belay and make fast an argument for fiscal policies directed toward the accumulation of publicly owned wealth. For those who are unmoved by this policy implication, these models can also stand alone as representations of the classical theory of growth.

1.1 Elements of the Classical Approach

This section presents some of the *differentia specifica* of the classical approach. While others may want to add, subtract, or quibble about this list, it is useful both pedagogically and heuristically. It addresses a question that conventionally trained economists are likely to raise. What does the classical approach have to offer by way of insights unobtainable by conventional means?

First, the classical theory insists that capitalist societies are class societies, and that any adequate model of accumulation needs class analytical foundations. Models populated by homogenous, hermaphroditic agents, both capitalist and worker, lack these foundations, making them inappropriate from the classical standpoint. The models developed in this book are two-class models descended from the work of Kaldor (1956) and Pasinetti (1962) that have been brought up-to-date by building them on stronger microeconomic foundations drawn from the literature on life-cycle and bequest saving.[2] Despite these cosmetic differences, they remain true to the Cambridge theorem discovered by Pasinetti: the relationship between the

2. This strategy was pioneered by Baranzini (1991) and adopted by Teixeira et al. (2002).

rate of growth and the rate of profit depends only on the saving behavior of capitalist agents and is independent of the workers' saving rate, the government saving rate, and technology. This remarkable theorem has illuminated the path in both the investigation and the exposition stages of this book.[3]

Second, capital accumulation is not necessarily constrained by fixed human resources; an eclectic approach that includes both a labor-constrained and capital-constrained closure fosters a more complete understanding of long-run growth. Because the growth rate is fixed outside the model in the former case but remains a free variable in the latter case, we adopt the terminology *exogenous* and *endogenous* growth. Rather than dogmatically asserting the full employment of a predestined labor force, the classical approach takes an agnostic view that has almost no counterpart in conventional economic discourse, with the possible exception of the New Endogenous Growth theory in which labor constraints are overcome by means of endogenous technical change.

Third, the modern classical economists envision capital as a social relationship rather than as a well-defined economic resource. One casualty of this vision has been the neoclassical production function and its offspring, marginal productivity theory, both the object of vigorous critiques by classical theorists. The classical models developed here make no use of this device, and as a result are able to bring the effects of fiscal policy on the class structure of capital accumulation into higher resolution. While many heterodox economists gainsay the validity of the neoclassical production function, for economists who are not convinced, the fixed coefficient assumption might be treated as a heuristic gambit that focuses on the question of accumulation itself. As mentioned above, Chapter 10 explores an alternative interpretation of the production function that motivates the structuralist treatment of technology, and Chapter 11 extends the discussion to the statistical record.

One might also argue that the neoclassical production function obscures the sources of endogenous technical change, which the classical tradition recognized well before it became fashionable in the New Growth theory. Starting with Smith's observations about the division of labor, Marx's dis-

3. This theorem is sometimes called the "Pasinetti paradox." From the neoclassical perspective, it is the independence of the rate of profit from technology and marginal productivity that renders it paradoxical. From a classical perspective, the idea that the workers' saving rate does not influence the steady state growth or profit rate might be seen as a paradox (it does to me). To the best of my knowledge, Pasinetti himself has never called this theorem a paradox, perhaps out of modesty or perhaps to avoid conceding to the neoclassical prejudice.

covery of the induced nature of technical change under conflictual relations of production, and Kaldor's pioneering resurrection of the dynamic returns to scale, economists in the heterodox tradition have kept the endogeneity of technical change at the forefront of their thinking. Yet this book stays away from these issues.[4] Where technical change is considered, it is taken to be exogenous, not because it is, but rather because of doubts that any of the existing theories are well enough understood to justify making them foundational supports for a useful growth model. This is more or less the same excuse that Solow (1994, 2000) gives for exogenous technical change.

All three of these distinguishing features of the classical tradition lead to specific results that are either obscured by or inaccessible from the neoclassical approach. In particular, the Cambridge theorem is a cynosure that provides the classical approach with distinctive explanatory powers.

There is a fourth significant feature of the heterodox tradition that plays only a supporting role in this book: the rejection of Say's law. The heterodox community continues to debate the question of how a complex modern economy generates sufficient aggregate or effective demand to maintain balanced growth. The resolution adopted here is to accept the general answer given by conventional economists, that the problem of effective demand can be analytically segregated to the short run, without accepting their specific theory of how supply factors govern the long run or, as discussed in Chapter 2, without accepting their indifference to the interactions between long-run and short-run factors. Because this "short-run Keynesian, long-run classical" separation fits in fairly well with the way the profession thinks, the results in this book debouch freely into the ongoing controversies about the long-run effects of social security and national debt. The models in Part II are designed to operate on the same level of abstraction as the neoclassical workhorses, the Solow-Swan and Diamond models. Wherever possible they cleave to a spirit of methodological pluralism, for example, by using modern techniques of optimization developed chiefly by neoclassical economists to motivate and animate the idealized economic agents.

Heterodox macroeconomics has evolved toward a classical-Keynesian synthesis over the last three decades.[5] Unlike the neoclassical-Keynesian

4. For a classical growth model that does address the endogeneity of technical change, see Foley (2003).

5. A reading list chronicling this evolution might include Harris (1978); Marglin (1984); Skott (1989); Dutt (1990); Palley (1996b); Foley and Michl (1999); Taylor (2004).

synthesis of the 1950s and 1960s, which proved to be an unstable equilibrium, the classical-Keynesian synthesis has grown stronger over time. The differences that leaven this community of discourse mainly concern the nature of the long-run constraints on growth. Economists who have taken up the Keynesian belief in the centrality of fundamental (Knightian) uncertainty are inclined to follow in the tradition of Kalecki, Robinson, and Steindl and emphasize the demand constraints on growth. For readers sympathetic to this tradition, Chapter 2 provides a fairly extensive discussion, including a heuristic exercise in modeling an economy that displays Keynesian characteristics in the short run but which gravitates toward a long-run growth path that combines classical and Keynesian features. This clears the decks for the investigation of the properties of a long-run classical economy that makes up the bulk of the book.

That the neoclassical-Keynesian synthesis of the 1950s and 1960s turned out to be ideologically labile is not necessarily surprising. It seems to have been a marriage of convenience designed to preserve the neoclassical doctrine by proposing that a political authority could guarantee full employment, allowing scarcity to remain the central preoccupation of economists. It appears with hindsight that the neoclassical influences acted as a universal acid, eroding the intellectual foundations for the Keynesians and forcing their heirs, the New Keynesians, to couch all their beliefs in some kind of rational decision-making process ("microeconomic foundations"). This has been accomplished with considerable ingenuity and skill, chiefly by recognizing the economics of information. The resulting New Classical–New Keynesian synthesis now exercises hegemonic influence over the economics profession, but that should not be allowed to crowd out competing points of view. The classical-Keynesian synthesis promises both greater stability and intellectual vibrancy than the old neoclassical synthesis. Rather than an arranged marriage designed to save the family fortune, it has the distinct advantage of originating in mutual attraction to some of the deeper enduring questions in political economy.

1.2 Harrod and Modern Growth Theory

It may help orient some readers to locate the classical growth model in the recent evolution of economic thought. Modern growth theory got its start with Sir Roy Harrod's (1939) projection of the Keynesian question of full employment into the long run. How does an economy with a growing labor force generate enough job growth to maintain full employment? To Harrod's argument that it doesn't, except by chance, there are three responses, two standard and one iconoclastic. The first, which has influenced this book materially, was given by Kaldor (1956), who pointed out that changes in the distribution of income could provide the answer. Because property owners tend to save at higher rates than wage earners, Kaldor pointed out, any imbalance between Harrod's "warranted" rate of growth and the natural rate of labor force growth could be eliminated by changes in the functional distribution of income. This answer places Kaldor firmly in the intellectual tradition of Ricardo, because it rests on the kind of class analysis of capitalist society that virtually all the classical economists took for granted. In fact, he turned Ricardo upside down insofar as the economic surplus that defines the classical approach for Kaldor is the residual left for wages after capitalists have taken what they need for luxury consumption and growth.

The second answer was given by Solow (1956) and Swan (1956), and in the Whig intellectual history that dominates the profession today, it is widely perceived as *the* answer. Solow's argument, in brief, is that Harrod's pessimism about full employment growth was premised on the special assumption of a fixed technology. Introducing variable coefficients, through the vehicle of a neoclassical production function, solves the problem. In a word, in the Solow model, the economy can never have too little (or too much) capital; changes in the wage can in principle bring into use a technique sufficiently labor (or capital) intensive to employ everyone. Solow's own statement of his achievement is still worth quoting:

> All theory depends on assumptions which are not quite true. That is what makes it theory. The art of successful theorizing is to make the inevitable simplifying assumptions in such a way that the final results are not very sensitive. A "crucial" assumption is one on which the conclusions do depend sensitively, and it is important that crucial assumptions be reasonably realistic. When the results of a theory seem to flow specifically from a special crucial assumption, then if the assumption is dubious, the results are suspect. (Solow 1956, 65)

When Solow wrote these words, both eloquent and true, he could have no way of knowing that they might be turned against his own growth model. A strong case can now be made that the neoclassical growth model itself rests on an assumption, the well-behaved production function, no less specialized than the Leontief technology that Solow complains about.[6]

The bill of particulars against the neoclassical production function begins with the Cambridge critique launched in the 1950s and 1960s by Joan Robinson (1953), Piero Sraffa (1960), and others. They pointed out that in a world with heterogeneous capital goods, the value of capital will depend on the distribution of income to such an extent that it is impossible to make any meaningful generalizations about movements of the capital-labor ratio in response to changes in wages, except under special conditions when the production function becomes "well behaved." After resisting this conclusion, neoclassical theorists finally had to concede the point (Samuelson 1966), although they continue to insist that this is merely an inconvenience to the broader neoclassical project.[7]

Yet after this decisive rejection of the production function, conventional growth theory continues to depend on its good behavior. To chalk that up to the empirical performance of the production function would be to ignore the devastating critiques in this area, some of them arising within neoclassical economics. For example, Shaikh (1974) showed that the method of fitting a production function by filtering out the "Solow residual" representing pure technical change effectively estimates an accounting identity, turning out the Cobb-Douglas form with arithmetic certainty. Recently, New Growth theorists (Romer 1987, 1994) have purchased inspiration from the large discrepancy between the actual profit share and that predicted by standard neoclassical theory. An hypothesis that lacks both internal and external consistency can hardly lay claim to generality.[8]

6. "But this fundamental opposition of warranted and natural rates turns out in the end to flow from the crucial assumption that production takes place under conditions of *fixed proportions* [emphasis in original]" (Solow 1956, 65).

7. The whole debate is beautifully reconstructed by Harcourt (1972) and revisited by Cohen and Harcourt (2003). For a thoroughgoing exposition of the theory, see Kurz and Salvadori (1995). One bit of delicious irony is that the technical conditions that make the aggregate production function well behaved also validate a pure labor theory of value.

8. Shaikh's finding has been reaffirmed by Felipe (2001), among others. An important response to the New Growth theorists in defense of the Solow model (Mankiw et al. 1992) has also been faulted (Felipe and McCombie 2005) for confusing an accounting identity with a production function. We revisit the discrepancy between marginalist theory and the evidence in Chapter 11.

Nonetheless, many economists will feel uncomfortable with the assumption of fixed proportions that supports the models in this book, and two chapters on an alternative framework (Michl 1999, 2002) for interpreting the historical and statistical record are included to address their concerns. The central idea is that biased technical change that is labor saving and capital using will create the impression of a well-behaved neoclassical production function where none exists. The technology (i.e., the set of known techniques) evolves as a fossil production function, so called by virtue of the presence of discarded, or fossil, techniques that are eligible for readoption. The fossil production function can explain the qualitative patterns that appear to confirm the neoclassical insistence on a law of (smoothly) diminishing returns as applied to capital (e.g., rising capital intensity, declining output-capital ratio).[9] And it can explain some of the quantitative anomalies that bedevil the marginal productivity theory of income distribution. A growth model that assumes, *pace* Solow, that only one technique dominates cannot be so easily dismissed.

This book focuses on the practical question of how fiscal policy, in particular regarding public debt and public pension systems like the Social Security system in the United States, affects the growth of the economy, the distribution of income, and the distribution of wealth. The main lesson is that public saving needs to be analyzed as one of many competing claims on future economic surplus (in the form of profit or, more generally, property income). It follows that fiscal policy has some of its most significant effects on the long-run distribution of income and/or wealth. By contrast, the dominant narrative, rooted strongly in the neoclassical tradition, focuses on the problem of crowding out investment in terms of its effects on the amount of capital per worker, relying heavily on the special assumption of a well-behaved production function. For example, Feldstein (1974) has argued that pay-as-you-go social security has reduced the amount of capital accumulated per worker.

Yet a third answer to Harrod's question was already available in the classical theory: the effective labor force adjusts to accommodate accumulation,

9. The classical critique originates in the sensible observation that marginal productivity theory is *au fond* an extension of Ricardo's theory of rent from the sphere of primary production (agriculture, mining, etc.), where diminishing returns are established by natural laws, to the sphere of general production using labor and capital goods, where machines are engineered or designed to be operated with specific crew sizes, making the marginalist framework less than convincing.

rather than the other way around. The classical economists regarded labor as an essentially reproducible input (Eltis 2000). This attitude has been adopted by some modern economists in the Keynes-Kalecki tradition. For Ricardo and Malthus, demographic forces provide the mechanism, but we do not have to accept the simplistic and counterfactual claims of Malthus to see other possibilities. For Marx, capital accumulation was constantly creating the reserves of labor it would need to satisfy an appetite for human labor power, either through technological displacement or through the erosion of precapitalist social formations such as peasant agriculture and the subsequent release of free laborers. If we take a global view of the accumulation process, it is hard to deny the continued importance of reserves of labor in this sense. We can often see how individual countries with access to labor reserves, for example, through immigration, can overcome labor constraints on their growth. The U.S. economy with its addiction to immigrant labor comes to mind, as does the Irish economy, with its returning diaspora. A modern classical treatment of growth would be incomplete if it did not consider both the traditional case of a labor-constrained economy together with the polar opposite case of an economy that enjoys access to labor reserves. Each particular question is worked out under both cases,[10] and Chapter 11 even presents a few shreds of empirical evidence on their relevance.

This agnosticism has practical significance. If the labor-constrained model holds, the current demographic transition associated with lower fertility and increased longevity is likely to put unprecedented pressure on global capitalist economies, and this has been the nearly unchallenged premise of the public debates about the effects of this shock on social security and other public programs. On the other hand, if the capital-constrained approach is more lifelike, the drama is likely to play out in a substantially different way. Pursuing this topic seriously would require a separate monograph, but this book may stimulate more inclusive research efforts and broaden the policy conversation.[11]

10. The effect of a demographic shock is one question that can only be attacked in an exogenous growth model. We will see that a slower rate of growth has positive effects on workers that are not often mentioned in public discussions that focus on intergenerational discord and ignore class conflict.

11. This book ignores the natural resource constraints on growth that occupied so much of Malthus's and Ricardo's attention and that are an ineluctable part of this conversation. For a modern classical treatment of the exhaustion of a nonrenewable resource, see Michl and

1.3 Rethinking Fiscal Surpluses

One distinctive feature of this book is that it appeals to heterodox economists to reexamine carefully their traditional aversion to fiscal surpluses. In the United States, at least, professional debates over fiscal policy have featured a prominent role for the "deficit hawks" such as Benjamin Friedman (1988), who have focused on the effects of crowding out on the future standard of living.[12] Progressive (left of center) economists have spent considerable intellectual capital repugning the doctrine that deficit reduction can be counted on to raise national investment (Eisner 1986; Pollin 1997; Galbraith 2005), while continuing the Keynesian mission of advocating judicious use of fiscal and monetary stimulus to maintain high employment levels. Such allegiance to the paradox of thrift has served as a guiding principle for the heterodox research program in macroeconomics. The price of this focus has been neglect of the potential long-run hazards of fiscal deficits and of the long-run benefits of public ownership achieved through fiscal surpluses. Both are accessible within the heterodox theory itself.

Heterodox growth models invite us to analyze public finance within the structure of the accumulation process. A fiscal surplus represents a financial claim by the public sector on future profits (economic surpluses) generated by the private sector. In an exogenous growth setting where the path of the capital stock has been fixed by assumption, ruling out any real crowding out, financial crowding occurs because these financial claims compete with the claims issued by the saving of capitalists and workers. A fiscal surplus can crowd out capitalist ownership claims, and indirectly crowd in workers' claims. Fiscal deficits fall into the same framework, with all the signs reversed.

As outlined in Chapters 5 and 6, in the long run public debt does have crowding-out effects, but these are not the standard textbook neoclassical effects on the capital intensity of production and the productivity of labor. Instead, the crowding-out effects that heterodox theory recognizes bear

Foley (2007). Wealth effects similar to those studied below and in Chapters 5 and 6 generate remarkable dynamic effects in this setting. In addition, we ignore the open economy issues that for good reason permeate discussions of public debt in the United States, and again, this is not because they lack importance.

12. One important version of this argument is that deficits crowd out net exports and run up the nation's foreign debt. The fact that this book maintains its focus on a closed economy should not be misinterpreted as a denial of the significance of this kind of crowding out.

on the distribution of wealth and/or the distribution of income between wages and profits. In short, debt funnels wealth upward and exacerbates the polarization between rich and poor. This conclusion is unambiguous when capitalists are assumed to have infinite planning horizons (Ricardian equivalence), and conditional (on the distribution of taxes) when they are assumed to be more myopic.

During the Clinton administration, the deficit hawks got their wish, in the form of large and to some extent unforseen fiscal surpluses. At the end of the 1990s, concern over the implications of paying off the national debt began to surface inside the beltway, as the Congressional Budget Office projections of current policy pointed toward that destination. If we accept the analysis of public debt just summarized (making the deficit hawks right for the wrong reasons), this raises the question, What should we do with fiscal surpluses? Of course, one perfectly acceptable position is that the government should not try to accumulate financial liabilities or assets but rather use its net asset position to stabilize aggregate demand, even if this is done through automatic stabilizers rather than discretionary fiscal policies.

But having gone to the trouble of identifying the hazards of public debt, we outline in Chapters 7 through 9 the potential benefits of public ownership of financial wealth and real capital. These chapters present an analytical framework for attacking the problem of public pensions, such as the U.S. Social Security system. The heterodox origin of this framework, particularly its explicit treatment of the class structure of accumulation, creates results that contrast with the standard neoclassical approach (Feldstein 1974), which suffers from its lack of a class-analytical foundation. In short, the standard overlapping generations model, by proposing that all saving derives from the life-cycle decisions of workers, misrepresents the effects of fiscal policy on aggregate saving by ignoring the dominance of capitalist saving brought into sharp relief by the Cambridge theorem. The conventional approach probably exaggerates the effects of social security on national saving.

Given the recent and historically significant increase in the concentration of income and wealth in the United States, particularly among the very top groups (Piketty and Saez 2003), we should be prepared for a brisk market in ideas that address the problem of polarization. These chapters elaborate an argument, situated within a well-defined analytical framework, for prefunding the public pension by means of progressive taxes on income and wealth.[13] The pension reserve fund (e.g, the Old Age and Survivors' Trust Fund in the United States) represents an ideal vehicle for effecting a progressive redistribution of wealth.[14] Under the conditions of endogenous growth, such a policy can increase the level (but not the long-run growth rate) of capital, employment, and output. Under exogenous growth where these effects are ruled out by assumption, this policy approach will have temporary effects on the distribution of income that permanently increase the workers' share of capital wealth. Once again, the heterodox approach reveals insights into the effects of policy on the distribution of wealth that are not accessible within the conventional classless macroeconomic model.

The classical approach to value, either in the traditional labor theory or in its modern Sraffian incarnation, recognizes the central role of the economic surplus (or, in the labor theory, surplus value) that constitutes a necessary condition for growth and capital accumulation. The classical vocabulary makes it natural to formulate the political question (and this is what makes classical theory a form of political economy) of control over the economic surplus. One can interpret the Marxian concept of exploitation in terms of the alienation of the direct producers from any control over the economic surplus that results from their efforts.[15] The policy proposals pursued in Chapters 7 through 9 explore a political vision whose historical objective it is to achieve a greater degree of popular, democratic control over the economic surplus of advanced capitalist societies. Regardless of one's opinion on the future of the socialist project (or its lack), it is hard to deny the historical imperative toward greater levels of political and perhaps economic democracy.

Ironically, the theoretical models that frame the argument are partly subversive to the classical labor theory of value because they acknowledge that workers control a nonnegligible amount of capital wealth acquired through

13. Along similar lines, Blackburn (2002) has proposed a share levy used to fortify social reserves and finance retirement.

14. But not necessarily the only vehicle. For example, similar arguments could be applied to the Medicare Trust Fund in the United States.

15. After all, as Marx points out in his *Critique of the Gotha Program*, a socialist society would require an economic surplus; the premise that this does not constitute exploitation must depend on the control over the surplus exercised by workers themselves. For further discussion, see Foley (2006) and for alternative conceptualizations of exploitation, see Roemer (1988).

their life-cycle saving. In practice, of course, much of this wealth takes the institutionalized form of the pension funds whose dual character Teresa Ghilarducci (1992) has captured in the expression "labor's capital." Despite the control over economic surplus bestowed upon workers by labor's capital, the Cambridge theorem explains why workers continue to occupy a subaltern position in the structure of accumulation.

Nothing is easier than criticizing a model. Economic theory is a bit like a well-worn sweater; if you pull on the loose ends too much, you will soon have nothing to keep you warm. There are some obvious loose ends in the middlebrow models presented here, but their construction required that the pulling stop, it is hoped at a point where these efforts contribute something useful to our understanding of the political economy of fiscal policy and the structure of capital accumulation.

— 2 —

The Nature of the Long Run

> . . . the long-run trend is but a slowly changing component of a chain of short-period situations; it has no independent entity, and the two basic relations mentioned above [*i.e., the multiplier and the accelerator*] should be formulated in such a way as to yield the trend cum business-cycle phenomenon.
>
> Michal Kalecki (1968)

> When Adam Smith explains the fall in the rate of profit from an over-abundance of capital . . . he is speaking of a *permanent* effect, and this is wrong. As against this, the transitory over-abundance of capital, over-production and crises are something different. Permanent crises do not exist.
>
> Karl Marx (1968)

A major premise of this book is that public saving can increase capital accumulation in the long run. This premise conflicts with the views of a very substantial (probably a majority) segment of the heterodox community of classical-Keynesian economists who subscribe in one form or another to the view that growth is demand-constrained. This chapter provides a brief overview of one of the main problems associated with demand-constrained growth, and a possible resolution. In particular, we limn out an illustrative model that underwrites the premise that saving can determine investment. In contrast to the polemical tone of some of the heterodox literature, this chapter aspires to be an exercise in what theologians call "irenics." It seeks to reconcile or at least clarify competing views on the long run.

Much of the recent literature on this topic accepts the classical conception of centers of gravity, and the distinction between a fast adjustment process that clears away imbalances in the short run and a slow adjustment process that provides the centripetal impulses at lower frequencies. The relationship between the long- and short-run behavior of a capitalist economy has been captured by the well-worn metaphor of a cyclist with a dog on a long leash. The cyclist chooses where the pair will go, but the dog enjoys relative autonomy. If we only saw the dog's path, we might conclude that it was the master of its destiny. In this metaphor, the bicycle represents the long-run position, or center of gravitation, while the dog represents the short-run position. The philosopher of science Mary Hesse (1966) points out that analogies and metaphors play a key role in scientific discovery both because they provide insight into the actual theories being analogized and because they contain gray areas that perform a heuristic function. This metaphor is useful because it illustrates that the short-run movements of a capitalist economy can exhibit relative autonomy, but it leaves open the question of whether and to what extent the dog can influence the path the cyclist chooses.

2.1 Effective Demand and Say's Law

The codiscovery by Keynes and Kalecki of the principle of effective demand puts them in the company of other Merton twins, such as Newton and Leibnitz (calculus), Lavoisier and Priestley (oxygen), or Darwin and Wallace (natural selection). This principle states that the level of planned investment spending determines the level of saving required for its realization, primarily through changes in the level of output in a short period with given capacity rather than, for example, through changes in the interest rate. The key conceptual breakthroughs appear to be the separation of investment and saving, each described formally by a distinct equation, and the distinction between planned and actual investment.

While prior economists had a good understanding of the fallacy of Say's law, which denies the possibility of overproduction or a general glut of commodities, the principle of effective demand deepened our understanding immeasurably. Marx, for example, identified the fallacy of Say's law as an error of omission, money having been ignored, for which he subjected Say to unmerciful ridicule. As Kenway (1980) showed, Marx did perceive the existence of "leakages" and "injections" but not the principle of effective demand that brings them together, and thus never went beyond the stage of a possibility theory of crisis. Malthus, whose opposition to Say's law singled him out for Keynes's praises, was never able to achieve even this, for as Bleaney (1976) points out, like most pre-Keynesian economists he was a prisoner of the belief that all saving would be automatically invested (aside from hoarding, which was regarded as irrational).

Kurz (1994) has observed that Say's law to the classical economists referred specifically to the tendency of capitalist economies to employ fully their available capital. It is only after the marginalist revolution that Say's law acquired its neoclassical identification with the full employment of labor. In this book, we stick to the classical usage and use Say's law as shorthand to refer to a situation in which it is permissible to ignore or suppress the distinction between planned investment and saving. Perhaps against better judgment, we will not use Say's law as a pejorative.

The principle of effective demand was extended into a more dynamic growth setting by Michal Kalecki, Joseph Steindl, Paul Sweezy and Paul Baran, and Joan Robinson, and their writings cast a long shadow over modern heterodox theory. In a neo-Kaleckian or neo-Steindlian model (Robinson 1962; Dutt 1990; Taylor 2004), the investment equation is typically written in terms of the rate of accumulation (rather than the level of investment) and includes the degree of capacity utilization as an independent variable. Saving is assumed to come primarily from profit, and the saving equation can also be written in growth terms with utilization as an independent variable. This system then determines a balanced growth equilibrium: output, capital, and capacity grow in parallel, and the degree of utilization (the ratio of actual output to capacity) is constant. Such a model can be modified to include worker, foreign, or government saving.

2.1.1 The Paradox of Thrift

The paradox of thrift is deeply embedded in the structure of the neo-Kaleckian model. While an increase in investment (either a shift or rotation in the investment equation) will increase utilization in order to generate sufficient saving to accommodate the plans of the entrepreneurs, an increase in saving, by rentiers, workers, or the government, for example, will not produce the converse effect on investment. Instead, it will reduce utilization and/or growth (depending on the details of the model). One can say without much fear of contradiction that in these models investment causes saving, but saving does not cause investment.

A related question is how this model responds to a greater equality of income distribution, or a decline in the profit share. Since workers are assumed to save less that rentiers, this redistribution is equivalent to a reduction in the social saving rate, which *ipso facto* should increase utilization and/or growth (again, depending on the model). This corollary to the paradox of thrift is sometimes called the paradox of cost. However, because the redistribution reduces the profit margin, it may discourage investment, which works against the paradox of cost. It is now widely recognized that the paradox of cost occurs only under a restricted set of conditions, skillfully catalogued by Blecker (2002). But the paradox of thrift appears to be an inescapable feature of this class of model.

Stagnationist theories of demand-constrained growth emerged out of the pervasive worldview in the aftermath of the Great Depression, a formative event in the lives of the economists mentioned above. Yet even after the Golden Age of Capital Accumulation, from 1950 to 1974, this worldview saturates the intellectual environment of heterodox economics, partly because it seems to offer some insights into the slowdown in growth since 1974, the formative event in the lives of the current generation of heterodox economists (Epstein and Schor 1990). Moreover, it has defined the heterodox position in the public debates (at least in the United States) over the direction of macroeconomic policy. An influential view among neoclassical economists has been that fiscal deficits crowd out investment in the long run, calling for a policy response directed toward increased national saving driven by fiscal surpluses; this, of course, was the theory behind the Clinton administration's policies. The heterodox response that an increase in national saving cannot be expected to raise investment spending dominates the contributions to Pollin (1997), a conference volume that includes commentary from prominent neoclassical economists on the work of leading heterodox economists.

Representative of the neoclassical reaction is Stanley Fischer's comment in this volume that "because neither the theory nor the empirical work addresses the issue of how the economy operates at full employment, the chapter [by David Gordon] does not get to grips with the orthodox presumption that an increase in government saving would increase investment" (Fischer 1997, 163). The reason, as Gordon makes clear, is that "it is not at all obvious . . . that capitalist economies *ever* approach the full utilization of resources upon which the long-run neoclassical argument is premised" (Gordon 1997, 150). This judgment is implicitly or explicitly endorsed by the remaining heterodox contributors to the volume.

We might also remark that this position is adopted by economists who have remained allegiant to the Keynesian aspects of the neoclassical-Keynesian synthesis, such as Robert Eisner (1986). In addition, some post-Keynesians who do not accept this synthesis, such as Palley (1996b), Setterfield (2002), and Thirlwall (2002) seem to accept this resolution as well, but unlike the Old Keynesians, they explicitly connect the theory of effective demand to long-run economic growth through its stimulative effects on endogenous technical change.

One reason why this position holds such a prominent place is that the neoclassical alternative is so unconvincing. On the theoretical level, Fischer's position harkens back to the Pigou-Modigliani-Patinkin denial of involuntary unemployment under flexible wages and prices. Their argument depends on the Pigou effect, whereby declining money wages and prices increase the wealth held (chiefly by rentiers) in the form of outside money, stimulating their consumption spending and leading to recovery from involuntary unemployment. In this theory, the capital stock will always be able to support any level of employment because the aggregate production function behaves itself along neoclassical lines. Say's law implies full employment of labor. Heterodox economists reject both of these arguments. The Pigou effect must contend with the Fisher debt-deflation effects that operate in the opposite direction, and these are likely to be overwhelming, as Japan's Great Recession attests. The well-behaved aggregate production function has been more or less thoroughly discredited as a scientific theory. Nonetheless, neoclassical macroeconomists remain committed to an unreal Walrasian model of the core capitalist economy, with various imperfections (sticky prices or wages, asymmetric information, etc.) accounting for any deviations from its fully adjusted state.[1]

Moreover, even accepting the standard neoclassical theory of the long run—the Solow growth model—the argument for sacrificing consumption today in order to increase output per worker in the future seems unconvincing; with most growth accounted for by technical change, the reward from capital deepening is small beer, as Baker and Weisbrot (1999, ch. 7) argue.

1. It is now customary to simply define the natural level of output as "the level of output that would arise if wages and prices were perfectly flexible" (Clarida et al. 1999 1665).

But the inadequacies of neoclassical economic theory do not constitute a valid excuse for evading the problem of excess capacity. One objective of this book is to redirect the discussion of national saving away from the production function framework with its focus on productivity and toward a political economy of the class structure of capital accumulation.

2.1.2 The Problem of Excess Capacity

The heterodox community has entertained a long-standing debate about the status of an equilibrium in which capitalist firms operate with excess capacity, or what Marx calls "permanent crises" in this chapter's epigraph.[2] Though he was discussing Baran and Sweezy's (1966) theory of monopoly capitalism in particular, Shaikh's comment that "they do not discuss why monopolists would persist in over-expanding productive capacity in the face of insufficient demand" (1978, 230) applies *a fortiori* to the whole class of neo-Kaleckian models. There are two broad types of answer to this question (which has been raised independently by many voices). The first endeavors to argue that demand-constraints operate in the short run while a more classical center of gravity regulates the system in the long run. The second endeavors to argue that demand-constraints operate at both high and low frequencies.

It is here that we come back to Harrod, this time in the guise of his instability hypothesis. Consider a neo-Kaleckian equilibrium, with capacity utilization below its normal or desired level. (There is widespread agreement that full utilization does not imply an engineering limitation but can include some spare capacity planned for strategic reasons, or as the by-product of technical change embodied in vintages of machine, or other reasons.) If we consider this a temporary equilibrium, what kind of error-correction mechanism might be reasonable? Clearly, if firms have excess capacity, they have overestimated the growth of the market and they are likely to reduce their expectation of growth. This can be modeled as a downward shift in the investment equation, which will push the system *away* from normal capacity utilization in the next period. As Kurz (1994) observes, this is a version of Harrod's celebrated knife-edge.[3] Clearly something must contain this instability.

2. For an overview, see Lavoie (1995), Lavoie et al. (2004), and Kurz (1990).

3. Many economists seem to operate under the misconception that Solow (1956) solved this problem by introducing substitution, but that is false. Harrod's instability problem arises only in a model with a separate investment equation, and substitution effects do not resolve

Shaikh's Resolution

Shaikh's resolution, presented in a remarkable series of papers (1989, 1991, 1992), reintroduces the distinction between circulating capital and fixed capital familiar to the classical economists. Circulating capital governs the growth of output through the input-output structure of production. In order to increase production in an expanding system, firms must increase inputs of materials and labor, or in effect, accumulate inventories of materials and works-in-progress. Let us call this form of investment in circulating capital A. Then short-run equilibrium (zero excess demand in product markets) is represented by the familiar equality between planned investment (fixed and circulating) and saving (assumed to be a constant proportion, s, of profits):

$$I + A = S$$

Dividing both sides by potential profit, P, and assuming a given propensity to invest in fixed capital out of profit, d, we have $d + A/P = s$. Shaikh is impressed (see, in particular, (1989, 76) and (1992, 287)) that the ratio A/P, which he calls the "rate of accumulation in circulating capital," is inversely related to d (holding s constant), but it is clear that this relationship can be satisfied by movements in A or P. In fact, holding A constant in a short-run setting and allowing the propensity to invest to increase would stimulate demand and raise the level of profits through the principle of effective demand, thus lowering A/P through the Keynes-Kalecki mechanism.

The central issue is how the system responds when utilization lies away from its normal level. If there is excess capacity, it is reasonable to assume with Shaikh that firms will reduce their propensity to invest in fixed capital. This, in itself, will tend to further depress utilization through Harrod's instability principle. Shaikh's resolution is that a decrease in the propensity to invest will automatically increase his rate of accumulation in circulating capital and that itself will cause an acceleration in the growth of output.

the problem. Solow's growth model assumes Say's law; it suppresses the distinction between saving and investment. The problem Solow can claim to have addressed is the existence of a growth equilibrium at a natural rate.

Utilization will thus be caught in a pincer and must rise.[4] But this conclusion seems to rest on an unstated premise that the increase in A/P will be brought about by an acceleration in A, presumably in anticipation of a corresponding burst in the growth of demand.[5] Since such a burst in demand is precisely what needs to be demonstrated, we will need to look elsewhere for a resolution to Harrod's instability problem that will satisfy economists in the Keynesian tradition.

A Keynesian Resolution

At the other extreme, some Keynesian economists have argued that in the long run, it is capacity alone that adjusts to demand. Cesaratto et al. (2003) present a simple Keynesian model of aggregate demand that makes three assumptions. First, the autonomous components of demand grow exogenously at the same constant rate. Second, all investment spending is induced; capacity only expands through investment spending. Third, the investment rate depends on the expected growth of demand, which adjusts adaptively and slowly to actual growth. With these assumptions, they argue that "the economy's productive capacity slowly gravitates towards a fully adjusted path in which capacity follows the trend of effective demand and the degree of capacity utilization is equal to the planned utilization rate" (Cesaratto et al. 2003, 44). A critical assumption is that expectations of growth do not change very quickly, for otherwise this model will display Harrodian instability.

To see the underlying mechanism, it will do no harm to simply assume that the expected rate of growth equals the rate of autonomous spending

4. Shaikh's own example takes up the opposing case of overutilization, leading to a rise in the propensity to invest: ". . . as the new short-run center of gravity is established, [A/P] will fall to accommodate the new higher short term level of [d]. Thus, an acceleration in the growth of capacity will end up decelerating the growth of actual production, *so that the capacity utilization level will tend to fall back toward normal (or even past it)*" (1989, 79).

5. We can formalize this argument for clarity by translating it into more neo-Kaleckian terms; readers are urged to consult the original (Shaikh 1989). Let u represent capacity utilization, $r = P/K$ the rate of profit, and note that $r = ur_n$, where r_n is the parametric profit rate at full utilization. Solving for the short-run equilibrium utilization rate, we have $u = (A/K)/((s - d)r_n)$. If u is less than normal, so that firms are induced to reduce d, we must have a sufficiently large increase in A/K to prevent utilization from spiraling downward. Now, since $A/P = (A/K)/(ur_n)$, it is clear that the incipient fall in utilization must raise A/P, but that is irrelevant since what is needed here is a conscious decision by managers to increase A sufficiently faster than K to offset the effects on A/P of an increase in utilization. This decision reflects an expectation that demand is accelerating.

growth. In this case, the investment function will remain stationary if it is expressed in growth terms. A temporary equilibrium with excess capacity can emerge if there is excess saving. But over time, autonomous consumption (normalized by the capital stock) increases, shifting the saving function (again, written in growth form) outward and raising the utilization rate. As the utilization rate approaches its normal level, the rate of growth of capital approaches the exogenously given steady state value. Autonomous consumption normalized by the capital stock will thus decelerate; its growth rate is the exogenous rate minus the actual rate of capital accumulation. In this way, the system will achieve the steady state that the quotation above describes.[6]

While this model does solve the problem of excess capacity, this comes at the price of treating all growth as exogenous in the final analysis. This resolution manages to be objectionable from both the classical and the Keynesian perspectives. The classical perspective sees capitalism as an inherently dynamic system prone to instability and crises that interrupt its progress. The idea that the system would simply stagnate in the absence of the external stimulus from autonomous consumer spending, government, net exports, and so on does not fit comfortably with that vision. The Keynesian perspective sees capitalism as prone to stagnation, but sees investment spending supported by the "animal spirits" of entrepreneurs as the key factor that explains periods of growth and stagnation. Treating *all* investment as induced by demand growth demotes the entrepreneur to a supporting role in the drama of accumulation, while elevating the rentiers and politicians who control private and public autonomous consumption to the status of prime movers. The assumption of exogenous growth of autonomous spending is even less intellectually appealing than the assumption of exogenous technical change, which at least can be rationalized by our inability to express the economics of invention and innovation in a satisfactory way.

6. We can formalize this argument for clarity by modifying the model presented in Cesaratto et al. (2003). The investment equation is $I/K = g^e u$, where g^e is expected growth of demand and u is the utilization rate, with normal utilization assumed to be unity. (We ignore depreciation of capital stock.) The saving equation is $S/K = -Z/K + \sigma_s \rho u$, where Z is autonomous consumption, σ_s is the social saving propensity, and ρ is the potential output-capital ratio. Now make the simplifying assumption that $g^e = g_Z$, where g_Z is the given rate of growth of autonomous spending. This model simplifies to a first-order nonautonomous nonlinear difference equation in u that converges to unity under reasonable parameter values.

A Neo-Kaleckian Resolution

Lavoie (1995) and Dutt (1997) offer a resolution more in tune with the neo-Kaleckian and neo-Steindlian approaches. We will focus on the former paper as there are some subtle differences between the two. Lavoie's central argument is that entrepreneurs form expectations adaptively about both the normal level of utilization and the rate of growth of sales. The former process guides the system to a fully adjusted state with normal utilization, so let us start there and, following Lavoie's own exposition, assume that sales expectations are constant. The idea is that in a temporary equilibrium with utilization below the normal rate (as that is currently perceived) entrepreneurs will revise their opinions of what constitutes "normal" utilization in the light of experience. In this case, they will lower their sights and redefine normal utilization. "This fall in the normal rate of capacity utilization . . . will in turn induce an *upward* [emphasis added] shift of the investment function" (Lavoie 1995, 807). Faced with utilization below their target rate, entrepreneurs choose to lower their aspirations concerning the target rate rather than reduce the growth of capacity. Entrepreneurs faced with excess capacity are thus inveterate optimists in the particular sense that they turn bad news into good. Formally, this tropism can be shown to be stabilizing, leading to the elimination of excess capacity.

While this device solves the problem of excess capacity, it robs the model of an important Kaleckian property because the long-run growth rate will be determined by the given expectations of sales growth. Lavoie solves that problem by proposing a similar adaptive expectations approach to sales expectations, which restores the endogeneity of growth as long as the expectations process is not so rapid that it destabilizes the system through the Harrod instability mechanism. The result is a neo-Kaleckian model that exhibits path dependency in both its growth rate and its rate of capacity utilization, yet always gravitates toward a fully adjusted state with utilization at its normal level and sales expectations realized.[7] This is an intellectually attractive result, but again it has been purchased at a high price. The entre-

7. We can formalize this argument for clarity by adapting the model laid out by Lavoie (1995). Let the investment equation be $I/K = g^e + d(u - u_n)$ and the saving function be $S/K = sp\pi u$, where s is the propensity to save out of profit and π is the (given) profit share. Note that this investment equation says that if utilization achieves the target rate, u_n, entrepreneurs will increase the capital stock at the expected growth of sales, g^e. Modeling first u_n and then including g^e with a standard adaptive expectations process generates two

preneurs in this world must be inveterate optimists possessed of a particular type of animal spirits.

Even though we find fault with the demand-constrained models surveyed here, the broader demand-based theory of the Keynes-Kalecki tradition does not stand or fall on any particular formal instantiation. Recalling the epigraph in Chapter 1, it is important to resist the temptation to reify models. This tradition's recognition of the role that radical or fundamental uncertainty plays in the investment decision, in particular, secures its position in the conversation of macroeconomics.

Duménil and Lévy's Resolution

The resolution offered by Duménil and Lévy (1999) comes closest to the standpoint of the rest of this book. They reintroduce money and finance into the model and propose that investment spending is constrained by finance or liquidity. In many ways, their model looks like the neo-Wicksellian models that now dominate monetary macroeconomics. The price level responds to the degree of capacity utilization. The money supply process is to some extent controlled or regulated by a monetary authority that is inflation averse. Thus, to return to our example, a temporary equilibrium with excess capacity would be deflationary (or disinflationary). The monetary authority would respond with accommodative policy, relaxing the financial constraint on investment so that the investment equation shifts upward. As a result, the system gravitates toward a fully adjusted position with normal utilization of capacity. We will return to this process and present a modified version of Duménil and Lévy's model below.

Joan Robinson's critique of Marxian economics contains one of the earliest statements of demand-constrained growth. Robinson correctly identifies the role that Say's law (in the nonpejorative sense defined above) plays in Marx's theory of the long-run cycle of accumulation. The theory she has in mind was later formalized by Richard Goodwin (1967), who assumes that all profits are saved and invested as befits Say's law. She writes:

> The confusion between this long-run cycle, which might be found in a world subject to Say's law, and the short-run cycle of effective demand,

models with the properties described in the text, as long as g^e does not respond too quickly to expectational error compared with u_n.

> accounts for the ambiguity of Marx's attitude to the problem of underconsumption. Part of the time he is accepting Say's law and part rejecting it. Push in the Say's law stop, and effective demand is dominant—the poverty of the workers is then seen to be the last cause of all real crises. Does it follow that a crisis would be relieved by increasing the consuming power of the workers? Pull out the Say's law stop, and the answer is no. (Robinson 1942, 86)

Robinson wants the stop to remain in, and she is not the only economist (Sweezy 1942; Steindl 1952; Kalecki 1971) to argue that had Marx developed his thoughts on underconsumptionism, he would have emerged a Keynesian through and through.

The Duménil-Lévy approach clears up this muddle by recognizing the value of both the classical and the Keynes-Kalecki approaches to growth. It assigns the problem of effective demand to the short run, where it rules the roost. Yet the long run, seen as the center toward which a sequence of temporary equilibria gravitate, is certainly subject to Say's law as defined above, and displays classical features. In particular, the paradox of thrift and that of cost prevail in the short run but not the long run. It is of some interest that this approach to an extent addresses Kalecki's frequently quoted statement that appears at the beginning of this chapter. This statement captures the truth that "long-run" is essentially an adjective, not a noun; the capitalist economy is always operating in the short run, even when it is in a fully adjusted state. Yet the "chain of short-period situations" does not wander randomly; long-run forces govern its evolution, perhaps slowly but persistently. From this perspective, the empirical chicken-and-egg question of whether investment causes saving or vice versa is poorly posed, and efforts to solve it, such as Gordon (1997), are not likely to succeed. The long-run center of gravitation conflates saving and investment constraints on growth; they have no independent identity at this level of abstraction.

This discussion represents the critical foundation for the work that follows. The premise of the growth models presented below is that they describe a long-run center of gravity that is a worthy object of analysis in its own right. While it would be foolish to expect all economists to accept this framework, it is important to communicate as precisely as possible why it might be persuasive so that the conversation can continue to generate more light than heat.

This framework bears only a superficial resemblance to the distinction neoclassical economists make between a New Keynesian short run with sticky prices and a neoclassical long run with full employment of labor. Here we have returned to the classical view that the long-run or fully adjusted state of a capitalist economy involves full utilization of capital; there is no compelling reason in the classical tradition to impose the assumption of full employment of labor, and in fact, there are plenty of good reasons to question that assumption. When we do adopt this assumption below, we will bracket it liberally with disclaimers.

2.2 A Classical-Kaleckian Model

In order to fix the idea of a model that operates along Keynes-Kalecki lines in the short run and more classical lines in the long run, we can write out a modified version of the Duménil and Lévy (1999) model, dispensing with their two-sector setup in favor of a corn model approach. We present the model under two alternative closures, first with an endogenous growth rate and second with an exogenous growth rate. One interesting conclusion is that, in the long run, the model exhibits both Keynesian and classical features. The aphorism "short-run Keynesian, long-run classical" is misleading to the extent that it implies that aggregate demand has no role to play in the long run.

2.2.1 Capital-Constrained Growth

Let us begin by assuming that labor supply does not confine economic growth. In effect, there is an infinitely elastic supply of labor at the existing real wage. In this world, we want to illustrate how capital constrains growth in the long run, even though effective demand governs the level and rate of growth of output in the short run. Our modifications move in the direction of the three-equation neo-Wicksellian macro model that is *au courant* in the mainstream. The central feature that we want to showcase is the hypothesis of two separate adjustment processes, one relatively fast (the short-run) and one relatively slow (the long-run). In the short run, firms achieve a temporary product market equilibrium by means of changes in capacity utilization, taking the fixed capital stock that anchors capacity as given. In the long run, firms adjust capacity and the monetary authority's influence ensures that it is utilized at its expected or normal level. The long run thus emerges at the end of a sequence of short-run or temporary equilibria.

Price inflation is assumed to depend on utilization, and the monetary authorities are assumed to be inflation averse. Thus, a period of high utilization induces a monetary response that takes effect in the next period, creating the centripetal forces that pull the system back toward normal utilization. While Duménil and Lévy work with the supply of money, we can express this mechanism just as effectively through the real interest rate, i. We will assume that the monetary authority targets the inflation rate, p, using the real interest rate as its policy instrument. The target inflation rate is $\bar{p}$, and the inflation-neutral rate of interest is i_n. The monetary authority reaction function is

$$i_{+1} = i_n + a(p - \bar{p}) \tag{2.1}$$

There is a long tradition of studying the reaction function of the central banks through an equation like (2.1). In this form, it could be interpreted as an example of inflation targeting. It could be augmented by some measure of utilization or employment,[8] in which case it would represent a version of the Taylor rule, or more broadly, the generic central bank reaction function. In our case, the assumption is that decisions taken in the short run take effect only in the next period. This, too, is fairly well established in the literature on central banking, where the lag between policy decisions and their effects is commonly placed from six months to two years (as originally suggested by Milton Friedman). One reason for this lag is that monetary authorities directly control only the rate on interbank lending, which is very short-term, typically in the form of overnight loans; whereas, the real interest rate that affects investment decisions is the long-term rate. Under the expectations theory of term structure, changes in the short-term rate will typically affect the long-term rate only after the markets have had time to digest them.

The reaction function implies that the monetary authorities recognize that the inflation process depends on the rate of utilization, u, through a Phillips curve–like relationship, and that the rate of utilization depends on

8. For an elaboration of the model, see Michl (2008). This paper shows that even with an employment target, the monetary authorities in this model will not be able to achieve both their inflation and employment goals except by fluke. In short, they have too few policy instruments.

the interest rate, through an IS-curve. We will model the inflation process through

$$p_{+1} = p + b(u - 1) \tag{2.2}$$

For convenience, we define the normal or desired rate of utilization as unity. Note that this does not represent full utilization in an engineering sense. Firms are assumed to build capacity slightly ahead of demand so as to accommodate fluctuations in orders without losing customers. The assumption is that they will respond to high demand partly by stepping up production and partly by raising prices in the next period. The utilization rate can exceed unity, and we will assume that firms operate well away from the engineering limits.

Money wages are assumed to respond to prices one-for-one so that their ratio, the real wage, remains constant. Thus, the distribution of income is parametric. We will use π to represent the profit share. For simplicity, we assume, without loss of much generality, that workers live hand-to-mouth and consume their real wage. (Most of the rest of this book is concerned with including worker saving in a macroeconomic model.)

To obtain an IS curve, we make use of an investment equation that is the staple of neo-Kaleckian modeling. Investment is responsive to the degree of utilization, on the grounds that high utilization signals that demand is expanding faster than capacity. We will include the interest rate, on the grounds that investment that cannot be financed through internally generated funds (profits) will be sensitive to credit conditions.[9] Normalizing by the capital stock, we have

$$\frac{I}{K} = d_0 - d_1 i + d_2 u$$

For simplicity, we will assume that a constant proportion, s, of profits is saved. (A more explicit treatment of saving is presented in the next chapter.) Thus, saving normalized by the capital stock is

$$\frac{S}{K} = s\pi\rho u$$

9. While some classical-Keynesian economists may object that economic theory and the empirical evidence do not support the existence of an interest-sensitive investment function, the position that investment completely lacks sensitivity to interest rates is hard to justify. For more discussion of this point, see Michl (2006b).

where ρ is the output-capital ratio, sometimes referred to as capital productivity.

The short run is assumed to be long enough to permit changes in utilization that eliminate any excess demand in the product market. Equating planned investment and saving, we obtain the IS curve

$$u = \frac{d_0 - d_1 i}{c} \tag{2.3}$$

where $c = s\pi\rho - d_2$ represents the marginal excess saving generated by an increase in utilization. Stability of the short-run adjustment mechanism requires that $c > 0$, and we will assume that this condition prevails. We also assume that the monetary authority knows the structure of the IS curve and can determine (probably with a lag) that the inflation-neutral rate of interest is

$$i_n = \frac{d_0 - c}{d_1}$$

Note that this model operates along standard Keynes-Kalecki lines in the short run (assuming the monetary authority does not change the neutral rate of interest instantaneously). The principle of effective demand reigns: investment determines saving through changes in utilization. An autonomous increase in investment (an upward shift in the intercept term of the investment equation) has a multiplier effect on utilization in the short run. An increase in the propensity to save has a deflating effect on utilization, exhibiting the paradox of thrift. A decrease in the real wage, or equivalently an increase in the profit share, also has a deflating effect on utilization, exhibiting the paradox of costs.

These three equations (2.1–2.3) form a dynamical system of linear, first-order difference equations:[10]

$$\begin{pmatrix} p_{+1} \\ i_{+1} \end{pmatrix} = \begin{pmatrix} 1 & -bd_1/c \\ a & 0 \end{pmatrix} \begin{pmatrix} p \\ i \end{pmatrix} + \begin{pmatrix} b(d_0/c - 1) \\ i_n - b\bar{p} \end{pmatrix}$$

The eigenvalues ($j = 1, 2$) of this system are

$$\lambda_j = \frac{c \pm \sqrt{c^2 - 4cbad_1}}{2c}$$

10. For a guide to the mathematics of dynamic systems, see Gandolfo (1997) or Elaydi (2005).

The stability of the equilibrium of the system requires that the eigenvalues lie within the unit circle, with modulus less than unity. This implies that

$$a < \frac{c}{bd_1}$$

This stability condition makes some sense. An increase in the slope of the IS curve (increase in c), an increase in the sensitivity of the inflation process (b), or an increase in the interest sensitivity of investment (d_1) all demand that the monetary authorities become less aggressive about inflation-fighting, lest they cross the tipping point and become a destabilizing influence on accumulation.

A more meaningful constraint on policy is probably the condition that separates a stable node from a stable focus, which is that the discriminant be positive. Ruling out over- and undershooting the steady state path imposes more restraint on the monetary authorities:

$$a < \frac{c}{4bd_1}$$

In light of the concern voiced by central bankers over achieving what Alan Greenspan has called a "glide path" to a "soft landing," this is probably the more relevant constraint.

It is easy to see that the fixed point, or equilibrium (assuming that it exists), of this little three-equation model occurs where inflation achieves its target level, $p = \bar{p}$, utilization achieves its normal level, $u = 1$, and the interest rate is neutral $i = i_n$. The growth rate of capital will then be given by the justly famous Cambridge equation,

$$g = s\pi\rho = sr_n$$

where r_n represents the normal rate of profit. It is also clear that the monetary authorities must know the neutral rate of interest, $i_n = (d_0 - c)/d_1$, in order to achieve their target rate of inflation, something that may not be that easy in practice.

Now we can substantiate the claim that this model operates along classical lines in the long run. An increase in capitalist saving, for example, will raise the rate of accumulation in the long run (even though its impact effect, in the short run, will be to reduce utilization and growth). Figure 2.1 illustrates a numerical simulation; the monetary policy parameters have been chosen to avoid oscillations. An increase in the profit share (i.e., a real-wage

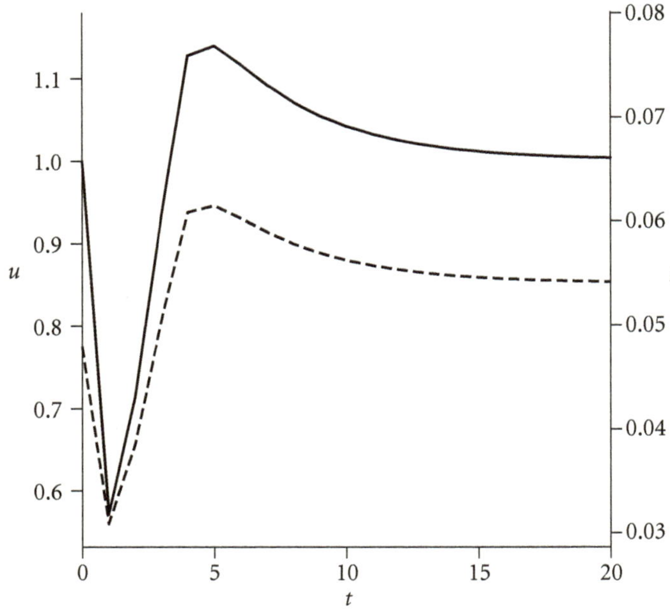

Figure 2.1 Short-run Keynesian, long-run classical models. In the short run, an increase in capitalist saving has Keynes-Kaleckian effects on the utilization rate (left scale, solid line) and rate of accumulation (right scale, dashed line) but classical effects in the long run. The system began in a steady state, with $u(0) = 1$ and $g(0) = 0.048$. The saving rate was increased in period 1 forward from 0.8 to 0.9, and the neutral rate of interest was recalibrated in three equal steps in period 2 forward. The parameters are $a = 0.05$, $\bar{p} = 0.05$, $\rho = 0.35$, $d_0 = 0.1$, $d_1 = 0.1$, $d_2 = 0.0375$, and $b = 0.5$. (Data have been joined by lines for visual effect only; the model is in discrete time.)

reduction) will similarly raise the long-run growth rate even though it engenders the paradox of costs in the short run.

An increase in public saving in a model extended to include government could be expected to have a similar effect, reducing effective demand in the short run. Policy makers and citizens should not find this prospect very attractive. The implication is that a successful implementation of a tight fiscal policy requires a loose monetary policy that offsets the fiscal restraint. We examine the effect of monetary accommodation below. Heterodox economists, already skeptical that flexible wages and prices can generate stabilizing forces, are similarly reluctant to believe that central banks can always be counted on to do the right thing. In addition, as several heterodox economists have pointed out, existing central bank operating procedures (mainly open marketing repos or similar securities, or running a Lombard facility) need to be modernized to keep up with the financial innovations that have redefined banking. One proposal, asset-based reserve requirements (Pollin 1993; Palley 2000), could improve the central bank's ability to direct stimulus to business fixed investment.

As we observed above, it is possible for a neo-Kaleckian model to generate profit-led growth, which would align it with the classical long run described here. However, the neo-Kaleckian models all display some version of the paradox of thrift. Increases in the saving rate do not stimulate accumulation but rather manifest themselves in lower capacity utilization. A numerical example of an increase in the saving rate has been chosen to illustrate the properties of this model in Figure 2.1 precisely because it is over this issue that the neo-Kaleckian and classical approaches are at swords' points.

Of course, it is formally possible that an equilibrium with normal utilization could fail to exist, if the IS curve is improperly positioned. To rule this out, the investment equation must satisfy the inequality $d_0 + d_1 > g$. If this inequality is violated, the system falls into a liquidity trap that requires the monetary authorities to target a negative real interest rate, something that has proved difficult to achieve in practice. Duménil and Lévy avoid this thorny issue by setting up their model in terms of the money supply, effectively taking the position that it is the availability of finance or liquid capital that constrains the investment process. One advantage of the present set-up is that it creates a bridge to the structuralist Keynesian models, which could be interpreted as applying to a world in which the investment inequality is persistently violated because of a deficit of entrepreneurial animal spirits.

2.2.2 Labor-Constrained Growth

As the model presented above contains no explicit reference to labor market conditions, it applies to the capital-constrained world of classical political economy in which labor is supplied elastically over the long-run horizon. It is possible to incorporate labor constraints, so that growth is exogenously determined by the natural rate of labor force growth, n. In order to make this exercise sensible, we will assume that the system's warranted rate of growth, $s\pi\rho$, has already adjusted to the natural rate of growth, perhaps through changes in distribution that are the subject of the remainder of this book.

Alternatively, we could interpret equality between the warranted and natural rates along endogenous-growth lines. If the rate of growth of labor supply adjusts, over some long horizon, to the warranted rate, then the results below would make just as much sense. Either way, with growth in the long run assumed to achieve the natural rate, the question that then confronts us is how the level of employment (dependent on the capital stock) will behave.

For ease of exposition, let us assume that the capital-employed labor ratio, k, equals unity; one unit of capital employs one unit of labor (we can always choose units so that this is true). We can define the employment rate, e, as the ratio of employed workers to the labor force, L. Finally, define the ratio of capital to the labor force (*not* to employment) as κ. Now we can see that the employment ratio depends on the utilization rate and the capital-labor force ratio, or

$$e = u\frac{K}{L} = u\kappa$$

We know that $u(i)$ evolves with the interest rate, converging on its long-run equilibrium, $u = 1$. Thus, to gain some appreciation of the dynamics of employment, we can concentrate on the capital–labor force ratio. Let $i(t)$ represent the solution to the system of difference equations above. Then we can obtain the nonautonomous linear difference equation

$$\kappa_{+1} = (\mathcal{A} - \mathcal{B}i(t))\kappa$$

where $\mathcal{A} = (1 + d_0 + d_0 d_2/c)/(1 + n)$ and $\mathcal{B} = (d_1 + d_1 d_2/c)/(1 + n)$.

We know that stability in the system above means that $i \to i_n$ as $t \to \infty$. Thus, this difference equation eventually becomes autonomous (time invariant). Substituting for i_n, we find that it reduces to

$$\kappa_{+1} = \kappa$$

which is to say, a pure unit-root process. This suggests that the capital–labor force ratio, and ultimately the employment ratio upon which it depends, are path dependent. They will settle down to whatever value they happen to have when the system enters its steady state. If the monetary authority imposes inflation targeting by choosing the current inflation rate as its target precisely when the system is in a steady state, then whatever the employment rate happens to be at that moment will remain the employment rate in the future.

Interestingly, the inflation rate and unemployment rate $(1 - e)$ will obey a Phillips-like relationship, complete with an apparent "natural rate" or NAIRU (nonaccelerating inflation rate of unemployment). Substituting into the true Phillips curve and solving for the change in inflation gives

$$\Delta p = b\left(\frac{1-\kappa}{\kappa}\right) - \frac{b}{\kappa}(1-e)$$

This could be called the pseudo-Phillips curve (in difference form) for this system. An unsuspecting econometrician might be tempted to estimate this relationship, thinking that it was generated by a stochastic process, when in fact, it is only reflecting the comovements in u, κ, and p. Unfortunately, our hapless econometrician would also be able to convince himself and others that a natural rate or NAIRU exists.

Monetary policy in this setting has all the expected properties in the short run. A switch to a more accommodating inflation target, for example, results in an immediate relaxation of the interest rate that has the usual Keynesian effects on demand and utilization; see Figure 2.2 for a numerical simulation, with monetary parameters again chosen to avoid oscillations. As inflation rises toward the new target level, the monetary authority restores normal utilization, and growth recovers the natural rate. Note that growth can increase temporarily because the system began with a capital–labor force ratio below unity, implying the existence of some unemployment. The period of supranormal growth, however, permanently raises the level of the capital stock, as is brought into sharp relief by the behavior of the capital–labor force ratio, κ, in Figure 2.2. The employment ratio similarly rises, initially buoyed up by both higher utilization and a higher capital stock but eventually held up by the higher capital stock alone. The ability of monetary policy to offset demand shocks, such as might be created by a fiscal tightening, seems secure in this model.

This example reveals the underlying syncretism of this model in the long run. A demand shock (in this case from a monetary regime change) has permanent effects on the level of the capital stock, a quality that is associated with the Keynes-Kalecki tradition. Nonetheless, the steady state growth rate remains obedient to the Cambridge equation, a quality associated with the classical tradition. More precisely, we have assumed a natural rate of growth here, to which the system returns. But running the same policy experiment

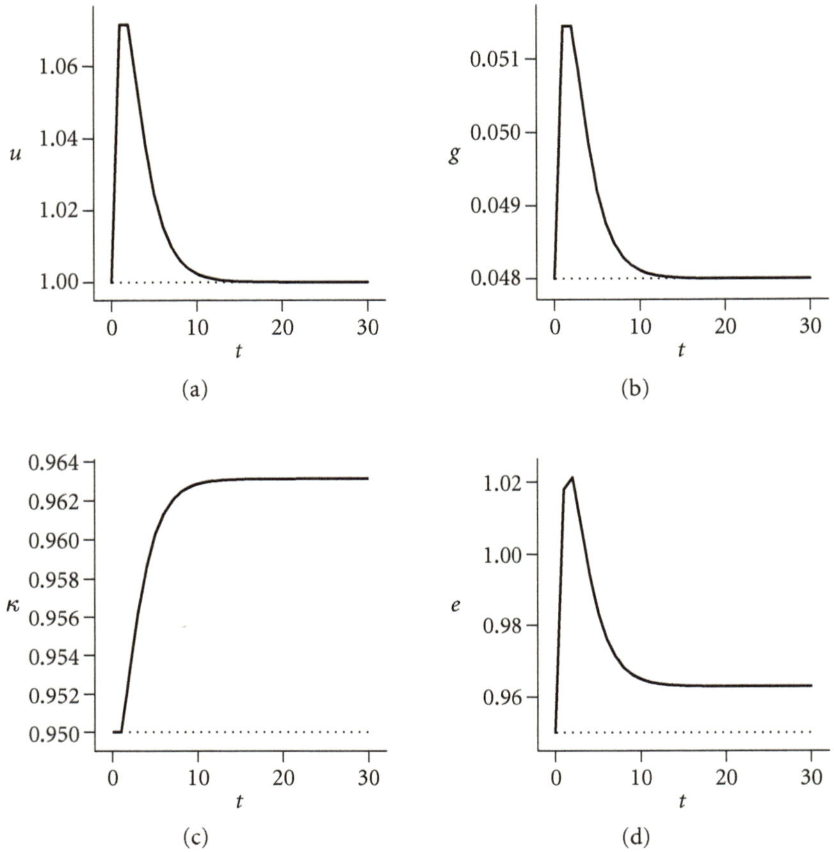

Figure 2.2 A classical-Keynesian long run. In the labor-constrained model, a shift to a more accommodating monetary policy leads to temporary increases in growth (g) and capacity utilization (u) but permanent increases in the capital–labor force (κ) and employment (e) ratios. Dotted lines show benchmark values without any policy change. Here the inflation target has increased (for dramatic effect) from 0.05 to 0.20 and the initial capital-labor force ratio is 0.95; for other parameters, see Figure 2.1. (Data have been joined by lines for visual effect only; the model is in discrete time.)

in the capital-constrained growth model would produce qualitatively similar results, and the growth rate would obey the Cambridge theorem in the long run. In either case, both demand and supply factors play a role in determining the path of the economic system.

2.3 An Intellectual Division of Labor

This model has been presented to convey the essential idea of an economic system that is Keynesian in its short-run characteristics but syncretic (classical-Keynesian) in its long-run characteristics. This idea underwrites the long period method of analysis that the rest of the book pursues. The working premise is that shocks due to changes in private or public saving can be stabilized by adroit monetary policy; we make no claim that automatic homeostatic forces in capitalist economies can perform the same duties.[11] The long period method studies the properties of the long-run equilibrium growth path by abstracting from the problem of achieving that growth path through a sequence of short-run equilibria. To refer to the metaphor above, we can determine where the cyclist is going by assuming she has an obedient dog. This intellectual division of labor has long been a staple feature of conventional macroeconomics, going back to the early days of the neoclassical-Keynesian synthesis, when the IS-LM model emerged as the choice for dealing with stabilization issues while the Solow model emerged as the choice for dealing with growth and accumulation. There is no reason why heterodox economists cannot build up the classical-Keynesian synthesis, in part at least, around a similar architecture to take full advantage of the benefits of specialization.

But we must not overlook the danger that this intellectual division of labor could become an excuse for ignoring the interactions between short- and long-run forces. Dutt and Ros (2007, 97) argue that "it is not acceptable to have a division in macroeconomics between the short and medium runs in which aggregate demand issues may be relevant, and the long run in which these issues can be completely forgotten. What happens in the short and medium runs can be expected to have long-run effects . . . ." If this statement is taken as a rejection of long-run models, then it seems excessive; but if it refers to an underlying theoretical attitude, then it well expresses one of the hallmarks of heterodox economics.[12] Nothing in the

11. There is no reason to dispute Dutt's (2006, 332) assertion that in light of the role demand plays under path dependency, "simple-minded efforts to increase the saving rate . . . will have to be rethought." The lesson of even this simple model is that an appropriate monetary-fiscal policy mix needs to be designed and implemented with careful attention to the limitations of monetary policy.

12. For other examples of heterodox models in which demand shocks have permanent growth effects through induced technical change, see Palley (1996a) and Dutt (2006).

subsequent theoretical exercises with strictly long-run models should be taken to imply that a government that single-mindedly pursues a tight fiscal policy without endeavoring to stabilize demand shocks (including the shock created by its own policies) will achieve objectives formulated within the framework of a long-run model, for these represent potential outcomes under idealized conditions. Indeed, heterodox theory enjoys a signal advantage over its neoclassical rival through its insistence on path dependencies such as those highlighted in the models above.[13] Bad policies do not merely create temporary deviations from an unchanged long-run trajectory, they permanently shift the whole path of the long-run center of gravity. This is particularly clear in the case of capital-constrained growth models that have no good counterparts in the neoclassical vocabulary. Like all tools, the long-run models that follow deserve to be handled with some care.

13. See, for example, Solow's (2005, 5) complaints about the lack of attention to the interactions between trend and cycle among neoclassical economists. As the current chapter attests, heterodox economists have been preoccupied with these interactions for some time.

— II —

Long-run Models of Fiscal Policy

— 3 —

A Two-Class Model

Accumulation of capital is therefore multiplication of the proletariat.

KARL MARX (1977)

. . . Tolstoy was by nature a fox, but believed in being a hedgehog.

ISAIAH BERLIN (1953)

This chapter outlines a pair of basic models of economic growth in the classical tradition that will be used as a platform in subsequent chapters to study some traditional macroeconomic questions concerning the long-run effects of fiscal policy. The models share the same underlying behaviorial assumptions but differ with respect to closure. The first model presented here assumes that the distribution of income is determined exogenously (and, in this sense, is truer to the original classical economists), leaving the system's growth rate a free variable. Since some changes in behavior, such as an increase in thrift on the part of capitalist agents, have permanent effects on the growth rate, this type of model is commonly referred to as an endogenous growth model. The second model makes the antipodean assumption that the rate of growth of the fully employed labor force is determined exogenously, leaving the distribution of income free to change so that the system can accommodate the natural rate of growth of the labor force. This closure has been the standard for modern growth theory since its inception in the 1950s. For obvious reasons, we refer to this type of model as an exogenous growth model.

Alternatively, it is sometimes more useful to recognize that in the endogenous growth model, growth is capital constrained while in the exogenous growth model, it is labor constrained. However, the full employment assumption is rather more specialized, because it is possible to imagine a world in which growth is constrained by the available labor supplies without full employment prevailing, as in the previous chapter. In the Goodwin (1967) model, the *ne plus ultra* of this genre, some background level of unemployment contains the conflict over the distribution of income so that accumulation can keep up with labor force growth. Cycles around this central rate occur through elegant predator-prey dynamics (workers, curiously, preying on the profits of the capitalists). The full employment assumption papers over all the drama of this disequilibrium model by asserting that the conflicts are resolved. Presumably, the payoff for this simplification comes in the form of insights that might be lost in the mathematical complexity of the Lotka-Volterra system.

Both these models assume that in the long run business enterprises operate fully utilized capital stocks. Full utilization occurs when the stocks are producing the output that the managers regard as normal, which may not be their maximum engineering capacity. The working premise is that the problem of achieving full utilization resolves itself over a short time scale, where more Keynesian methods are not only appropriate but own all the best real estate. As discussed in the previous chapter, some economists reject this intellectual division of labor for shortchanging demand considerations. This is an unresolved and ongoing conversation, but it can only move forward if the interlocutors elaborate on their own personal research projects.

Finally, one should not lose sight of the turbulence and complexity of actual capitalist production and accumulation. Attacking such a foxy world with the single-mindedness of a hedgehog, the models presented in this chapter and put to work in subsequent chapters should be appreciated as analytical frameworks useful for clearing up logical issues in the theory of accumulation, not necessarily as behavioral descriptions of real economies.

3.1 Elements of the Growth Models

We begin by developing the foundations for our growth models with overlapping generations of workers and a class of agents referred to as "capitalists" since they manage to subsist on their holdings of physical capital wealth alone. The model is set in discrete time, and the time subscript on dated variables will be left implicit to minimize clutter. Thus, for the capital stock at time $t+1$, we will write K_{+1}. As in similar one-sector models, output can be either consumed or accumulated as capital stock.

3.1.1 *Wages and Profits*

In a one-commodity system with Leontief technology, the technique of production is described by any two of three parameters: labor productivity (or the output-labor ratio), $x = X/N$, capital productivity (or the output-capital ratio), $\rho = X/K$, and capital intensity (or the capital-labor ratio), $k = K/N$. The determination of r, the net rate of profit (the gross profit rate after depreciation, δ) follows directly from the wage-profit equation, or

$$r = \frac{x - w}{k} - \delta \tag{3.1}$$

It is also useful to define the maximal rate of profit, $R = \rho - \delta$, since it crops up frequently in the analytical expressions we will encounter.

In a world of multiple commodities, although the rate of profit remains a monotonic function of the wage, this equation would not be linear unless by fluke, even under the single technique assumption, owing to the presence of price Wicksell effects: changes in distribution alter the whole vector of prices at which capital goods are evaluated, changing the capital-labor ratio (Harcourt 1972). Care must always be taken to avoid the temptation to conclude that results obtained under the one-commodity assumption would automatically carry over into the richer multicommodity framework. Nonetheless, the one-commodity assumption is so convenient that it remains a staple of economic reasoning 200 years after Ricardo first proposed his famous Corn model. The Leontief technology, however, is not standard among neoclassical economists and deserves some explanation. The neoclassical growth theorists are nearly unanimous in assuming the existence of a well-behaved neoclassical production function, meaning one in which price Wicksell effects do not create any difficulties. As we have argued, this appears to be a more specialized and less defensible assumption than is commonly recognized.

The Leontief function treats the existing technique of production as part of the underlying structure of the economy. This assumption is perhaps less specialized and more defensible than is commonly recognized. It does not require that we treat technology as being fixed or the existing technique as the only available way of doing things. Rather, it rests on the belief that the existing technique dominates the alternative techniques, at least within the range of wage rates that the model encompasses. In real capitalist economies, technical changes push out the frontier more or less continuously as the dominant technique evolves.

Growth models routinely abstract from technical change, as we are doing, in order to get a clear understanding of the structure of capital accumulation. It is possible to add technical change and if it is purely labor-saving, or Harrod-neutral (meaning that it leaves the capital productivity of each technique intact), the resulting growth model can have a steady state solution because Harrod-neutral technical change is equivalent to an increase in the effective labor force. Thus, with appropriate redefinition of per-worker variables (expressed per effective worker), most of the results carry over to a growth model augmented by neutral technical change. We return to technical change in Chapters 10 and 11.

3.1.2 Capitalists

In this book, we consider two alternative treatments of the capitalist agents. In the first, capitalists are intergenerationally altruistic and can be conceptualized as an infinitely lived dynasty in the manner of Barro (1974). These capitalist dynasties derive utility from consumption. In the second, capitalists derive utility from their own consumption and from the wealth they leave behind as a legacy. It is possible to interpret the utility from their bequest as an expression of their altruism (the joy of giving), but other interpretations make sense. For example, their legacy wealth can express their success as capitalists, from which they derive pleasure (Carroll 2000).

Altruistic Bequest Motive

Capitalists solve a constrained optimization problem over an infinite time horizon, discounting consumption by the factor β_c $(0 < \beta_c < 1)$. (We will premultiply the utility summation by $(1 - \beta_c)$ to simplify the arithmetic, making the discounting terms sum to unity.) The usual explanation for such dynastic behavior is that each generation cares about its offspring, becoming linked across time and behaving like one infinitely lived household.[1] This may not be the primary reason that households in the wealthiest percentiles (where most real capitalists can be found) accumulate so dili-

1. In the standard Ramsey-Cass-Koopmans growth model, the household optimizes over the discounted utility per person, multiplied by the number of members of the household

gently, but it does lend a familiar structure to the problem and impose needed intellectual discipline. Capitalists' end-of-period wealth consists of undepreciated capital plus net end-of-period profits. The net rate of profit after depreciation is denoted r. We assume that the number of capitalist households remains constant, and we normalize it to 1 in the formal presentation. (But when it is awkward to speak of a singular capitalist, we slip into more natural terminology in the informal discussions in this book.) The capitalist programming problem in period 0 is to choose consumption levels, C, so as to

$$\max\,(1-\beta_c)\sum_{t=0}^{\infty}\beta_c{}^t \log C$$

$$\text{subject to } C + K^c_{+1} \le (1+r)K^c$$

$$\text{given } K^c_0,\ \{r\}_0^\infty$$

The solution can be obtained relatively easily and, as is well known, turns out to have a straightforward form.[2] Capitalists consume a constant proportion of their end-of-period wealth and save the rest. Their saving function is written as follows:

$$K^c_{+1} = \beta_c(1+r)K^c \tag{3.2}$$

A convenient mathematical expression of the capitalist saving function is the dynamic form that we will call the *Cambridge equation*:[3]

$$(1+g) = \beta_c(1+r) \tag{3.3}$$

(Romer 1996, ch. 2). This treatment implies that the saving rate depends on the growth rate of the household. Lower fertility will result in less saving, since fewer children require smaller bequests. The implications of this alternative treatment are discussed further below.

2. Write the Lagrangian $\mathcal{L} = (1-\beta_c)\sum_{t=0}^{\infty}\beta_c^t \log C - \sum_{t=0}^{\infty}\mu(C + K^c_{+1} - (1+r)K^c)$, where μ are the Lagrangian multipliers (with time subscripts suppressed, as they are for the other dated variables). Then, from complementary slackness and the first-order conditions, $\mathcal{L}_C = 0$, $\mathcal{L}_{K^c_{+1}} = 0$, and $\mathcal{L}_\mu = 0$, it follows that $C = (1-\beta^c)(1+r)K$. Details of this solution can be found in Foley and Michl (1999) and an elaboration of the advantages of using the Lagrangian method versus, for example, dynamic programming, can be found in Chow (1997).

3. The original Cambridge saving equation is written $g = sr$, where s is the capitalist's average propensity to save out of profits. For the variant in the text, the propensity to save out of wealth, β_c, is constant and the average propensity to save out of profits is an increasing function of the rate of profit.

In this equation, $1 + g$ represents the growth factor for capitalist wealth, K^c_{+1}/K^c, or 1 plus its growth rate. We elide any identifying superscript on g to reduce notational clutter.

With the log utility function, we can afford to neglect expectations of future profit rates because substitution and wealth effects always offset one another. Thus, the Cambridge equation describes capitalist saving over any dynamic path taken by the rate of profit.

Pure Legacy Motive

As an alternative, consider a capitalist agent who receives an inheritance, lives for one period, and values her legacy wealth. We are assuming that the agent leaves her wealth to an heir who repeats this behavior. Continuing to assume a logarithmic felicity function, the programming problem is

$$\max\ (1 - \beta_c) \log C + \beta_c \log K_{+1}$$

$$\text{subject to } C + K^c_{+1} \leq (1 + r)K^c$$

$$\text{given } K^c_0, r$$

Once again, we can easily solve this problem using the Lagrangian method. The solution turns out to be identical to the previous problem for an altruistic dynasty of capitalists. Capitalist saving will be described by equation (3.2) or (3.3).

It follows that in this chapter we have no need to write out a special model in order to examine the pure legacy motive. (We should note, however, that the discount factor represents different subjective time preferences in these two treatments; it should always be clear from context which bequest motive is operational.) However, when we take up the issue of government debt in subsequent chapters, this will no longer be true. The altruistic dynasty has an infinite planning horizon and will regard its future taxes servicing the debt as an offset against any government bonds it holds, while the agent motivated by a pure legacy motive has a finite horizon and will ignore future taxes.

3.1.3 Workers

Workers solve a two-period optimization problem, discounting consumption by the factor β_w $(0 < \beta_w < 1)$. The present value of their consumption, comprising spending during their active period, c^w, and spending during retirement, c^r, cannot exceed their lifetime wealth, which comprises their wage. Any saving they achieve during their active period earns interest at the expected market rate r^e. Thus, we write

$$\max\ (1-\beta_w)\log c^w + \beta_w \log c^r$$

$$\text{subject to } c^w + \frac{c^r}{1+r^e} \leq w$$

$$\text{given } K_0^w,\ w,\ r,\ r^e$$

The solution can easily be obtained.[4] During their working period, workers will consume a constant fraction of their lifetime wealth:

$$c^w = (1-\beta_w)w$$

Thanks to the Cobb-Douglas utility function, changes in the expected profit rate do not affect individual worker saving (income and wealth effects just cancel out), which is

$$s^w = w - c^w = w\beta_w$$

Finally, workers consume all their accumulated wealth (including interest at the actual rate of profit) during retirement, completing the worker's consumption demand system:

$$c^r = \beta_w(1+r_{+1})w$$

An expression for aggregate workers' saving, K_{+1}^w, corresponding to equation (3.2) for capitalist saving, can be derived by multiplying individual worker saving, s^w, by employment, N. The aggregate saving of workers is thus

$$K_{+1}^w = \frac{w\beta_w}{k}K \tag{3.4}$$

It is interesting to note that the life-cycle theory of saving, as applied to workers, does not leave any doubt about the hoary question of the worker saving propensity from wages (i.e., β_w) versus from property income (i.e., unity). And the theory does not seem as remote from the experience of real workers as, say, the theory of dynastic capitalist saving does with respect

4. Write the Lagrangian $L = (1-\beta_w)\log c^w + \beta_w \log c^r - \mu(c^w + c^r/(1+r^e) - w)$, where μ is the Lagrangian multiplier. The solution for c^w follows from the first-order conditions, $L_{c^w} = 0$, $L_{c^r} = 0$, and $L_\mu = 0$.

to real capitalists. We now have, in equations (3.1) through (3.4), all the elements for constructing a fully specified growth model, provided we can close the model with an assumption about the labor market.

3.2 Endogenous Growth

The main classical economists, such as Ricardo or Marx, took the real wage to be socially and historically determined by the subsistence or conventional standard of living, as established by the historically given social environment. They believed, each for different reasons, that the supply of labor was highly elastic in the long run, a sentiment captured by the Marx epigraph at the chapter's beginning. For Ricardo, this was true because he accepted a version of the Malthusian population theory. For Marx, the flexibility of labor supply was attributed to the tendency for capitalist economies to generate reserves of underutilized labor (the reserve armies of labor), either by dissolving precapitalist modes of production and proletarianizing the victims or by deracinating workers through labor-saving technical changes.

Modern economists have used a similar approach, most notably in development economics, in which the dual economy model of Arthur Lewis (1954) has influenced generations of economists. Lewis himself explicitly denied that his approach was relevant to developed economies, but there is good reason to think that, to the contrary, it does teach us something about how a developed economy such as the United States operates, at least at the low frequencies of 15 to 25 years appropriate to a growth model. The developed economies of the North have access to the global reserves of labor, many of them located in the less developed South.

Recent research on the effect of immigration on wages in the United States lends qualified support to this interpretation. Studies of immigration and local labor markets find almost uniformly that the wage effects of immigration are small or nonexistent (Borjas 1994, 1697–1700), which is consistent with the hypothesis that immigration is demand induced in the context of a labor surplus economy. Subsequent efforts to rescue the standard model of the labor market in a labor-constrained context have focused on the hypothesis that out-migration by natives smooths out the local effects and requires a general equilibrium approach using time series data. Using that approach, Borjas (2003) has found modest but hardly negligible effects on the wages of low-skilled workers at the aggregate level. Unlike the use of cross sections of local labor markets that have the quality of a natural experiment with areas unaffected by immigration serving as controls, time series methods require strong assumptions about the control. The relative wage of low-skilled (high school education or less) has remained roughly constant over a period of rising immigrant density in the United States, leading Card (2006) to observe that "while the counterfactual is unknown, it is hard to argue that the aggregate time series evidence points to a negative impact of immigration unless one starts from that position *a priori*" (2006, 25).

In addition, economies like the United States have historically been able to grow by tapping into the web of internal noncapitalist activities, notably the unpaid labor of women in the home, that Marglin (1997), in an endorsement of the endogenous approach, calls "social migration." There are some reasons to believe that this and other sources of labor reserve may continue to play an important role in supporting growth (Cesaratto 2005, ch. 8).

The viewpoint that labor constraints are not decisively binding in the long run has also been explicitly adopted by some Keynesian economists, such as Kaldor (1996) or Thirlwall (2002), and stands in the background implicitly for many others. There is a distinct niche for the endogenous growth model in the classical-Keynesian tradition.

With the assumption that the labor force adjusts to satisfy the demand for workers, the wage is determined exogenously and we close the growth model with

$$w = \bar{w} \tag{3.5}$$

One can imagine that $\bar{w}$ represents the reservation wage attached to a horizontal labor supply function. Or we might argue that the distribution of income is regulated by social, political, and economic forces that are separate from the forces regulating price formation. In a more realistic setting with technical change, the assumption of a fixed conventional wage is observationally inconsistent with the visible tendency for wages to rise more or less *pro tanto* with labor productivity, at least over most long historical periods. In a model with technical change, a more appropriate assumption suggested by Foley and Michl (1999) is that of a conventional wage share.

As important as this assumption is to the endogenous growth models, the main point in its favor is the sheer fact that the profit and wage shares are remarkably constant over time and across countries.[5] We might rely on the theory of imperfect competition to provide some support for a belief in the stability of the markup over costs that can help explain the empirical constancy of the profit share, but that only begs the question of why the underlying factors identified by that theory, chiefly the elasticity of product demand, should be so stable.[6] In the end, we are no farther along than we were in 1942 when Joan Robinson wrote that "the mystery of the constant relative shares remains as a reproach to theoretical economics" (1942, 81).

Equations (3.1) and (3.5) fully determine the wage rate and profit rate. Let us denote these variables as w and r (without the bar) with the understanding that in the endogenous growth model they are postulates of the model.

3.2.1 Dynamics of Capital Accumulation

Capitalist saving and worker saving, equations (3.2) and (3.4), form a dynamic system of first-order difference equations. Using boldface to indicate vectors (lowercase letters) and matrices (uppercase letters), the system is compactly represented by[7]

$$\tilde{\mathbf{k}}_{+1} = \mathbf{A}\tilde{\mathbf{k}}$$

where $\tilde{\mathbf{k}}' = (K^c, K^w)$ and

$$\mathbf{A} = \begin{pmatrix} \beta_c(1+r) & 0 \\ \frac{w\beta_w}{k} & \frac{w\beta_w}{k} \end{pmatrix}$$

5. See Chapter 11 for more discussion of variations across countries. Over time, "constancy" should not be taken too literally. It is well known that the 1970s was a period of rising wage shares (profit squeeze) in the advanced capitalist countries, and there is now substantial evidence that the period since 1980 has been characterized by falling wage shares, both among advanced countries (Carter 2007) and on a global scale (International Monetary Fund 2007).

6. The *locus classicus* for this explanation of the stability of the profit share is Kalecki (1971), whose theory has been criticized for its tautological character, for example, by Kaldor (1956) and by Joan Robinson in the location cited in the text. Besides the marginalist explanation based on the Cobb-Douglas form of the production function, discussed in Chapters 10 and 11, an alternative technological explanation invokes the theory of induced technical change (Duménil and Lévy 1995; Foley 2003).

7. Again, readers seeking guidance on the mathematics of dynamic systems are urged to consult Gandolfo (1997) or Elaydi (2005).

The characteristic equation of this system is

$$(\beta_c(1+r)-\lambda)(\frac{w\beta_w}{k}-\lambda)=0$$

with eigenvalues λ_1 and λ_2 having obvious solutions at

$$\lambda_1=\beta_c(1+r) \qquad \lambda_2=\frac{w\beta_w}{k}$$

We can see immediately that the nature of this model depends on which eigenvalue is dominant. The first eigenvalue is equivalently the steady state growth factor, $1+g$. It should not go unnoticed that λ_1 represents the justly famous Cambridge equation.

Two-Class Solution: $\lambda_1 > \lambda_2$

The two-class model requires $\lambda_1 > \lambda_2$. Out of respect for the pioneers of modern classical economic theory, we will call this the Kaldor-Pasinetti-Robinson regime. If this condition is violated, the saving of a thrifty working class will eclipse that of the capitalists, whose wealth will thus become vanishingly irrelevant. The maximum value of the worker discount factor consistent with a two-class steady state solution, $\bar{\beta}_w$, is an increasing function of the capitalist saving propensity, or using $w/k=R-r$,

$$\bar{\beta}_w=\frac{\beta_c(1+r)}{R-r}$$

Assuming that $\beta_w < \bar{\beta}_w$ and starting from an arbitrary initial condition, (K_0^c, K_0^w), the system will converge monotonically on the eigenvector associated with the dominant eigenvalue, λ_1. By normalizing this eigenvector on $K^c=1$, it is clear that its second element represents the distribution of wealth. Define the workers' share of capital by

$$\phi=\frac{K^w}{K}$$

The second element then becomes $\phi^*/(1-\phi^*)$, where the asterisk represents the steady state value of a variable.

We can highlight the distribution of wealth by recasting the system around the total capital stock, $K=K^c+K^w$, and the vector $\mathbf{k}'=(K, K^w)$. The system is now written

$$\mathbf{k}_{+1}=\mathbf{Bk}$$

where $\mathbf{B} = \mathbf{PAP}^{-1}$ using the permutation matrix

$$\mathbf{P} = \begin{pmatrix} 1 & 1 \\ 0 & 1 \end{pmatrix}$$

Since **A** and **B** are similar, they have the same eigenvalues. The normalized eigenvector associated with λ_1, which we can call $\mathbf{k}^*$, will be given by $(1, \phi^*)$ where

$$\phi^* = \frac{\lambda_2}{\lambda_1} = \frac{w\beta_w}{\beta_c(1+r)k}$$

The dynamic behavior of this system can easily be visualized in Figure 3.1. Starting from some initial level and distribution of capital, the trajectory of the system will take it on a journey that converges on the eigenvector $\mathbf{k}^*$. In subsequent chapters, as we complicate the model by adding various fiscal policies, we will see that such extensions can be analyzed fruitfully in terms of their impacts on these matrices, their eigenvalues/vectors, and the dynamics they beget.

Another way of representing the dynamics of this model is to focus on the behavior of the distribution of wealth. Dividing the second row of **Bk** by the first row, we arrive at the nonlinear first-order difference equation for ϕ, which simplifies to

$$\phi_{+1} = \frac{\phi^*}{\phi^* + (1-\phi)}$$

This equation has fixed points at ϕ^* and 1. The former is stable, since at $\phi = \phi^*$ it is easy to show that $d\phi_{+1}/d\phi = \phi^*$, which is less than unity by assumption. Since the workers' share of capital cannot exceed 1, the system must be (almost) globally stable: starting from any initial value ($\neq 1$), the system will converge on ϕ^*. It is also easy to see from Figure 3.2a that the convergence will be monotonic, with no overshooting or alternations.

One-Class Solution: $\lambda_2 > \lambda_1$

The other possible solution will converge asymptotically on a one-class equilibrium with $\phi = 1$. Out of respect for the seminal contributions of two eponymous neoclassical economists, we will call this a Samuelson-Modigliani regime. This configuration is illustrated in Figure 3.2b.

In this case, the fixed point at $\phi^* > 1$ will be unstable, and the system will converge on its other fixed point, which is clearly a stable equilibrium

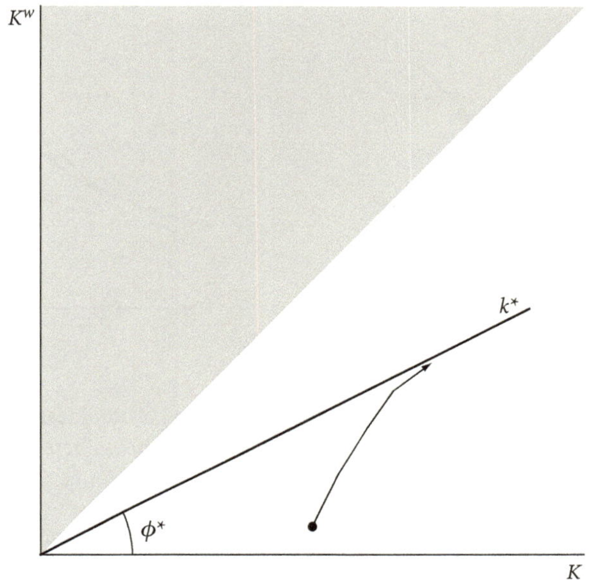

Figure 3.1 The eigenvector $\mathbf{k}^*$ associated with the dominant eigenvalue (i.e., the Cambridge equation) will function as the attractor in the two-class regime. Its slope measures the steady state workers' share of capital wealth. The arrow identifies a representative path taken from some initial level and distribution of capital. (The shaded area is not economically meaningful since workers' capital cannot exceed total capital.)

point because $d\phi_{+1}/d\phi = 1/\phi^* < 1$ evaluated at $\phi = 1$. A thrifty working class will eventually own all the capital wealth. In terms of Figure 3.1, the dominant eigenvector will lie along the 45-degree line that borders the shaded area.

For completeness, we should also consider the nonhyperbolic equilibrium point that occurs when $\phi^* = 1$. In this case, the difference equation will be tangential to the 45-degree line in the phase diagram. Mathematically, this case is regarded as unstable (Elaydi 2005, 29), but it is actually stable from the left, which has an economically meaningful interpretation since $\phi > 1$ is not economically possible. In other words, from an economic standpoint, it is stable.

We will focus on the two-class solution to the near exclusion of the one-class regime, as befits the classical-Keynesian vision of capitalist economies. One justification for this asymmetric treatment is that the one-class regime

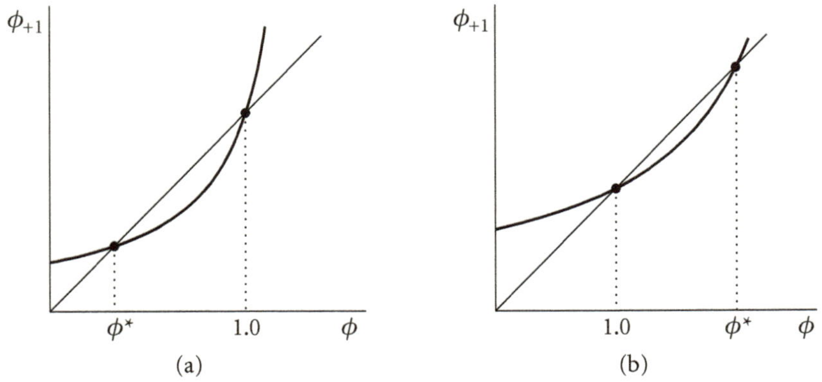

Figure 3.2 The workers' share of capital wealth obeys a nonlinear first-order difference equation in the endogenous growth model, shown here on the phase diagram. The stable equilibrium point is the first point of contact with the 45-degree line. (a) The two-class, or Kaldor-Pasinetti-Robinson regime, prevails when $\phi^* < 1$. (b) The one-class, or Samuelson-Modigliani regime, prevails when $\phi^* > 1$.

arguably is observationally inconsistent (Michl and Foley 2004) with the statistical and historical record of modern capitalist economies.

3.2.2 Comparative Dynamics

To conduct a comparative equilibrium analysis of alternative steady states, one could work with the equations in the previous section directly. Sticking closely to the two-class regime as promised, the most important results are given by the signs of the derivatives:

$$\frac{d\phi^*}{d\beta_c} < 0 \qquad \frac{dg^*}{d\beta_c} > 0$$

$$\frac{d\phi^*}{d\beta_w} > 0 \qquad \frac{dg^*}{d\beta_w} = 0$$

These relations illustrate in inverted form what Luigi Pasinetti has called the Cambridge theorem, and what others have dubbed the Pasinetti paradox. Changes in the worker propensity to save have no effect on the long-run growth rate; they can affect only the distribution of capital. The long-run dynamics are controlled through the Cambridge equation. (The Cambridge theorem states that given the growth rate, the rate of profit is determined by the capitalist saving propensity, independently of worker saving. We will encounter this theorem in the next section.)

One way to visualize these results is to consider the relationship between growth and the distribution of wealth implied by the capitalist and worker saving functions, each taken separately. Dividing equations (3.2) and (3.4) by K, and using the fact that $K = K_{+1}/(1 + g_K)$ by definition, we recover the general relationship. By substituting in the steady state growth rate, g^*, we recover the particular relationship between the distribution of wealth and growth consistent with capitalist and worker saving behavior. In the case of capitalist saving, it is clear that the relationship collapses to the Cambridge equation. The distribution of wealth consistent with capitalist saving behavior (call it $\tilde{\phi}$) can be any number ($\neq 1$) between 0 and 1. In the case of workers, the distribution of wealth consistent with worker saving behavior (call it $\hat{\phi}$) is given by

$$\hat{\phi} = \frac{\beta_w}{1 + g^*}(R - r)$$

The steady state equilibrium is formed by the equality, $\tilde{\phi}(g^*) = \hat{\phi}(g^*)$, giving us a tool for visualizing the comparative dynamics. Figure 3.3 illustrates how increases in the capitalist and worker saving propensities

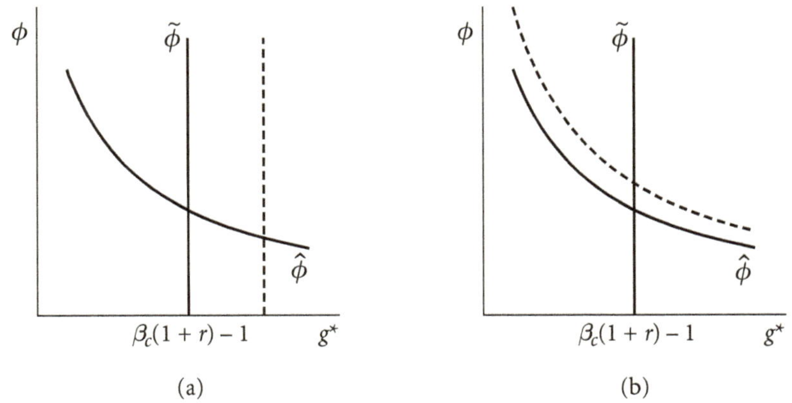

Figure 3.3 The steady state in the endogenous growth model with a two-class equilibrium. (a) An increase in the capitalist propensity to save, β_c, shifts out the $\tilde{\phi}$ function representing wealth distributions consistent with capitalist saving (the Cambridge equation). Accumulation rises and the workers' share of wealth declines. (b) An increase in the workers propensity to save, β_w, shifts out the $\hat{\phi}$ function representing wealth distributions consistent with worker saving. This increases the workers' share of wealth. The rate of accumulation remains constant in accordance with the Cambridge theorem.

affect the steady state. This graphical apparatus will serve us well in subsequent chapters when we consider fiscal complications.

3.3 Exogenous Growth

At the other extreme stands the traditional closure for growth models, in which the labor force is predetermined and fully employed by assumption. A typical implementation is that the workforce grows at a constant rate, called the natural rate of growth, n. Under the Leontief technology, a necessary condition for full employment is that the capital stock must also grow at the natural rate,[8] so that we can complete the growth model by the equation

$$g_K = n \tag{3.6}$$

In this case, we are in the realm of exogenous growth, in which labor constraints are decisive. How can a capitalist economy possibly achieve the precise amount of growth required by equation (3.6)? That question was famously posed by Roy Harrod. The two-class growth model emerged as one answer in the writings of Nicholas Kaldor, Joan Robinson, and Luigi Pasinetti. Changes in the distribution of income, operating mainly through the Cambridge equation, can enforce this equality.

It is worth reflecting in advance on what we can and cannot hope to learn from an exogenous growth model of this type. A good starting point is Pasinetti (1974, 119), who regarded models of this type "as a logical framework to answer interesting questions about what *ought* to happen if full employment is to be kept over time, more than as a behavioral theory expressing what actually happens." In the present context, we impose full employment on a model even when it is not necessarily in a fully adjusted steady state by asserting that there must be some underlying economic process that could render this possible by means of changes in income distribution sufficient to maintain accumulation at the natural rate. In an overlapping generations setting, this requires that the amount of investment in the current period adjust to the growth of labor resources, despite the evident fact that any imbalance between capital and labor will not manifest itself until the next period. Far from being an argument that full employment is the

8. The necessary and sufficient condition is that the capital stock is at all times large enough to fully employ the given workforce N^s, or $K = N^s/k$.

natural condition under capitalist development, this kind of model raises troubling questions about what the nature of the economic process could be that would fulfill these requirements. The neoclassical theorists have made their own lives easy by routinely adopting the assumption of a well-behaved production function that sweeps all these difficult questions under the rug, asserting in effect that we can never have too much or too little capital. This may be the most damaging aspect of the uncritical use of this theoretical metaphor.

Economists working in the classical tradition do not routinely assert that the economies they are studying are in a state of perpetual equilibrium. The best historical investigations in this tradition, such as Duménil and Lévy (2004), Brenner (2002), or Armstrong et al. (1991), artfully journey back and forth between the concrete details of material life and the abstractions of theory. By imposing the assumption that the economies they study remain in an equilibrium state, neoclassical economists cannot help but overlook the social tension and drama that punctuate the processes of over- and under accumulation and economic development.

3.3.1 Temporary Equilibrium

In any given period, the capital stock and its distribution are inherited from the past and can be treated as predetermined variables. By using equations (3.2), (3.4), and (3.6), we can derive an expression for the income distribution needed to sustain growth at the natural rate. This expression, together with equation (3.1), the wage-profit curve, form the compact system

$$\begin{pmatrix} \frac{\beta_w}{k} & \beta_c(1-\phi) \\ 1 & k \end{pmatrix} \begin{pmatrix} w \\ r \end{pmatrix} = \begin{pmatrix} \psi \\ y \end{pmatrix}$$

where $\psi = 1 + n - \beta_c(1-\phi)$ is just a consolidating term and $y = x - \delta k$ represents net output per worker. We will call the matrix on the left-hand side of this expression **C**. It is useful to realize that the determinant of **C** governs the sign of the derivative of g_K with respect to w. This derivative plays an important substantive role in Stephen Marglin's critique of the standard OG model of growth. Marglin (1984) argues that without an elasticity of substitution (weakly) greater than 1, this derivative will be positive, a sign that does not conform to standard intuition about labor market stability. (If $g_K > n$, we would expect an excess demand for labor to emerge, driving up wages, and reducing accumulation in order to maintain balanced growth.) The two-class model solves this problem by asserting capitalist control over the accumulation process, as discussed in Michl (2007). In the present setting, we have

$$\frac{dg_K}{dw} = \frac{1}{k}(\beta_w - \beta_c(1-\phi)) = \frac{1}{k}\,|\mathbf{C}|$$

and we can appeal to the labor market stability condition to assert that

$$|\mathbf{C}| < 0$$

The equilibrium rate of profit and wage rate follow by applying Cramer's rule:

$$r = \frac{\frac{\beta_w y}{k} - \psi}{|\mathbf{C}|}$$

$$w = \frac{\psi k - y\beta_c(1-\phi)}{|\mathbf{C}|}$$

These expressions can be used to recover the equations governing the sequence of temporary equilibria over time.

3.3.2 Dynamics of Wealth Distribution

From equations (3.4) and (3.6), we can pin down the motion of the workers' share of wealth, and substituting the temporary equilibrium wage just derived gives us the equation of motion for the workers' wealth share:

$$\phi_{+1} = \frac{\beta_w}{1+n}\left(\frac{1+n-\beta_c(1+R)(1-\phi)}{\beta_w - \beta_c(1-\phi)}\right) \tag{3.7}$$

This is a first-order autonomous nonlinear difference equation. Equation (3.7) has fixed points at

$$\phi = 1$$

and

$$\phi^\dagger = \frac{\beta_w(1+R)}{1+n} - \frac{\beta_w}{\beta_c}$$

The former solution represents the "no capitalists," or one-class, case. The equation of motion for workers' wealth generates two qualitatively different regimes. In a Samuelson-Modigliani regime, the one-class economy constitutes the steady state. In a Kaldor-Pasinetti-Robinson regime, the steady state is the two-class economy, with $\phi^* = \phi^\dagger$ and $0 < \phi^\dagger < 1$. Let us consider each of these cases in turn. They are distinguished in the first instance by the thriftiness of workers in relationship to the critical value of the worker discount factor,

$$\bar{\beta}_w = \frac{1+n}{1+R}$$

that separates the one- and two-class regimes.

In both cases, we can make use of the condition for $\phi^\dagger < 1$, which is

$$\beta_w < \frac{\beta_c(1+n)}{\beta_c(1+R) - (1+n)} \quad (3.8)$$

In the one-class regime, this turns out to be a stability condition, and in the two-class regime, it turns out to be useful for characterizing the effect of a demographic shock.

One-Class Solution: $\beta_w > (1+n)/(1+R)$

This is a necessary condition for the Samuelson-Modigliani regime. When it prevails, the difference equation slopes upward in the phase diagram and cuts the 45-degree line twice, first from below and then from above, with one intersection at $\phi = 1$ (see Figure 3.4a). If the first intersection lies below 1, then this point will be asymptotically unstable and the system will converge on $\phi = 1$. This is the realm of a Samuelson-Modigliani economy (Samuelson and Modigliani 1966), in which worker saving ultimately overwhelms capitalist saving, collapsing the class structure of accumulation.

It is worth reflecting on the economic meaning of an upward sloping difference equation. Starting from some initial value, ϕ will increase monotonically over time in this case. Why? The share of capital owned by workers, ϕ, represents the wealth of retirees, which is destined for consumption under the life-cycle theory of saving. Thus, when the share of worker-owned wealth increases, it implies a higher level of retiree consumption. In order to maintain capital accumulation at the natural rate, there must be a compensating change in the distribution of income that favors saving. In the one-class regime, accumulation is wage led so the compensating change must take the form of a wage increase. Since this further shifts resources toward life-cycle saving, it results in a further increase in the workers' share

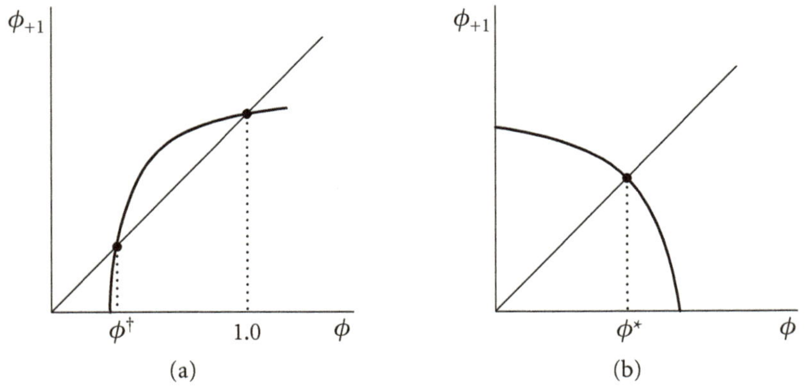

Figure 3.4 Phase diagrams for two regimes in the exogenous growth model. (a) The one-class, or Samuelson-Modigliani solution at $\phi^* = 1$ is the point of attraction when $\beta_w > (1+n)/(1+R)$. The fixed point at $\phi^{\dagger}$ is not stable. (b) The two-class, or Kaldor-Pasinetti-Robinson regime prevails when $\beta_w < (1+n)/(1+R)$. The steady state occurs at $\phi^* = \phi^{\dagger}$.

of wealth in the next period. This story line raises Marglin's question of the plausibility of the labor market dynamics, since the change in distribution has been initiated by an incipient excess *supply* of labor (too little investment to keep up with population growth).

We can formalize this point by setting $|\mathbf{C}| > 0$ and substituting $\phi^{\dagger}$. From this we recover the necessary condition for the one-class regime, $\beta_w > (1+n)/(1+R)$.

The difference equation (3.7) is governed by the condition for asymptotic (local) stability, $\left|d\phi_{+1}/d\phi\right| < 1$ (the nonhyperbolic case when this derivative equals 1 is discussed below). Evaluated at $\phi = 1$, this condition requires

$$\beta_w(\beta_c(1+R) - (1+n)) < \beta_c(1+n)$$

which is, of course, condition (3.8) restated. This implies that the stable values for the two saving propensities are

$$\text{for } \beta_c < \frac{1+n}{1+R} \qquad \beta_w > \frac{\beta_c(1+n)}{\beta_c(1+R) - (1+n)}$$

$$\text{for } \beta_c > \frac{1+n}{1+R} \qquad \beta_w < \frac{\beta_c(1+n)}{\beta_c(1+R) - (1+n)}$$

With an upward sloping difference equation, there are just four possibilities, depending on the placement of $\phi^\dagger$:

1. When $\beta_c \leq (1+n)/(1+R)$, the first intersection of the 45-degree line occurs at $\phi^\dagger \leq 0$. The intersection at $\phi = 1$ clearly represents a stable equilibrium for any permitted value of β_w.
2. When $\beta_c > (1+n)/(1+R)$, and $0 < \phi^\dagger < 1$, the fixed point at $\phi = 1$ remains a stable equilibrium.
3. When $\phi^\dagger = 1$, the difference equation is nonhyperbolic, and the equilibrium point will be unstable (Elaydi 2005, 29).
4. When $\phi^\dagger > 1$, the fixed point at $\phi = 1$ is unstable. Thus condition (3.8) is a stability condition.

The fact that saving is wage-led also points toward the feasibility of the steady state. It must be possible to achieve a wage sufficient to support the natural rate of growth. Substituting $\phi = 1$ and solving for w yields $w = (1+n)k/\beta_w$. The feasibility condition that $w \leq x$ then requires

$$\beta_w \geq \frac{1+n}{\rho} \tag{3.9}$$

Figure 3.5a illustrates the space of stable (and feasible) parameter values for the Samuelson-Modigliani one-class regime. As we have seen, the labor market stability requirement, $|\mathbf{C}| < 0$, cannot prevail at or near the stable equilibrium, calling the one-class model into question as an economically meaningful representation of capitalist society. This does not mean that the one-class model lacks entirely in theoretical value, however. We will see in subsequent chapters that it provides a useful benchmark case for studying the interface between the conventional neoclassical literature on the overlapping generations model (which is, after all, almost exclusively devoted to the one-class case) and the classical model. One can always invoke some sort of benevolent dictator assumption to overcome the theoretical incoherence of the one-class model.[9]

9. In fairness, we should point out that the standard neoclassical resolution to this problem is to posit a sufficiently large "elasticity of substitution of capital for labor" in the well-behaved production function, as is explained by de la Croix and Michel (2002), Marglin (1984), and Taylor (2004).

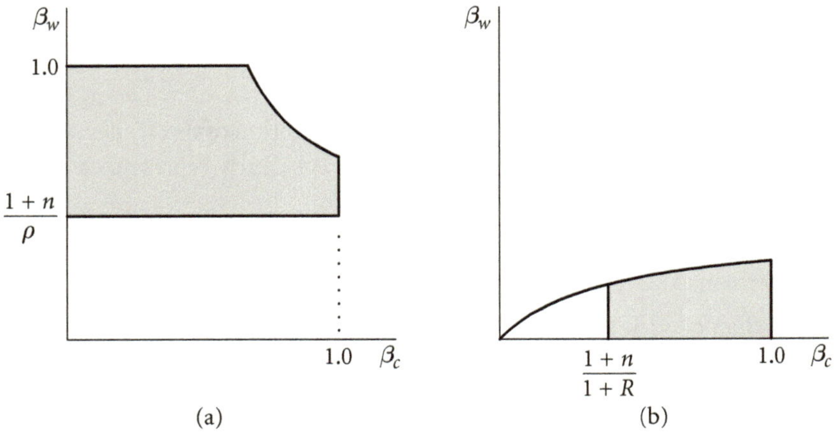

Figure 3.5 The space of saving propensities that support an asymptotically stable equilibrium in the two cases of the exogenous growth model. (a) In the one-class, or Samuelson-Modigliani, regime. (b) In the two-class, or Kaldor-Pasinetti-Robinson, regime.

Two-Class Solution: $\beta_w < (1+n)/(1+R)$

This is a necessary condition for the Kaldor-Pasinetti-Robinson regime. We will use the notation $\bar{\beta}_w$ to identify this first-line boundary for the two-class regime. The economically relevant steady state occurs at $\phi^* = \phi^\dagger$. Figure 3.4b illustrates the properties of equation (3.7) in the phase diagram under the assumption that this condition prevails. Clearly, this difference equation gives rise to cycles, or to be more precise, alternations. This kind of motion is not particularly appealing or intuitive, but it is not uncommon in overlapping generations models (de la Croix and Michel 2002).

Again, it is worth reflecting on the underlying economic meaning of these alternations and the negatively sloped difference equation. When workers own more than the steady state share of wealth, we know that consumption by retirees will tend to be high as well. In order to maintain capital accumulation at the natural rate, there must be a compensating change in the distribution of income that favors saving. In the two-class regime, accumulation is profit led so the compensating change must take the form of low profits and high wages relative to steady state values. Since this shifts resources away from life-cycle saving, it results in a subsequent decline in the workers' share of wealth in the next period. (Obviously, this process now repeats itself in reverse from this point, and we get alternations.) This story line invokes quite plausible labor market dynamics, since the decline in wages has been initiated by an incipient excess supply of labor (too little investment to keep up with population growth). We can formalize this point by setting $|\mathbf{C}| < 0$ and substituting $\phi^{\dagger}$. From this we recover the necessary condition for the two-class regime, $\beta_w < (1+n)/(1+R)$.

It follows from the definition of $\phi^{\dagger}$ that for a solution with positive workers' wealth, $\phi^* > 0$, we must have

$$\beta_c > \frac{1+n}{1+R} \tag{3.10}$$

A solution with positive workers' wealth requires that capitalists save enough to generate the natural rate of growth even when they receive less than the maximal rate of profit.

In addition, it is clear that condition (3.8) for $\phi^{\dagger} < 1$ must be satisfied (workers cannot own more wealth than exists). This restriction will obviously be satisfied by virtue of the condition for the two-class regime, $\beta_w < (1+n)/(1+R)$.

Asymptotic (local) stability at $\phi^* = \phi^{\dagger}$ in the two-class regime requires

$$\beta_w < \frac{\beta_c(1+n)}{\beta_c(1+R)+(1+n)} \tag{3.11}$$

This restriction will dominate the necessary condition for a two-class regime. For $\beta_c = 1$, the right-hand side becomes $(1+n)/(2+R+n)$, which is clearly less than $(1+n)/(1+R)$; for $\beta_c = 0$, the right-hand side is zero; and the right-hand expression increases monotonically between these two points. Figure 3.5b illustrates the boundaries of the space of saving propensities defining asymptotically stable two-class equilibria with positive ϕ^*.

One final issue concerns the sequence $\{\phi_t\}_0^{\infty}$. We need to rule out paths that include any negative values, or ensure that $\inf\{\phi\} \geq 0$. Therefore, it is necessary that $0 \leq \phi_0 \leq \bar{\phi}$, where

$$\bar{\phi} = 1 - \frac{\beta_c(1+R)}{1+n}$$

The role of $\bar{\phi}$, the zero value of equation (3.7), is to rule out a negative value for ϕ_1. It is easy to show that as an added bonus this condition also implies that the labor market operates along conventional lines, or to show that $|\mathbf{C}| < 0$ is satisfied even if ϕ_0 is as large as $\bar{\phi}$.

But the workers' wealth share also must stay within these limits, which means that $\sup\{\phi\} < \bar{\phi}$. If this can be ensured, we will have also established a sufficient condition for $\inf\{\phi\} \geq 0$. Consider the boundary case represented by the sequence $\{\bar{\phi}, 0, \phi_2, \ldots\}$. Clearly, for this path to be viable, it is required that $\phi_2 < \bar{\phi}$. (The inequality must be strict to rule out an endless 2-cycle.) Substituting from equation (3.7) and using the definition of $\bar{\phi}$, we find that

$$\beta_w < \frac{\beta_c(1+n)}{\beta_c(1+R) + (1+n)}$$

which is just the asymptotic stability condition (3.11). Thus, provided the system is asymptotically stable, we can be sure that it will stay within the limits over the first two iterations. The same argument can then be repeated to prove by induction that it will stay within the limits indefinitely.

We also want assurance that the system converges on the steady state value, ϕ^*, or that

$$\limsup_{t\to\infty} \phi = \liminf_{t\to\infty} \phi = \phi^*$$

Fortunately, this is not hard to show because equation (3.7) is in the form of a Riccati equation and can be transformed into a second-order linear difference equation that is solvable (Elaydi 2005, 100–101). First, rearrange the equation to bring out its Riccati form:

$$\phi_{+1} = \frac{\mathcal{A}\phi + \mathcal{B}}{\mathcal{C}\phi + \mathcal{D}}$$

where $\mathcal{A}$, $\mathcal{B}$, $\mathcal{C}$, and $\mathcal{D}$ are consolidating terms.[10] Then define a new variable

$$\frac{v_{+1}}{v} = \mathcal{C}\phi + \mathcal{D}$$

This variable obeys a linear second-order difference equation,

$$v_{+2} + p_1 v_{+1} + p_2 v = 0$$

10. In other words, $\mathcal{A} = \beta_w\beta_c(1+R)$, $\mathcal{B} = \beta_w(1+n) - \beta_w\beta_c(1+R)$, $\mathcal{C} = \beta_c(1+n)$, and $\mathcal{D} = \beta_w(1+n) - \beta_c(1+n)$.

where

$$p_1 = -(\mathcal{A} + \mathcal{D})$$
$$p_2 = \mathcal{A}\mathcal{D} - \mathcal{B}\mathcal{C}$$

(We need to ensure that $p_2 \neq 0$ by ruling out the singular case where $\beta_w = (1+n)/(1+R)$.) Solving this equation for its characteristic roots gives

$$\lambda_1 = \beta_c(\beta_w(1+R) - (1+n))$$
$$\lambda_2 = \beta_w(1+n)$$

In the two-class case, it is easy to show that the stability condition (3.11) is necessary and sufficient to establish that $|\lambda_1| > |\lambda_2|$, or that λ_1 is the dominant root.[11] The solution to the transformed system is

$$v_t = A_1\lambda_1^t + A_2\lambda_2^t$$

where A_i are constants that can be definitized by the initial conditions.

Substituting in the definition of v, we obtain the solution to the original system:

$$\phi_t = \frac{A_1\lambda_1^{t+1} + A_2\lambda_2^{t+1}}{\mathcal{C}A_1\lambda_1^t + \mathcal{C}A_2\lambda_2^t} - \frac{\mathcal{D}}{\mathcal{C}}$$

By multiplying through the numerator and denominator of the first fractional term by $1/\lambda_1^t$, and using the fact that λ_1 is the dominant root (which makes $(\lambda_2/\lambda_1)^t$ vanish as $t \to \infty$), we can see that ϕ converges:

$$\lim_{t\to\infty} \phi_t = (\lambda_1 - \mathcal{D})/\mathcal{C} = \phi^*$$

Thus, the initial condition $0 \leq \phi_0 \leq \bar{\phi}$ defines the basin of attraction for this system, provided the stability condition is also satisfied.

Figure 3.5b sums all this up by showing the economically relevant space for a two-class steady state.[12] When the two panels are overlayed on one another (they have been scaled to make this possible), it is clear that this general model not only has the two reasonably well-behaved regimes that we

11. In the one-class case, these roles are reversed and λ_2 will be dominant, offering us one more way to see the class structure reflected in the mathematical structure of the roots of a dynamical system.

12. For discussion of the feasibility condition that $w < x$, see Michl (2007).

have described but also a kind of no-man's-land of instability. The boundaries in the two-class case instruct us that given a capitalist propensity to save sufficient to support growth at the natural rate, an increase in worker saving will eventually jeopardize the stability of the two-class model.

3.3.3 Comparative Dynamics

It remains to consider the effects of changes in underlying parameters on the steady state equilibrium. We will restrict the investigation to the two-class model. The steady state distribution of wealth is given by $\phi^* = \phi^\dagger$.

The steady state distribution of income can be found easily by applying the Cambridge equation, equation (3.3). In a steady state, capitalist wealth must grow at the natural rate, which gives us the steady state profit rate, r^*:

$$r^* = \frac{1+n}{\beta_c} - 1$$

and the steady state wage rate, w^*, follows from equation (3.1).

Saving Propensities

As in the endogenous growth model above, let us write out the signs of the relevant derivatives, which are easily obtained from the equations describing the steady state solution:

$$\frac{d\phi^*}{d\beta_c} > 0 \qquad \frac{dr*}{d\beta_c} < 0$$

$$\frac{d\phi^*}{d\beta_w} > 0 \qquad \frac{dr*}{d\beta_w} = 0$$

We can visualize the steady state as we did earlier by focusing on the relations between the distribution of wealth and the steady state profit rate implied by the workers' and capitalists' saving equations, each taken separately. In the case of the capitalists, the function connecting the distribution of wealth to the rate of profit, $\tilde{\phi}(r^*))$, degenerates to the Cambridge equation. Any distribution of wealth is consistent with this equation.

In the case of workers, the distribution of wealth consistent with any given rate of profit, $\hat{\phi}$, will be given by

$$\hat{\phi} = \frac{\beta_w}{1+n}(R - r^*)$$

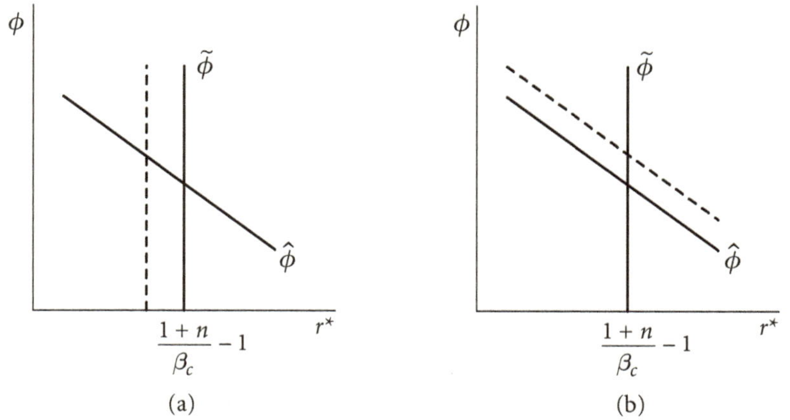

Figure 3.6 The steady state in the exogenous growth model. (a) An increase in the capitalist propensity to save, β_c, shifts inward the $\tilde{\phi}$ function representing wealth distributions consistent with capitalist saving (the Cambridge equation). The rate of profit falls and the workers' share of wealth rises. (b) An increase in the workers' propensity to save, β_w, shifts out the $\hat{\phi}$ function representing wealth distributions consistent with workers' saving. The workers' share of wealth increases while the rate of profit remains constant in accordance with the Cambridge theorem.

Graphing these functions in Figure 3.6 provides a handy apparatus that fixes visually the basis for the pattern of signs above. It seems evident that an increase in the worker saving propensity should raise the workers' share of wealth. But it may not be quite so intuitive that an increase in the capitalist saving propensity should have the same effect. The underlying reason is immediately obvious from the figure: a higher capitalist propensity to save lowers the rate of profit and raises the wage, and this supports more worker saving.

As in the endogenous growth model, the Cambridge theorem remains central to understanding the two-class model. In the exogenous growth model, the rate of profit is determined by the natural rate of growth, independent of worker saving (which does, as before, affect the distribution of wealth if not the distribution of income). This theorem, we shall see in subsequent chapters, continues to play a central role even when the model is complicated by the existence of a fiscal system, debt, and taxes. The two-class models outlined in this chapter provide sturdy platforms from which to launch an investigation of fiscal policy and other issues in macroeconomic theory.

Demographic Shock

As a final comparative equilibrium drill, consider a demographic shock, an important issue given the widespread concern over declining fertility and population growth in the advanced countries, and elsewhere. The relevant effects are summarized by

$$\frac{d\phi^*}{dn} > 0 \qquad \frac{dr*}{dn} > 0 \qquad \frac{dw^*}{dn} < 0$$

A demographic shock will put upward pressure on wages and reduce the rate of profit, resulting in an increase in the share of capital wealth owned by workers. Will this make workers better off? The answer is not obvious since workers care not only about their wage but also about the return they receive on their retirement saving.

Consider $V(c^w(w), c^r(w, r))$, the indirect utility function of the representative worker, where consumption levels satisfy the worker's consumption demand system (i.e., consumption functions for c^w and c^r). Restricting the system to steady state positions and differentiating V yields the following condition for a demographic shock to be welfare improving:

$$\frac{dV}{dn} < 0 \Leftrightarrow \beta_w < \frac{1+n}{\beta_c(1+R) - (1+n)}$$

We can see from this condition that it is possible in principle for workers to be made worse off by a decline in the natural rate of growth only if they care sufficiently about future consumption, as reflected in a discount factor large enough to violate the inequality above. But this inequality, like condition (3.8) for a workers' wealth share below unity, must be satisfied since it is dominated by the necessary condition for the two-class regime. We conclude that in the two-class regime a decline in the natural rate of growth must always be welfare improving in the steady state for workers under laissez-faire conditions. We will see later that this statement needs to be qualified in the presence of some fiscal policies, such as a public pension system.

As a matter of algebra, from the Cambridge equation it is clear at a glance that a decline in the natural rate of growth could be accommodated, partially or wholly, by a decline in the capitalist saving propensity, β_c. Indeed, in the basic (classless) Ramsey-Cass-Koopmans growth model, the representative household will reduce its saving rate so that the steady state rate of profit remains equal to its pure rate of time preference.[13] With fewer children to provide for, there is simply less need for saving. As Baker et al. (2005) point out, this strong result assumes that each new family member contributes the same to family welfare as the existing members; there is no diminishing marginal utility to family size. By including diminishing returns to family size, they show that a lower natural rate of growth will reduce the rate of profit, but by less than it would in the present model. Thus, even with this emendation, the comparative equilibrium results above could be jeopardized. Having duly noted this complaint, we need not pursue the issue further as it requires investing the dynastic fiction with more credibility than it perhaps deserves. From the perspective of the capitalist with a pure legacy motive, of course, there is no obvious reason to believe a change in the natural rate of growth would prompt a recalibration of the discount (saving) rate. One can also question the social and political stability of the combined effects of slower population growth and a lower capitalist propensity to save, which necessarily implies greater polarization in the distribution of consumption, even as the distribution of income remains invariant. We will conduct further explorations of the comparative dynamics of a demographic shock under the conditional assumption that the capitalist saving propensity remains fixed.

3.4 Intuition and Alternative Closures

The endogenous and exogenous growth models present very different aspects of the accumulation process. One might be tempted to embrace an Aristotelian mean between them, but it seems likely that an economy sharing properties of both of these models would respond to parameter changes through some combination of distributional shifts and changes in growth, making growth endogenous as that term is understood by economists; being partially exogenous compares to being partially pregnant. For this reason, the order of exposition in this book (as well as the order of investigation that preceded it) runs from capital-constrained to labor-constrained growth.

13. See the discussion in Romer (1996, 46ff).

Both models exhibit some version of the Cambridge theorem in their two-class forms, and that is the key to understanding them. In the endogenous model, the number of workers depends on the amount of capital that has accumulated. If capitalist saving generates a higher rate of accumulation than workers would be able to sustain in the absence of capitalists, then the Cambridge equation defines the long-run growth rate. The growth of workers' capital will depend on their share of capital. Only retired workers own capital since workers save during their active years. If workers initially own a small share of capital relative to the steady state distribution, the active workers generate a large amount of saving relative to the capital stock that retirees own. In other words, the growth rate of workers' capital will exceed the long-run growth rate in this circumstance. If workers own a relatively large share of capital, of course, exactly the opposite outcome emerges. In either case, as the growth of workers' capital converges on the long-run rate, their share of capital stabilizes. In this setting, even though workers are saving and enjoying the benefits of some of the economic surplus they have produced, they are ultimately subsidiary to the capitalists who occupy the commanding heights of the structure of accumulation. Capitalist saving determines the long-run growth rate that workers' capital must accommodate, given the distribution of income.

In the exogenous model, the number of workers is predestined by the natural growth rate and initial conditions. In the two-class case, the wage adjusts to any incipient excess demand for labor, and the workers' share of capital will converge on its steady state value. If workers initially own less wealth, the consumption of retired workers will be low (relative to its steady state value) and social saving will be high, creating an incipient excess demand for labor that is resolved by a rise in the wage and a decline in the profit rate. This response is stabilizing because accumulation is profit led through the Cambridge equation in the two-class case. Again, the capitalist agents occupy a privileged position in the structure of accumulation. Capitalist saving determines the steady state rate of profit and the wage, given the natural rate of growth.

3.5 Appendix: Dynamic Programming

As the text points out, the altruistic capitalist's optimization problem can be solved as a standard concave nonlinear programming problem using the method of Lagrange. But it also lends itself to dynamic programming methods, and illustrates very nicely the basic idea behind Bellman's (1957) principle of optimality. Since most textbook expositions[14] illustrate the solution techniques by solving a neoclassical growth model, it seems appropriate to include an appendix illustrating how dynamic programming can be applied to the similar problem of an altruistic capitalist. Let us restate the problem without the $1 - \beta_c$ term in the objective function.[15] Dropping the subscript on β and superscript on K since there is no danger here of confusing capitalists and workers, the problem is

$$\max \sum_{t=0}^{\infty} \beta^t \log C$$

$$\text{subject to } C + K_{+1} = (1 + r)K$$

$$\text{given } K_0, \{r\}_0^{\infty}$$

We have also replaced the inequality in the wealth constraint on the economic grounds that no agent with an always-increasing utility function will throw wealth away. The wealth constraint now performs as an equation of motion: any choice of C automatically entails a choice of K_{+1}.

Dynamic programming makes use of the value-function, which is defined as

$$\mathcal{V}(K_0) = \max \sum_{t=0}^{\infty} \beta^t \log C$$

The challenge is to find the function that satisfies this definition (subject to the constraints in the original problem, of course). The key insight exploited by dynamic programming is that the value function satisfies a functional equation, commonly called the *Bellman equation*:

$$\mathcal{V}(K) = \max_{C} \{\log C + \beta \mathcal{V}(K_{+1})\}$$

If we can find this function, we can also find the rule that describes consumption and saving, which will take the form of a policy function. In this

14. See, for example, Stokey and Lucas (1989) and Ljungqvist and Sargent (2000), which also provide the prototype for the solution pursued here.

15. Recall that this term makes the Lagrangian problem slightly easier to solve because $(1 - \beta_c) \sum_0^{\infty} \beta_c^t = 1$, but it does not change the solution since it is just a linear displacement of the utility function.

case, the policy function will simply be the capitalist consumption (or saving) function. Note that the Bellman equation instructs us to decide how much to consume today (which gives us instant utility) and how much to keep in the program (which gives us value in the future and has been suitably discounted).

To solve this problem, we employ two techniques. First, we will iterate on the Bellman equation to establish the form of the value function. Second, we will use the method of undetermined coefficients to finish the job.

Iterating on the Bellman equation has an economic interpretation that helps clarify how it works. Suppose there is a terminal date for our capitalist agent. We know this is a fiction since the planning horizon is infinite, but we are going to increase the horizon in steps, so let us start by imagining that our agent has one year to live. What is the value of any saving, expressed by our first iteration for the value function, $\mathcal{V}_0(K)$? Clearly, it is zero since the agent gets no utility from wealth after death ("You can't take it with you"). If we substitute $\mathcal{V} = 0$ into the RHS (right-hand side) of the Bellman equation and solve it (trivially, since the solution is to consume all our initial wealth), we arrive at our next iteration,

$$\mathcal{V}_1(K_0) = \log(1 + r_0) + \log K_0$$

Now we can replace the value function on the RHS of the Bellman equation with $\mathcal{V}_1$ and solve for the maximizing values of K_{+1} and C_0. The optimality principle tells us that the value function optimally evaluates any wealth we leave in the program. Thus,

$$\mathcal{V}_2(K_0) = \max\{\log C + \beta \mathcal{V}_1(K_1)\}$$

The maximizing solution can then be substituted back into the Bellman equation to obtain the expression for $\mathcal{V}_2$ in the next iteration, which is

$$\mathcal{V}_2(K_0) = \log \frac{1 + r_0}{1 + \beta} + \beta \log \frac{\beta(1 + r_0)^2}{1 + \beta} + (1 + \beta) \log K_0$$

We are implementing Bellman's principle of optimality. Instead of trying to solve the whole multistage problem, we break it down into the simpler problem of choosing between consumption today and the optimal value generated by the wealth (saving) we leave in the program. Whatever decision we make today at t about consumption, the remaining subproblem that starts at $t + 1$ will be solved optimally by the value function; this is the essence of the principle of optimality. Of course, at this iteration the problem has only three stages, but as we add periods, the signal advantage of this approach becomes apparent. Each time we add a stage, we come closer to solving the original problem.

At this point, the character of the value function is beginning to take shape. It looks like a good guess might be the log-linear form $\mathcal{V}(K_0) = \mathcal{A} + \mathcal{B} \log K_0$. Pursuing that hunch, we find that as we continue the iteration process the ith iteration of the coefficient, $\mathcal{B}_i$, emerges like a nested matryoshka doll:

$$\begin{aligned}
\mathcal{B}_1 &= 1 \\
\mathcal{B}_2 &= 1 + \beta \\
\mathcal{B}_3 &= 1 + \beta(1 + \beta) \\
\mathcal{B}_4 &= 1 + \beta(1 + \beta(1 + \beta)) \\
\mathcal{B}_5 &= 1 + \beta(1 + \beta(1 + \beta(1 + \beta))) \\
&\vdots \\
\mathcal{B}_i &= \ldots
\end{aligned}$$

These expressions suggest that as we push the horizon out to infinity the coefficient $\mathcal{B}$ converges on

$$\mathcal{B} = \lim_{T \to \infty} \sum_{0}^{T-1} \beta^t = \frac{1}{1 - \beta}$$

It turns out that as the number of iterations approaches infinity this procedure will in fact converge on a unique solution for the value function under certain well-defined conditions (Ljungqvist and Sargent 2000), so we can promote this suggestion to a solid result. With it, we have enough information to determine the policy function (here, the saving function). Substituting $\mathcal{V}(K) = \mathcal{A} + (1/(1 - \beta)) \log K$ into the Bellman equation and solving for the maximizing decision gives us the Cambridge equation,

$$K_1 = \beta(1 + r_0)K_0$$

Since every period is identical to the first period, this function can be stripped of its specific time subscripts and written in time invariant form.

Some readers may be curious about the convergence of the other coefficient. It turns out not to have such a clear solution, so we turn to a second strategy for finding the value function, the method of undetermined coefficients. Simply substitute $\mathcal{V} = \mathcal{A} + \mathcal{B} \log K$ into the RHS of the Bellman equation and perform the maximization. The result is

$$K_1 = \frac{\beta\mathcal{B}}{1+\beta\mathcal{B}}(1+r_0)K_0$$

$$C_0 = \frac{1}{1+\beta\mathcal{B}}(1+r_0)K_0$$

Replacing C and K_{+1} in the RHS of the Bellman equation with these optimum values, and putting $\mathcal{A} + \mathcal{B} \log K_0$ on the LHS (left-hand side) lets us recover expressions for the still undetermined coefficients. It quickly becomes evident on rearranging that $\mathcal{B} = 1/(1-\beta)$ (as we already determined using the iteration strategy). Using that result, the solution for $\mathcal{A}$ follows:

$$\mathcal{A} = \left(\frac{1}{1-\beta}\right)^2 \left(\log(1+r_0) + (1-\beta)\log(1-\beta) + \beta \log \beta\right)$$

These techniques are fairly easy to apply in this case of logarithmic preferences, but it turns out not to be true more generally where "it is typically impossible analytically to compute even *one* iteration" (Ljungqvist and Sargent 2000, 33) and researchers are forced to resort to computational methods and other strategies. As Chow (1997) points out, there is little inherent advantage to recovering the value function and, consequently, the Lagrangian method used in the text turns out to be more direct and in many cases preferable to dynamic programming.

— 4 —

Saving and the Class Structure

Wealth is not without its advantages and the case to the contrary, although it has often been made, has never proved widely persuasive.

JOHN KENNETH GALBRAITH (1958)

Accumulate, accumulate! That is Moses and the prophets!

KARL MARX (1977)

This chapter begins by presenting some evidence that supports (or at least informs) the two-class interpretation of modern capitalist societies and closes by producing some thoughts on the value of a class analysis of the structure of accumulation. It can be skipped without loss of continuity. Galbraith's lambent epigraph points us toward evidence on the concentration of wealth.

4.1 Critical Values of the Discount Factor

Both the endogenous and exogenous growth models identify a clear dividing line between the one-class and two-class regimes that we have represented by $\bar{\beta}_w$, the maximum worker discount factor consistent with the two-class equilibrium (see pages 53 and 61). In order to measure this separatrix, we need data for the wage (profit) share, the productivity of capital, and the rate of capital accumulation.[1] Table 4.1 exhibits some calculations

1. Note that $R - r = (1 - \pi)\rho$, where $1 - \pi$ is the wage share, w/x. Obviously, π is the profit share.

Table 4.1 Mean values of $\bar{\beta}_w$, cross section of selected countries

Sample	Endogenous Model $\frac{1+g}{R-r}$	Exogenous Model $\frac{1+n}{1+R}$
Full	0.295	0.188
High-income	0.305	0.199
Low-income	0.285	0.177

Notes: Assumes a generational period of 30 years and $\delta = 1$. The rate of growth is measured by the rate of capital accumulation. The full sample has 56 observations; the subsamples are defined by median per capita income and each have 28 observations. *Sources:* ρ and g from Extended Penn World Tables, π from Bernanke and Gürkaynak (2001), Gollin (2002), and the United Nations' System of National Accounts.

using the Extended Penn World Tables for the latter two variables and the United Nations' System of National Accounts for the wage and profit share. The full sample includes only the 56 countries for which good profit share data are available, observed from 1963 to 1998. (These data are described more fully in Chapter 11.)

Following a common practice in calibrating overlapping generation growth models (de la Croix and Michel 2002, 338), the generational period has been set at 30 years and the depreciation rate has been set to unity. The depreciation rate over such a long period presents some conceptual difficulties, but if we assume that depreciation is an exponential process ("radioactive decay"), even small rates will come close to unity over a generation.[2]

The sample has also been split into two income groups based on per capita income. Curiously, there are minimal differences between rich and poor countries. As is discussed further in Chapter 11, the profit share is fairly constant across countries at different levels of development; any variation in the critical discount rate must therefore be due to the other variables. Evidently, economic development lowers both capital productivity and growth in offsetting ways.

It is clear that the statistical record sets the bar for entry into the Samuelson-Modigliani regime quite high. If labor constraints are not binding, the workers' saving rate would have to be well over 25 percent. While

2. If $\delta = 0.1$ per year, the depreciation rate over a generational period is $1 - (1 - 0.1)^{30} = 0.96$. It is also necessary to recalibrate capital productivity by multiplying annual output per worker by 30, and to scale the growth factor by exponentiation: $(1 + g)^{30}$.

that is far from an impossibility, most observations of average saving rates out of personal income are below this value by a comfortable margin. If labor constraints are binding, the bar is a little lower but still lies well above observed saving rates (typically in single digits). We will see in subsequent chapters that the existence of fiscal factors (debt, social security) probably raises these bars even higher than the laissez-faire levels assumed here.

On the other hand, the fact that the critical saving rates are not an order of magnitude from observed rates makes the question of a transition between regimes approachable. Because, as we will see, fiscal policies directed toward greater public ownership of wealth reduce these critical saving rates, such a transition could command serious attention.

4.2 Saving

Several branches of the empirical literature on saving and consumption have added to our understanding of the class structure of accumulation, including the debate over saving motives, the direct observation of saving propensities by social class, and the study of the institutional structure of saving.

4.2.1 Saving Motives

The two-class model and the literature on the distribution of wealth by saving motive are mutually informative. It has long been known that wealth is far more concentrated than can be explained by the existing distribution of income together with the life-cycle theory of saving (Atkinson 1971). We now know from the literature on the distribution of wealth by saving motive that the range of estimates is quite broad (Kessler and Masson 1988). Kotlikoff and Summers (1981), for example, find that as little as 20 percent of the wealth stock originated in saving out of earnings. This estimate has been challenged, most notably by Modigliani (1988), who insists that life-cycle saving accounts for the great bulk of capital accumulation in the United States, perhaps as much as 80 percent. Not surprisingly, more recent research has tended to report estimates mid-range between these extremes. Many of the methodological assumptions advocated by Modigliani have proved unpersuasive, as in his treatment of saving out of property income earned on inherited wealth as life-cycle saving. Blinder (1988) provided an influential and balanced assessment of the debate, and it has largely stood the test of time, judging from the survey of Davies and Shorrocks (2000,

655–657). For example Gale and Scholz (1994) find that over 50 percent of wealth originates in bequest saving, while Davies and Shorrocks's (2000) widely cited survey places the consensus range of bequest wealth between 35 and 45 percent.

Subsequent research in this field has drifted away from the accounting exercise summarized here, and toward a classless, eclectic focus on distinguishing between life-cycle, precautionary, and bequest motives (Gale and Potter 2003). As so often happens in economics, the first relatively naive impressions often remain the most pungent. Kotlikoff, for example, acknowledges that "my prior view was that life-cycle saving would explain essentially all of private wealth holdings" (2003, 341), an admission that puts his finding to the contrary in the category of a revealing first impression. From the perspective of the two-class model, the accounting framework captures important information about the class structure of wealth ownership, at least to a first approximation. One problem is that it does seem to ignore the creation of entrepreneurial wealth through capitalization of founder's profits, which would be categorized as life-cycle wealth under some accounting conventions.

4.2.2 Saving Propensities

The central premise of the classical approach is that the rich save more, and this has been confirmed repeatedly, most recently by Dynan et al. (2004). At the other end of the distribution, Wolff (1981) has shown that a significant proportion of workers do no significant saving and even carry negative net worth; the class division of saving is tripartite. To that extent, our use of a representative worker who saves for life-cycle purposes oversimplifies. Marglin (1984) observes that the life-cycle theory describes the consumption problem of a well-established white-collar worker, such as the professors (including your author) who make such free use of the theory. Yet it is hard to think of a better way to model the saving of the working classes (or, perhaps, noncapitalist class might be more accurate) in a macroeconomic setting.

4.2.3 The Institutional Structure of Saving

Another useful perspective on the class structure of saving is provided by Table 4.2, which shows the relative importance of corporate saving in total

Table 4.2 U.S. corporate saving as share of private saving, 1960–2004.

	Average	
Years	Net	Gross
1960–1969	0.414	0.664
1970–1979	0.310	0.629
1980–1989	0.281	0.655
1990–1999	0.421	0.767
2000–2004	0.625	0.894

Notes: Column 2 is undistributed corporate profit divided by net private saving. Column 3 is undistributed profit plus private consumption of fixed capital divided by net private saving plus consumption of fixed capital. *Source:* Council of Economic Advisors (2006, Table B32) and author's calculations.

U.S. private saving. Net private saving probably overstates the importance of household (noncorporate) saving because it does not include depreciation of household capital stock. Gross private saving is more meaningful, and it is clear from either measure that the household sector in the national income and product accounts does not dominate the saving process. An even more dramatic accounting has been provided by Ruggles and Ruggles (1992) who remove institutions from the household sector, eliminate rental imputations for owner-occupied housing, and emend the data in several other ways. They demonstrate that the household sector appears to be self-reliant, generating just enough saving to finance its own (mostly residential) investment. Similarly, the business sector appears to finance its investment spending from its own cash flows. Given the high degree of concentration of financial wealth among households, one might conclude that the saving decision more or less originates in the dividend policies of business enterprises, which function as an extension of the capitalist household. On the whole, then, the class structure of accumulation finds expression in several different dimensions.

4.3 The Distribution of Wealth

One implication of the dynamics of both the endogenous and exogenous growth models outlined above is that the workers' share of wealth should be increasing (not necessarily monotonically) if the system is destined to achieve a one-class equilibrium. The research on saving motives surveyed

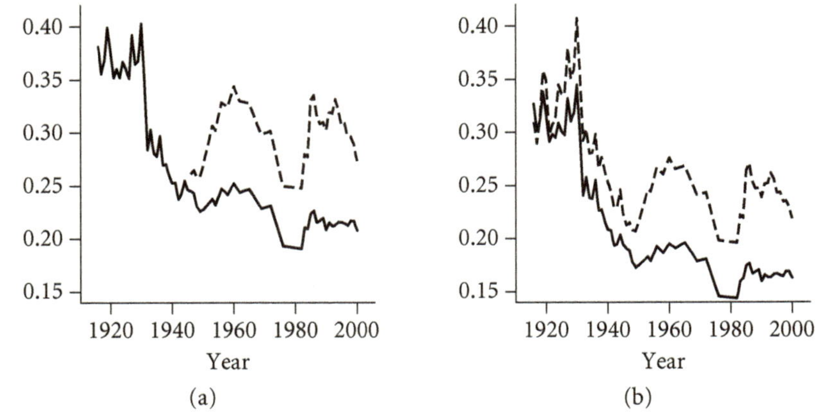

Figure 4.1 Shares of total wealth (solid lines) and financial wealth (dashed lines) for top groups from 1916 to 2000 are shown. (a) Top 1 percent. (b) Top 0.5 percent. *Source:* Kopczuk and Saez (2004) and author's calculations.

above does not have much to say about historical trends; it would probably be asking too much of the scanty data available.[3]

We can, however, observe the behavior of wealth concentration on the supposition that the top shares are good proxies for the holdings by capitalist agents in the theoretical model. Figure 4.1 shows the behavior of wealth shares in the United States developed from estate tax records by Kopczuk and Saez (2004).

In addition to the shares of total wealth that the authors focus on, these figures also show the shares of financial wealth derived from their data on the grounds that it more closely corresponds to the capital wealth that animates economic growth in our theoretical model. Financial wealth is total wealth minus real estate holdings and consists chiefly of equities, bonds, and life insurance, net of personal debt.[4]

These data do show signs of a declining top share of wealth over the twentieth century, in both the total and financial series. Most of the decline is concentrated in the Depression/World War II period from 1930 to 1945.

3. But see DeLong (2003), a delightful essay that argues, using *inter alia* Jane Austen's *Pride and Prejudice*, that bequests have receded quantitatively and changed qualitatively.

4. My methodology for measuring a group's share of financial wealth was to calculate:
$$\text{group share of total wealth} \times \left(\frac{\text{share of financial in group wealth}}{\text{share of financial in total wealth}} \right).$$

Table 4.3 Wealth shares in the United States, 1983–1998

	Net Worth		Financial Wealth	
Years	Top 5%	Top 10%	Top 5%	Top 10%
1983	0.561	0.682	0.680	0.803
1989	0.590	0.706	0.708	0.824
1992	0.600	0.718	0.706	0.821
1995	0.603	0.718	0.718	0.830
1998	0.594	0.709	0.683	0.797

Source: Wolff (2003).

Kopczuk and Saez (2004, 468–470) argue that this decline was mostly the result of the rise of progressive income and estate taxation, abetted by the stock market collapse. Since this period, neither series indicate any strong trend; the total wealth shares do seem to have declined modestly but the financial shares have increased modestly. Both series exhibit some oscillations whose periods are roughly consistent with a generational period of perhaps 15 to 20 years, but these movements can be explained by historical contingencies such as the changes in tax law.

If we take Modigliani's lower-range estimate for bequest saving and make the (heroic?) assumption that almost all bequest saving is concentrated among top groups, the top 1 percent, holding between 20 and 25 percent of the total wealth, makes a good candidate for a capitalist class. (The top 2 percent holds between 25 and 30 percent of total wealth; the series for this group resembles those shown in Figure 4.1.) On the other hand, if we take a mid- or upper-range estimate for the fraction of wealth due to bequests, we will need to examine the wealth share of a larger top group. Table 4.3 presents estimates based on the Federal Reserve Board Survey of Consumer Finances (SCF) that align with the mid- and upper-range estimates. There are discrepancies between SCF data and the estate tax data used in Figure 4.1, so it is hazardous to compare the levels directly. In particular, the SCF data report household wealth whereas the estate tax data report individual wealth. In these broader data series, we find the same time pattern observed earlier.

The systemic concentration of wealth that characterizes modern U.S. capitalism shows no signs of retreat. This stylized fact is consistent with the two-class Kaldor-Pasinetti-Robinson model and gainsays the one-class

Samuelson-Modigliani regime. The distribution of wealth expresses the class structure of accumulation, and it does not seem to be merely an artifact of an unequal distribution of wage income.[5]

4.4 On Class Analysis

Both models presented above offer the choice of the Pasinetti (two-class) regime or the Anti-Pasinetti (one-class) Dual theorem, whose discoverers opined perhaps somewhat disingenuously that "it is with some regret that we must confess to most serious qualms over the empirical relevance of these assumptions—notably that relating to the existence of identifiable classes of capitalists and workers with 'permanent membership'—even as a rough first approximation" Samuelson and Modigliani (1966, 271). Their first "qualm" was that the assumption of permanent classes "completely disregards the life cycle"(ibid., 297); but we have seen in the previous chapter that incorporating life-cycle saving presents no problem, and even enriches the two-class model. Their more serious complaint is that

> in a modern industrial society the capitalist's class is not a hereditary caste: its membership at any point of time is far from limited to people who were born into it by virtue of inherited wealth. . . . But even the assumption that class membership and saving propensity do not change during one person's lifetime is not enough for our purposes. Since people do not live forever, one would have to extend the assumption to one's heirs, and their heirs, and so on, until Kingdom-come. . . . For, the moment that one admits transfers of wealth between classes, either through living persons switching class membership or by virtue of death, *it is no longer true that* . . . [the changes in K_c and K_w] . . . *are equal to the rate of saving of the respective classes*. . . . (Samuelson and Modigliani 1966, 297)

Subsequent economic research discussed above has diminished the force of these comments. In particular, we now know that a substantial proportion, perhaps around half, of wealth in the United States can be attributed to bequest saving, despite Modigliani's best efforts to hold that number down to one-fifth. (And even if Modigliani is closer to the truth, in the theory we have just presented, the quantity of wealth owned by capitalists does not

5. Indeed, Kopczuk and Saez (2004, 483) observe that the failure of the wealth shares to rise in the 1990s is not inconsistent with the well-documented increases in income inequality in this period, partly because of the shift of top incomes toward compensation and away from capital income.

itself distinguish between the two-class and one-class regimes.) Barro has taken care of Kingdom-come and the extent to which the elite fortunes are reproduced over very long periods has been well documented (Atkinson 1981). Yet even if these facts are admitted, the cavils expressed above still resonate with economists trained in the hegemonic paradigm of methodological individualism and for that reason demand some response.[6]

From the classical perspective, this quotation exhibits a reductionist attitude toward class that seems to rob it of much potential scientific or categorical value. It sets up a straw man, an historian, sociologist, or political economist who would cleave to a hereditary theory of class, excluding even Adam Smith, whose own focus on the problem of "rank" betrayed a deep appreciation for the mystery of behavioral patterns that reproduce class structure.[7] Novelists (Jane Austen, William Thackery, Edith Wharton, Henry Green, or Tom Wolfe, say) who make a living by penetrating appearances return repeatedly to the theme of social class in modern industrial society, as do journalists (New York Times (correspondents of) 2005). Even the Greco-Roman social structure, founded as it was on a continuum of masters and slaves, admitted a surprising degree of social mobility (Finley 1981). Does that mean the political economy of the Roman *latifundia* must renounce the concept of an economic surplus produced by unfree labor, and base itself on strict methodological individualism? Or that former slaves somehow carried their behavioral characteristics with them like baggage, as the former workers who are blessed to join the capitalist class in the quotation above seem to do?

The classical approach treats class as a social relation of production embedded deeply in the structure of society, providing theoretical justification for replication of the class structure at the foundational level in macroeconomic models of capitalism. The individuals who participate in class society do so according to its rules (including those that govern switching

6. For example, Lucas (2002, 144) writes: "In view of the way capitalist economies have evolved in the last 200 years, however, assumptions designed to maintain rigid class lines have become increasingly dubious empirically as well as hard to reconcile with individual rationality. I will deal here with models of classless societies only." It is not clear what empirical evidence the author had in mind.

7. Referring to the rich in pursuit of "their own vain and insatiable desires," Smith (1976, 184–185) writes that "they are led by an invisible hand to make nearly the same distribution of the necessaries of life, which would have been made, had the earth been divided into equal portions . . . ". Interestingly, this first use of the invisible hand metaphor by Smith makes no mention of the magic of markets; it is all about class.

class membership); however, if the class structure reproduces itself, it is because their behavior makes such an outcome inevitable and consequently commands our attention as political economists. In Marx's theoretical formulation, economic agents personify social relations: the capitalist appears as the personification of capital. Idiosyncratic capitalists (Robert Owen in Marx's day; Ben Cohen and Jerry Greenfield in ours) only bring systemic patterns of behavior into sharper relief as exceptions that prove the rule. Even if the capitalist class were as fluid as implied by Schumpeter's metaphor of a "capitalist hotel" that is always full but whose occupants change, this would not diminish the need to embed social relations of production in an economic model.

The models presented here rely on a weak form of methodological individualism that respects the value of modeling individual behavior where this is appropriate either for enforcing some theoretical discipline or for rhetorical effectiveness in communicating with economists trained in the neoclassical tradition. But we have not conceded to a strong form of methodological individualism that would demand the wholesale rejection of structural categories like social class. Our focus on the two-class model represents an attempt to implement a classical theory of the political economy of capitalism through its characteristic property relation. In this approach, the decisive characteristic of the capitalist agents is their compulsion to accumulation ("Moses and the prophets"), which translates, somewhat imperfectly, into the language of modern economic theory by way of the modeling devices rehearsed above. If these efforts are too simplistic, that is not because they ignore the individual but because they pay insufficient attention to the corporate structure of modern capitalism, with its division of capitalist functions among managers, financial capitalists, and rentiers.[8] At the risk of a solecism, it might be more accurate to say that the business enterprise personifies capital in advanced capitalist societies. In any event, to speak of capital and labor without recognizing the presence of people in specific roles has the unfortunate effect of reifying and distorting these useful economic categories.

8. The tradition of incorporating corporate structure into classical-Keynesian models starts with Kaldor (1966) and continues through Marglin (1984).

— 5 —

Debt and Endogenous Growth

> The public debt becomes one of the most powerful levers of primitive accumulation. As with the stroke of an enchanter's wand, it endows unproductive money with the power of creation and thus turns it into capital, without forcing it to expose itself to the troubles and risks inseparable from its employment in industry or even in usury.
>
> . . . The great part that the public debt, and the fiscal system corresponding with it, has played in the capitalisation of wealth and the expropriation of the masses, has led many writers . . . to seek here, incorrectly, the fundamental cause of the misery of the people in modern times.
>
> Karl Marx (1977)

This chapter presents the basic elements of a treatment of government debt and then develops two endogenous growth models with public debt. In the first, the capitalists have an infinite planning horizon, and Ricardian equivalence prevails. In the second, the capitalists have a finite planning horizon, and Ricardian equivalence does not prevail. The next chapter applies these elements to an exogenous growth model.[1] While we will not seek in public debt the fundamental cause of misery, in these two chapters we will examine Marx's claim in the vivid passage above that debt becomes a powerful lever of wealth redistribution.

1. These chapters build on Michl and Georges (1996) and Michl (2006a). The material on finite planning horizons is new.

5.1 Public Debt in a Growth Model

The first order of business is to introduce public debt into the saving functions of the capitalists, workers, and of course, the government itself. For analytical simplicity, nothing beats the *Gedankenexperiment* pioneered by Evsey Domar for studying the pure burden of debt: a government whose sole task is debt servicing. The saving functions that we derive here will also be enlisted in the subsequent chapter, which develops an exogenous growth model with public debt.

5.1.1 Government

Since the central issue is how debt itself affects macroeconomic performance in the long run, let us consider a highly stylized government whose sole function is to service a debt inherited from the past. The premise is that some temporary government expenditure in the past (say, a war) has been financed by borrowing; the subsequent debt burden can then be managed by growth, inflation, or taxation. This set-up, originally proposed in a classic paper by Domar (1944), lets us interpret the tax needed to service the debt as a measure of the burden of debt.

As a stylized description of U.S. public debt over the last two centuries, this is not too far from the truth, as Figure 5.1 illustrates for the U.S. debt–GDP ratio.[2] Most of the spikes are clearly related to major wars: the Revolutionary War, the War of 1812, the Civil War, WWI, and WWII are all represented. The Great Depression presents an exception, illustrating the newly found power of Keynesian fiscal policy, and the most recent cycles seem to represent a new pattern of peacetime debt financing, unless we permit both the escalation in the Cold War that started under President Carter and the second Gulf War in Iraq to qualify as major wars. A more likely and interesting hypothesis is that these are political debt cycles. We return to this issue in the next chapter.

Government debt, B, will be assumed to be a perfect substitute for private capital, K, an assumption not uncommon in the literature (Pasinetti 1989, 34). Both are risk free and earn a rate of return equal to the net rate of profit, r. The bonds mature in one period, so that there are no complicating

2. The U.K. public debt–GDP ratio follows a similar pattern, but with substantially higher peaks, reaching a level over 2 after the Napoleonic Wars (Buiter 1990).

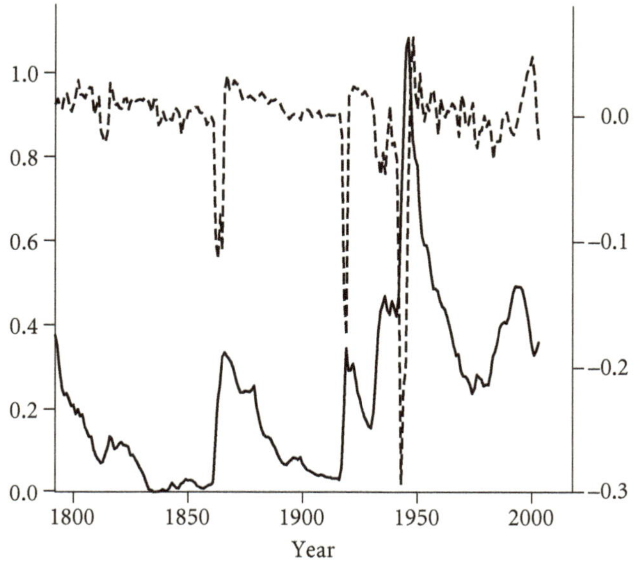

Figure 5.1 The debt–GDP ratio (left scale, solid line) in the United States has generally increased during major wars and declined subsequently through some combination of primary surpluses (right scale, dashed line), real growth, and inflation. The recent debt cycle may be an exception. *Source:* Bohn (2004).

problems with the price of these instruments, which is definitionally 1. The government collects lump-sum taxes, T, of which ΩT is paid by the capitalist agents and $(1-\Omega)T$ is paid by active workers, as discussed in Michl and Georges (1996). Retirees live tax-free. Each of the N workers pays an equal share of worker taxes, or $\tau = (1-\Omega)T/N$.

The government's one-period budget constraint (sometimes called simply the budget identity, since it doesn't do much constraining) is simply

$$B_{+1} = (1+r)B - T \tag{5.1}$$

Note that T represents the primary fiscal surplus. Later, it will be convenient to normalize the primary fiscal surplus by the capital stock and represent it by $\theta = T/K$. Similarly, we will normalize debt and represent it by $\sigma = B/K$.

With debt and capital perfect substitutes, it should not matter if workers happen to choose the corner solution with no debt such that all government debt resides in the portfolio of the capitalists, subject to the obvious limitation that the government debt can at no time exceed the gross wealth of the capitalists. This shortcut simplifies the bookkeeping considerably with no loss of generality.[3]

Summing the government budget constraint forward through time, starting at $t = 0$, and using R_S to represent the total return factor[4] over the horizon S, we write

$$B_0 = \frac{B_S}{R_S} + \sum_{t=0}^{S-1} \frac{T}{R_{+1}}$$

The usual assumption is that the government cannot borrow indefinitely to service its debt, because forward-looking agents will not lend to it, subjecting the government to the No-Ponzi Game restriction:

$$\lim_{S\to\infty} \frac{B_S}{R_S} = 0$$

This restriction implies that the current value of the government debt, in the limit as $S \to \infty$, must be equal to the present discounted value of all future expected primary surpluses, and these in turn can be parsed into the contributions of capitalist and worker taxes (assuming a constant tax distribution parameter, Ω), or

$$B_0 = \sum_{t=0}^{\infty} \frac{T}{R_{+1}} = \sum_{t=0}^{\infty} \frac{\Omega T}{R_{+1}} + \sum_{t=0}^{\infty} \frac{(1-\Omega)T}{R_{+1}} \tag{5.2}$$

Armed with this knowledge, capitalists who plan over an infinite horizon should internalize this infinite-horizon budget constraint (often referred to as the intertemporal budget constraint). We will see in the next section exactly at which stage in the solution of the capitalist program this occurs.

On the other hand, capitalists who plan only over their own lifespan are indifferent to this budget constraint. And, in fact, it is not clear that there is any intertemporal budget constraint facing the government in a world in which all the agents have finite horizons. We will assume, in our modeling exercises below, that even in this world, the government operates through fiscal rules that eventually stabilize the debt ratios. For example, in

3. For further elaboration, see Michl (2006a, 456).

4. Defined as

$$R_S = \prod_{t=0}^{S-1} (1+r)$$

the European Union (EU), the Maastricht criteria limit the ratios of debt and the overall deficit to GDP, whereas in the United States, economists frequently counsel the government to maintain a unified budget balance (or surplus) over the business cycle for stabilization purposes.

How well they have succeeded can be judged from Figure 5.1, which shows the (nominal) U.S. debt and the primary surplus, both scaled by nominal GDP. The debt figure snakes along to the right, with periods of rising debt followed by periods of decline. The primary surplus plays some role in this and, as discussed below, weakly responds to the increases by rising in subsequent periods. For example, the Reagan-Bush increase in the debt ratio leads to the Clinton surpluses.

5.1.2 On the Government Budget Constraint

The intertemporal government budget constraint has been the center of several loosely related controversies. One issue is whether the fiscal authorities (chiefly in the United States) have obeyed this constraint historically, particularly over recent decades when fiscal deficits have apparently been the rule rather than the exception.[5] The second issue is whether the fiscal authorities must obey this constraint (Buiter 2002), or whether it represents merely an equilibrium condition (Cochrane 1999) that is enforced systemically, for example, by movements in the price level (which we have abstracted from). The equilibrium interpretation forms a key ingredient in the fiscal theory of the price level, by which the price level adjusts in order to equate the real value of debt with the present value of future expected primary surpluses. In this case, inflation is tied to general government liabilities rather than just to the liabilities of the monetary authority, as in the monetarist, or quantity theoretic, tradition. Since this latter controversy lies outside the scope of this book (in particular, we abstract from money, the price level, and monetized debt held by the central bank), let us turn to the former debate.

At issue, fundamentally, is the No-Ponzi restriction that, in the limit, the debt will not grow faster than the interest rate, so that the discounted

5. But note that the intertemporal budget constraint refers to the primary or noninterest surplus, whereas the official accounts typically report the surplus inclusive of interest. A permanent negative surplus (i.e., a deficit) inclusive of interest is consistent with the budget constraint; it is only a permanent primary deficit that is ruled out when the interest rate on debt exceeds the growth rate.

value of future debt vanishes at some long horizon. The government cannot promise to service future debt by simply issuing new debt; at some point, it must commit real resources (tax revenues) to this task. The assumption here is that the financial markets insist that current debt is backed up by future primary surpluses. It can be demonstrated that this behavior is the only kind consistent with an optimal consumption program over an infinite horizon. If the No-Ponzi restriction were violated, consumers with infinite planning horizons could do better by simply consuming all their principal and interest at some point and then refusing to continue to lend to the government.

But what if the financial markets do not always insist on this restriction? For example, suppose agents have finite horizons (a possibility we explicitly consider below); in this case, the No-Ponzi restriction does not apply. Another alternative is that current bond holders believe a version of the greater fool theory: there will be someone in the future willing to lend money to service past debts. The market for debt could have the characteristics of a self-fulfilling speculative bubble, and the current value of the debt will be equal to the expected future surpluses, as in equation (5.2), *plus* some term representing the lending from greater fools. In a seminal paper, Hamilton and Flavin (1986) test this hypothesis and are able to reject it for U.S. debt from 1960 to 1984. However, using methods putatively less restrictive, Wilcox (1989) finds evidence in the same data that fiscal policy after 1974 has been unsustainable, meaning that the greater fool term is statistically and economically significant. (Incidentally, his prediction that such an unsustainable fiscal regime would be forced to change was validated shortly after he made it, as is evident in Figure 5.1; although, the extent to which the Clinton administration's fiscal surpluses were a boon of good fortune, an exit response to market discipline, or a voice response to Robert Rubin, the investment banker who served as Clinton's treasury secretary, remains an open question.)

These tests have been criticized by neoclassical theorists for their treatment of risk. In particular, Bohn (1995) argues that in a risky world, the safe interest rate on public debt can be lower than the rate of growth, and that sustainable fiscal policies do not require permanent primary surpluses; in this context, he proposes an alternative test of sustainability as explained below. In fact, in the United States, both of these conditions characterize fiscal policy historically. The average ex post real interest rate on government debt from 1792 to 2003, for example, was 3.1 percent, while the average growth rate of real GDP was 3.8 percent and the primary surplus, as a share of GDP, was -0.3 percent (Bohn 2004, table 2). Interestingly, as can be seen visually from Figure 5.1, a few large fiscal deficits associated with major wars dominate the average primary surplus. The median, a more robust statistic that may be more appropriate, was +0.4 percent of GDP in these data. The conventional intertemporal budget constraint's requirement that debt be validated by fiscal surpluses thus seems to have been respected historically in the United States. Nonetheless, a major discrepancy between the theory presented in this chapter and the real economy is that public debt and capital are far from being perfect substitutes. The rate of profit on capital substantially exceeds the rate of interest on public debt.[6]

Using data over a longer historical period than the earlier debt sustainability literature, Bohn (1999) shows that fiscal policy has indeed been sustainable, once the effects of fiscal shocks (e.g., WWII) and business cycles are properly represented in a tax-smoothing framework. His test is that from 1916 to 1995 the primary fiscal surplus does respond positively to the debt-income ratio. To be more precise, he fits a regression of the primary surplus to the lagged debt ratio, a constant, and controls for high government spending and the cyclical component of output. The coefficient on debt in this equation is in the range 0.028–0.054, implying that a $100 increase in debt stimulates a $2.80 to $5.40 increase in the primary fiscal surplus in the next period. If the growth rate exceeds the real interest rate on average, Bohn (1999, 955) shows that a positive coefficient is sufficient to make the debt-income ratio stationary and mean-reverting, and Bohn (2004) finds that this relationship holds over the even longer time span represented in Figure 5.1.

Just as the intertemporal budget constraint instructs us, periods of deficits that run up the debt ratio imply future periods of larger primary surplus (or at least smaller primary deficits) to validate the debt. The hypothesis maintained in this and the subsequent chapter is thus supported to some extent by economic research. The U.S. government, at least, appears to follow sustainable fiscal policies that respect its intertemporal budget constraint.

6. The fact that this difference seems to exceed by a wide margin the predictions of the standard Capital Asset Pricing model with plausible levels of risk aversion is the basis of the "equity premium puzzle."

5.1.3 *Capitalists with Infinite Horizon*

The capitalists are assumed to be altruistic toward their children so that a capitalist household can be reconceptualized[7] as an infinitely lived dynasty along the lines of Barro (1974). We will represent capitalist gross wealth by $W = K^c + B$, taking advantage of the assumed absence of government bonds in the portfolios of workers. We can simplify by normalizing the number of capitalist households to unity while continuing to speak informally of capitalists (plural) to keep the language natural. The capitalist one-period budget constraint (assuming no wealth is ever wasted or destroyed) is

$$W_{+1} = (1 + r)W - C - \Omega T$$

and by the same procedure that we used on the government's budget constraint, we arrive at the conclusion that the present discounted value of future consumption plus taxes equals gross wealth, or

$$W_0 = \sum_{t=0}^{\infty} \frac{C + \Omega T}{R_{+1}}$$

Since the capitalist share of the present value of taxes appears on both sides, it is clear that the present value of consumption must equal private capital plus the workers' share of the present value of taxes, or

$$\sum_{t=0}^{\infty} \frac{C}{R_{+1}} = K_0^c + \sum_{t=0}^{\infty} \frac{(1 - \Omega)T}{R_{+1}}$$

The RHS of this expression represents the net wealth of capitalists, which we can define as

$$W_N = K^c + (1 - \Omega)B$$

7. Since this is such a bizarre assumption from a classical-Keynesian perspective, let it be said that this framework does establish a benchmark or ideal case, within which we can legitimately ask specific logical questions under controlled conditions without necessarily endorsing the economic model we have constructed as a description of any real economy. Just as Marx erected schemes of reproduction that can never be satisfied in real economies in order to understand the conditions that must prevail to permit balanced growth, so too can we construct idealized models of growth in order to understand the conditions that govern the structure of accumulation. As always, making the journey from the abstract to the concrete requires judgment.

We can now write down the capitalist program, assuming that capitalists maximize the discounted logarithmic consumption function, with discount factor $0 < \beta_c < 1$:

$$\max\ (1 - \beta_c) \sum_{t=0}^{\infty} \beta_c{}^t \log C$$
$$\text{subject to } W_{+1} + C + \Omega T \leq (1 + r)W$$
$$\text{given } B_0, K_0^c, \{r, T, B\}_{t=0}^{\infty}$$

As is well known, the solution to this type of problem specialized by a log utility function is to consume a constant fraction of end-of-period net wealth, but it is well worth the effort to show that net wealth conforms to the definition given above in this case. To solve this program using conventional techniques, we follow Foley and Michl (1999, ch. 5) and first write out the Lagrangian function with shadow prices μ_t:

$$\mathcal{L} = (1 - \beta_c) \sum_{t=0}^{\infty} \beta_c^t \log C - \sum_{t=0}^{\infty} \mu(W_{+1} + C - (1 + r)W + \Omega T)$$

The penalty function (i.e., the last term on the RHS) can be rewritten:

$$-\sum_{t=0}^{\infty} \mu C - \sum_{t=0}^{\infty} (\mu - \mu_{+1}(1 + r_{+1}))W_{+1} + \mu_0(1 + r_0)W_0 - \sum_{t=0}^{\infty} \mu \Omega T$$

Using this expansion in the Lagrangian makes it easy to derive the first-order conditions for C, W_{+1}, and μ, which are

$$\frac{(1 - \beta_c)\beta_c^t}{C} - \mu \leq 0 \tag{5.3}$$

$$-\mu + \mu_{+1}(1 + r_{+1}) \leq 0 \tag{5.4}$$

$$-(W_{+1} + C - (1 + r)W + \Omega T) \geq 0 \tag{5.5}$$

where the inequality applies only if the relevant constraint is slack (complementary slackness).

We know from the saddlepoint property of the solution that the penalty function must be zero, so that

$$\sum_{t=0}^{\infty} \mu C = \sum_{t=0}^{\infty} (-\mu + \mu_{+1}(1 + r_{+1}))W_{+1} + \mu_0(1 + r_0)W_0 - \sum_{t=0}^{\infty} \mu \Omega T$$

and we can then use expressions (5.3) and (5.4) to obtain

$$1 = \mu_0(1 + r_0)W_0 - \sum_{t=0}^{\infty} \mu\Omega T$$

It is at this point that we invoke the government's infinite-horizon budget constraint as embodied in equation (5.2), from which it is clear that

$$(1 + r_0)B_0 = T_0 + \frac{T_1}{(1 + r_1)} + \frac{T_2}{(1 + r_2)(1 + r_1)} + \cdots$$

This can be used to eliminate the summation of future taxes valued at the shadow prices, which rearranges to

$$\sum_{t=0}^{\infty} \mu\Omega T = \Omega\mu_0 \sum_{t=0}^{\infty} \frac{\mu T}{\mu_0}$$

Iterating forward[8] using expression (5.4), which we know will be an equality from the strict positivity of wealth, we can see that the sum of future taxes, evaluated using the shadow prices μ_t, will be

$$\sum_{t=0}^{\infty} \frac{\mu T}{\mu_0} = T_0 + \frac{T_1}{(1 + r_1)} + \frac{T_2}{(1 + r_2)(1 + r_1)} + \cdots$$

Because capitalists take the government's infinite-horizon budget constraint into account in their own program, we can replace this expression with $(1 + r_0)B_0$ in the penalty function in order to solve for the shadow price in period 0 (recalling that $W = K + B$):

$$\mu_0 = \frac{1}{(1 + r_0)(K_0 + (1 - \Omega)B_0)}$$

Further substituting into the first-order condition (5.3) for $t = 0$ gives us the familiar result that consumption will be a fraction of end-of-period wealth (or in this case, net wealth).[9] Since every period will be like period 0, this argument generalizes to the capitalist consumption function:[10]

8. In other words, derive

$$\mu_S = \frac{\mu_0}{\prod_{t=1}^{S}(1 + r)}$$

9. This was shown for the two-period case in Michl and Georges 1996 in a model without worker saving.

10. One might motivate this consumption function on intuitive grounds as a reasonable rule of thumb for capitalist agents who recognize that some of their bond holdings will be

$$C = (1 - \beta_c)(1 + r)W_N$$

This consumption equation leads to the following equations for gross saving and capital accumulation:

$$W_{+1} = \beta(1 + r)K^c + \beta'(1 + r)B - \Omega T \tag{5.6}$$

where $\beta' = (\beta_c - \Omega\beta_c + \Omega)$, and using equation (5.1),

$$K^c_{+1} = \beta_c(1 + r)K^c - (1 - \beta')(1 + r)B + (1 - \Omega)T \tag{5.7}$$

This equation is a version of the Cambridge equation, modified to accommodate fiscal policy in the case of capitalists with infinite horizons.

5.1.4 Capitalists with Finite Horizons

Another, perhaps more lifelike, way to model the capitalist agents is to assume that they live for one period and optimize over their own consumption and the size of the legacy they leave behind. One can interpret this kind of utility function in various ways (Carroll 2000). For example, it might be a modern restatement of Marx's gnomic observation that "accumulate, accumulate, that is Moses and the Prophets" to the capitalist.

The capitalist's program in this case is

$$\max\ (1 - \beta_c)\log C + \beta_c \log W_{+1}$$
$$\text{subject to } W_{+1} + C + \Omega T \leq (1 + r)W$$
$$\text{given } B_0, K^c_0, \{r, T, B\}$$

Using the Lagrangian method to solve this problem leads to the consumption function:

$$C = (1 - \beta_c)((1 + r)W - \Omega T)$$

The capitalists consume a constant fraction of their after-tax wealth. With a finite planning horizon, they do not consider the taxes on their descendants to be a liability, and they treat all the public debt in their portfolio as net worth, in contrast to the dynastic agents in the previous section. Ricardian equivalence does not prevail.

The accumulation function in this case can be found by substituting the consumption function into the capitalist budget constraint, using the

offset by taxes charged against their estates in the indefinite future. But it is useful to know that this behavior could be the solution to a traditional optimization problem.

government's one-period budget constraint, equation (5.1), to eliminate B_{+1}:

$$K^c_{+1} = \beta_c(1+r)K^c - (1-\beta_c)(1+r)B + (1-\Omega\beta_c)T \tag{5.8}$$

This equation is also a version of the Cambridge equation, modified to accommodate fiscal policy for the case of a finite planning horizon. We will see that equations (5.7) and (5.8) lead to growth models (both endogenous and exogenous) with distinct and interesting features.

5.1.5 Workers

Workers are assumed to plan only for their own consumption, without the implicit altruism toward future generations of the dynastic capitalists, and therefore workers do not need to take into account the government budget constraint. Their programming problem is

$$\max\ (1-\beta_w)\log c^w + \beta_w \log c^r$$

$$\text{subject to } c^w + \frac{c^r}{1+r_{+1}} \leq w - \tau$$

The solution to this problem is that workers consume a constant fraction of their wealth, or

$$c^w = (1-\beta_w)(w-\tau)$$

and save the rest:

$$s^w = \beta_w(w-\tau)$$

From the worker's individual saving function we can derive, with some substitutions, the aggregate worker saving function (recall that we are assuming that workers hold no government debt):

$$K^w_{+1} = \frac{w\beta_w}{k}K - \beta_w(1-\Omega)T \tag{5.9}$$

The burden of debt on workers (taxation to service debt) reduces their ability to save both individually and in the aggregate.

5.2 Debt in the Infinite Horizon Case

Recall from Chapter 3 that the endogenous growth model takes the distribution of income to be exogenously determined with respect to the accumulation process, so that the wage and the rate of profit are parametric. The question that confronts us is what effect public debt has in the model when capitalist dynasties plan over an infinite horizon and Ricardian equivalence prevails.

5.2.1 *Temporary Equilibrium*

The first order of business is to characterize the properties of a temporary equilibrium for some arbitrary fiscal policy. At generational frequencies, the temporary equilibrium bears no relationship to ordinary conceptions of a short run that might involve business cycle frequencies. From the capitalist and worker accumulation functions, equations (5.7) and (5.9), and the government's one-period budget constraint, equation (5.1), we can derive the accumulation equation for the growth factor K_{+1}/K:

$$\begin{aligned} 1 + g_K = &\beta_c(1+r)(1-\phi) - (1-\beta')(1+r)\sigma \\ &+ (1-\beta_w)(1-\Omega)\theta + \beta_w(R-r) \end{aligned}$$

From this equation, we turn to the effects of changes in the fiscal variables, θ and σ. Since the former measures the primary fiscal surplus, we can express the flow effect of fiscal policy on accumulation through the following:

$$\frac{\partial g_K}{\partial \theta} = (1-\beta_w)(1-\Omega) \geq 0$$

An increased level of government saving, that is, a larger primary surplus, contributes to higher levels of capital in the next period. Notice that this assumes that workers pay at least some of the taxes. If not, then Barro neutrality reigns: the timing of taxes to service debt has no real consequences.

For this formulation of the fiscal crowding-out effect to make any sense, there must implicitly be some process within the period to translate changes in saving into changes in capital formation, presumably operating through interest rates and investment. Empirical evidence for this mechanism has been mixed, but Gale and Orszag (2004) provide a survey of the literature and some persuasive evidence of a negative correlation between fiscal surpluses and interest rates.[11] Their key innovation is to use projected measures of fiscal policy and forward interest rates.

The stock crowding-out effect from an increased ratio of debt to capital is (recalling that $\beta' = \beta_c - \beta_c\Omega + \Omega$):

$$\frac{\partial g_K}{\partial \sigma} = -(1 - \beta_c)(1 - \Omega)(1 + r) \leq 0$$

Because some debt is regarded by capitalists as net wealth, it will crowd out real capital in their portfolios, and thus retard the accumulation of capital. Once again, if capitalists pay all the taxes that support the debt, they will not regard any of their bond holdings as net wealth and the timing of taxes will be completely Barro-neutral.

5.2.2 Steady State

In a steady state, the gross wealth of the capitalists must grow at the same rate as the capital stock. By dividing both sides of the capitalist saving equation (5.6) by W, using $\theta = (r - g^*)\sigma$ and the definition of β', and making some decisive substitutions,[12] we obtain

$$1 + g_W = \beta_c(1 + r) - \frac{\Omega\sigma}{1 - \phi + \sigma}(\beta_c(1 + r) - (1 + g^*))$$

Now set $g_W = g^*$ and remarkably we arrive at the unalloyed Cambridge equation:

$$1 + g^* = \beta_c(1 + r)$$

This confirms the finding of Pasinetti (1989) that the Cambridge theorem applies to a model with government debt, provided that Ricardian equivalence prevails. Here, however, we have the Cambridge theorem in inverted form, since this theorem in its original form refers to the rate of profit in an exogenous growth setting.

To complete the picture of the steady state, the workers' share of the capital stock can be derived from equation (5.9):

$$\phi^* = \frac{\beta_w(R - r - (1 - \Omega)(r - g^*)\sigma)}{(1 + g^*)} \tag{5.10}$$

11. But see the Keynesian rebuttal by Galbraith (2005).

12. The following expressions were useful:

$$\frac{K^c}{W} = \frac{1-\phi}{1-\phi+\sigma} \quad \frac{B}{W} = \frac{\sigma}{1-\phi+\sigma} \quad \frac{T}{W} = \frac{\theta}{1-\phi+\sigma}$$

The workers' burden of debt at a social level manifests itself in a smaller share of capital, a result of the lower after-tax wealth of a smaller workforce.

Curiously, from the capitalist dynasty's perspective, the debt burden of workers does not represent any net gain. Since the government's debt management strategy cannot affect the distribution of income (by assumption), it cannot bring about any favorable changes in the net worth of the capitalists. If the government allows a large debt to accumulate, capitalists will wind up receiving a larger portion of their net income through the fiscal system (as taxes on workers that are used to service the debt) and less of their net income through the private market, in the form of profits on invested capital. As was pointed out in a similar endogenous growth model by Michl and Georges (1996), the path of capitalist consumption is invariant with respect to the government's debt management strategy. But capitalist investment is not invariant, because bonds crowd out capital in their portfolios.

5.2.3 Comparative Dynamics

The quickest path to a comparative equilibrium analysis of the steady state is simply to differentiate the above equations for ϕ^* and g^*:

$$\frac{d\phi^*}{d\sigma} = \frac{-\beta_w(1-\Omega)(r-g^*)}{1+r} \leq 0$$

$$\frac{d\phi^*}{d\Omega} = \frac{\beta_w \sigma (r-g^*)}{1+r} > 0$$

Unless capitalists pay all the tax to service the debt, an increase in the debt-capital ratio depresses the share of capital owned by workers. Similarly, an increase in the share of taxes paid by capitalists will increase the share of worker capital. Moreover, from the Cambridge equation, we can see that steady state growth is invariant to both σ and Ω.

We can visualize these effects using the $\tilde{\phi}$ and $\hat{\phi}$ functions illustrated in Figure 5.2. As in the basic laissez-faire model, the $\tilde{\phi}(g^*)$ function, which describes the relationship between growth and the distribution of capital wealth consistent with capitalist behavior, reduces to the Cambridge equation.

The $\hat{\phi}(g^*)$ function, which describes the growth-distribution relationship consistent with workers' behavior, takes on the same form as equation (5.10) above. Thus, an increase in the debt-capital ratio shifts $\hat{\phi}(g^*)$

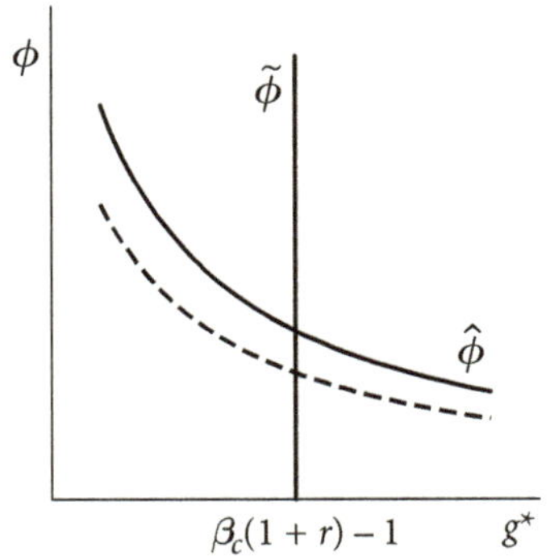

Figure 5.2 A larger debt-service burden in the infinite horizon case, either from an increase in the share of taxes borne by workers or from an increase in the debt-capital ratio, will depress worker saving, and reduce the steady state workers' share of capital wealth, ϕ^*. With an infinite capitalist planning horizon, the Cambridge theorem is in effect, and the rate of accumulation is invariant to fiscal policy in the long run.

down, a reflection of reduced worker saving consequent upon the burden of debt-service payments. As a result, the equilibrium share of capital wealth controlled by workers declines. An increase in the share of debt serviced by capitalists has the opposite effect.

5.2.4 Transitional Dynamics and Class Structure

Economists have explored several fiscal policy rules, including a constant debt per capita and constant deficit per capita, and both of these work well with the present model. We begin with the former assumption, which turns out to be convenient for exploring the boundary between a one- and two-class solution.

Constant Debt Ratio

Let us treat the debt-capital ratio, $\sigma = \bar{\sigma}$, as the target for fiscal authorities. We can see immediately from equation (5.1), the government's one-period budget constraint, that this makes $T = (r - g_K)\bar{\sigma}K$. The tax, in other words, becomes an endogenous variable along with the rate of capital accumulation.

With this fiscal policy in place, we can compactly represent the system in the familiar form:

$$\mathbf{k}_{+1} = \mathbf{B}_1\mathbf{k} \tag{5.11}$$

where the subscript on **B** will be used to distinguish between the various incarnations of this matrix encountered in this chapter. (The elements of $\mathbf{B}_1$ are presented in the appendix at the end of this chapter.)

The eigenvalues of $\mathbf{B}_1$ are

$$\lambda_1 = \beta_c(1+r)\ \lambda_2 = \frac{\beta_w(R - r - (1-\Omega)\bar{\sigma}(1+r))}{1 + (1-\Omega)(\bar{\sigma}(1-\beta_w))}$$

The (normalized) eivenvector associated with λ_1 is, of course, $(1, \phi^*)$.

From λ_2 we can see immediately that the debt burden reduces the second eigenvalue and moves the system away from a one-class solution. The maximum worker saving propensity consistent with a two-class solution satisfies $\lambda_1 > \lambda_2$ and is now written:

$$\bar{\beta}_w = \frac{\beta(1+r)(1+(1-\Omega)\bar{\sigma})}{R - r - (1-\beta_c)(1+r)(1-\Omega)\bar{\sigma}}$$

Here we can see that if $\Omega = 1$ or $\bar{\sigma} = 0$, the ceiling on the worker saving propensity is identical to the ceiling in the laissez-faire model of Chapter 3. As the tax burden on workers increases, either through reductions in the share of taxes paid by capitalists or through outright increases in the debt ratio, the ceiling on the worker saving propensity rises monotonically. By reducing workers' ability to save, the burden of debt reduces the threat that thrifty workers will jeopardize the class structure of accumulation in this model.

The presence of a debt target does not fundamentally change the character of the transitional dynamics. In the laissez-faire model, the workers' share of wealth was seen to obey a nonlinear first-order difference equation. By dividing the first row of equation (5.11) by the second row, we can see that the recursion

$$\phi_{+1} = \frac{b_{21} + b_{22}\phi}{b_{11} + b_{12}\phi}$$

now describes the path of the wealth distribution (where b_{ij} is an element of $\mathbf{B}_1$). This equation has a fixed point at ϕ^*, where its slope is less than unity. The distribution of wealth will converge monotonically on this fixed point as in the laissez-faire model.

Constant Deficit Ratio

If the fiscal authorities target the overall or unified budget surplus, they will add a constant amount of new debt per unit of capital, or

$$\frac{B_{+1} - B}{K} = a$$

which, using equation (5.1), implies that the tax satisfies

$$T = rB - aK$$

and that the steady state debt-capital ratio will be

$$\sigma^* = \frac{a}{g^*}$$

With this fiscal policy, the key vector expands to $\tilde{\mathbf{k}}' = (K^c, K^w, B)$ and the full model is

$$\tilde{\mathbf{k}}_{+1} = \mathbf{A}_2\tilde{\mathbf{k}}$$

(The $\mathbf{A}_2$ matrix is presented in the appendix.)

This model can be rearranged to describe the vector $\mathbf{k}' = (K, K^w, B)$ using the permutation matrix,

$$\mathbf{P} = \begin{pmatrix} 1 & 1 & 0 \\ 0 & 1 & 0 \\ 0 & 0 & 1 \end{pmatrix}$$

to find $\mathbf{B}_2 = \mathbf{P}\mathbf{A}_2\mathbf{P}^{-1}$, giving us the system

$$\mathbf{k}_{+1} = \mathbf{B}_2\mathbf{k}$$

The eigenvalues of $\mathbf{B}_2$ are

$$\lambda_1 = \beta_c(1 + r)\ \lambda_{2,3} = c \pm \sqrt{\Delta}$$

where c and Δ (the discriminant) are functions of β_w, w, a, k, and Ω. For sufficiently large β_w, $\Delta < 0$ and the two nondominant roots are complex conjugates. Thus, this model is capable of generating oscillations.

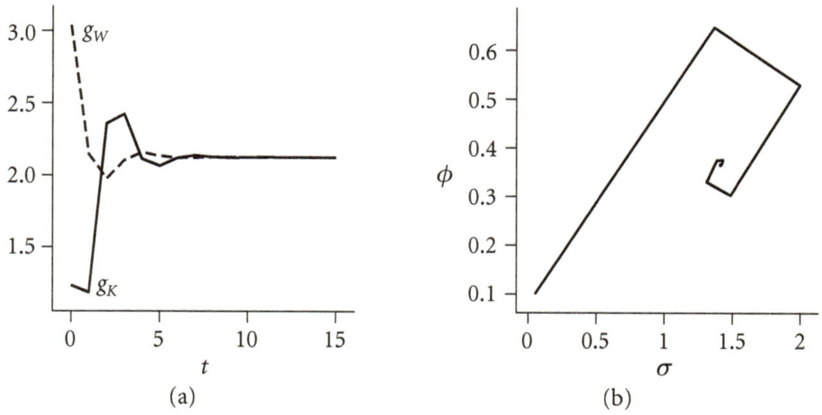

Figure 5.3 A numerical example of the transitional dynamics of an endogenous growth model with a constant deficit rule in the infinite horizon case. The parameter values are $w = 750$, $x = 1000$, $k = 60$, $\delta = 1$, $\beta_w = .1$, $\beta_c = .75$, $\Omega = .3$, $a = 3$, $K_0 = 100$, $K_0^w = 10$, $B_0 = 5$. (a) The path of capital accumulation, g_K, and the rate of growth of capitalist wealth, g_W. (b) The trajectory of the distribution of capital ownership, ϕ, and the debt-capital ratio, σ.

The normalized eigenvector associated with the dominant eigenvalue, assuming the two-class solution prevails, is $(1, \phi^*, \sigma^*)$.

We can get a better view of the dynamics by dividing the whole system by its first row to shrink the model down to the nonlinear first-order difference equations (here b_{ij} is an element of $\mathbf{B}_2$):

$$\phi_{+1} = \frac{b_{21} + b_{23}\sigma}{b_{11} + b_{12}\phi + b_{13}\sigma}$$
$$\sigma_{+1} = \frac{a + \sigma}{b_{11} + b_{12}\phi + b_{13}\sigma} \tag{5.12}$$

Figure 5.3a shows a numerical example with damped oscillations along the transitional path, focusing on the rate of accumulation and the growth of capitalist wealth. Notice how the rate of accumulation overshoots its long-run level along the transient. This illustrates the interplay of the flow effect of the primary surplus (which crowds in capital) and the stock effects of debt itself (which crowds out capital). Figure 5.3b shows the trajectory in the phase plane for this model, continuing the same numerical example.

5.3 Debt in the Finite Horizon Case

We can now confront the effect of public debt in a model with capitalists who optimize over the finite horizon of their own lifespan. As in the previous section, we first examine the temporary equilibria and steady state before we impose specific fiscal policy rules to bring out more properties of the model.

5.3.1 Temporary Equilibrium

From the capitalist and worker accumulation functions, equations (5.8) and (5.9), and the government's one-period budget constraint, equation (5.1), we can obtain the accumulation equation:

$$\begin{aligned} 1+g_K &= \beta_c(1+r)(1-\phi) - (1-\beta_c)(1+r)\sigma \\ &\quad + (1-\Omega\beta_c - \beta_w(1-\Omega))\theta + \beta_w(R-r) \end{aligned}$$

From this equation, we turn to the effects of changes in the fiscal variables, θ and σ. The flow effect of fiscal policy on accumulation is given by

$$\frac{\partial g_K}{\partial \theta} = 1 - \Omega\beta_c - \beta_w(1-\Omega) > 0$$

As in the previous model with an infinite capitalist horizon, an increased level of government saving (a larger primary surplus) contributes to higher levels of capital in the next period. But now, even if capitalists pay all the taxes, public saving has a positive effect on accumulation; Ricardian equivalence does not obtain. All else equal, an increase in the primary surplus has a smaller effect here than in the infinite-horizon example because capitalists regard all their bondholdings as net wealth.[13]

The stock crowding-out effect from an increased ratio of debt to capital is

$$\frac{\partial g_K}{\partial \sigma} = -(1-\beta_c)(1+r) < 0$$

Because all debt is regarded by capitalists as net wealth, it will crowd out real capital in their portfolios, and thus retard the accumulation of capital.

13. This comparison and the one just below treat β_c as the capitalist saving propensity and ignore the fact that it has a different conceptualization as a discount factor in the infinite and finite horizon cases.

All else equal, a given increase in the debt ratio will have a larger absolute effect on accumulation here than in the infinite-horizon example. (Recall that $\beta' = \beta_c - \Omega\beta_c + \Omega$ so $1 - \beta_c \geq 1 - \beta'$.)

5.3.2 Steady State

Finding the steady state solution using the accumulation function of the capitalists and workers is slightly more involved because the Cambridge theorem does not go through in its unalloyed form. Instead, working from equation (5.8), we arrive at a modified form of the Cambridge equation, to wit,

$$1 + g^* = \beta_c \left(1 + r - \frac{\Omega\theta}{1 - \phi + \sigma}\right)$$

where the parenthetical term on the RHS is the after-tax rate of profit. But since ϕ remains an endogenous variable, this equation is not sufficient to determine the rate of accumulation unless capitalists pay no taxes.

The best strategy to recover the solution and analyze its properties is to enlist the $\tilde{\phi}$ and $\hat{\phi}$ functions that describe the steady state relationship between the distribution of capital ownership and the rate of growth consistent with capitalist and worker behavior. The former function, relating to capitalist behavior, is

$$\tilde{\phi} = 1 + \sigma - \frac{\Omega\beta_c(r - g^*)\sigma}{\beta_c(1 + r) - (1 + g^*)}$$

We must be careful to remember that in case $\Omega = 0$, this equation degenerates to the Cambridge equation, and the denominator on the RHS vanishes.

The latter equation, relating to worker behavior, is

$$\hat{\phi} = \frac{\beta_w}{1 + g^*}(R + (1 - \Omega)g^*\sigma - (1 + (1 - \Omega)\sigma)r)$$

The steady state solution occurs where $\tilde{\phi}(g^*; \Omega, \sigma) = \hat{\phi}(g^*; \Omega, \sigma)$. There are multiple solutions to this system, and the relevant solution will be given by the largest value of g^*. There is nothing transparent about the algebraic expressions for (ϕ^*, g^*), but the comparative equilibrium features of the system can be retrieved using the implicit function theorem.

5.3.3 Comparative Dynamics

To see how changes in the debt burden and the distribution of taxes affect the equilibrium growth rate and distribution of capital ownership, first we write out the equations at the steady state:[14]

$$\begin{aligned} \hat{\phi}(g^*; \Omega, \sigma) - \phi &= 0 \\ \tilde{\phi}(g^*; \Omega, \sigma) - \phi &= 0 \end{aligned} \tag{5.13}$$

We make use of the following signs of key partial derivatives:[15]

$$\begin{array}{ll} \hat{\phi}_\Omega > 0 & \tilde{\phi}_\Omega < 0 \\ \hat{\phi}_\sigma \leq 0 & \tilde{\phi}_\sigma \leq 0 \\ \hat{\phi}_g \leq 0 & \tilde{\phi}_g < 0 \end{array}$$

The Jacobian determinant of equations (5.13) can be evaluated at the steady state equilibrium to establish that

$$|J| = \tilde{\phi}_g - \hat{\phi}_g < 0$$

This inequality reveals that the $\hat{\phi}$ function cuts the $\tilde{\phi}$ function from below at the steady state.

Debt Ratio

Totally differentiating equations (5.13), setting $d\Omega = 0$, and applying Cramer's rule gives us

$$\frac{dg^*}{d\sigma} = \frac{|J_1|}{|J|} = \frac{\hat{\phi}_\sigma - \tilde{\phi}_\sigma}{|J|} \leq 0$$

evaluated at the steady state equilibrium. The subscript on J_1 indicates the column of the Jacobian matrix that has been replaced by the vector of relevant partial derivatives, in this case $(-\hat{\phi}_\sigma, -\tilde{\phi}_\sigma)$. This derivative is zero when $\Omega = 0$, and then $\tilde{\phi}(\,\cdot\,)$ degenerates into the Cambridge equation. We

14. For an accessible introduction to the mathematical techniques used in this section, and again in the next chapter, see Chiang (1974, ch. 8).

15. We will impose the condition for $\hat{\phi}_g \leq 0$, which is

$$\sigma \leq \frac{R - r}{(1 - \Omega)(1 + r)}$$

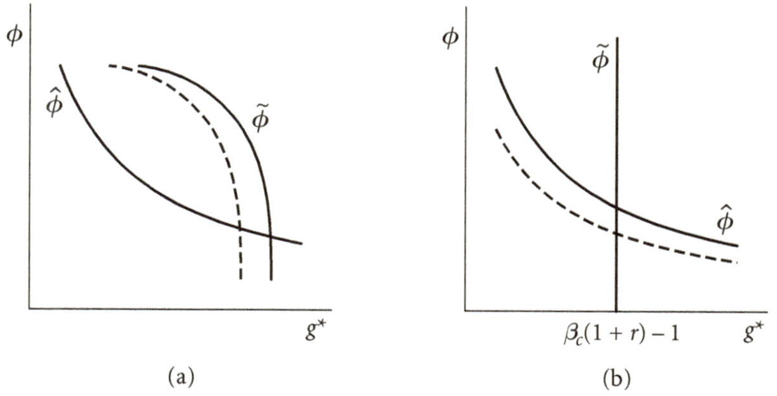

Figure 5.4 The effects of an increase in the debt ratio, σ, are conditional on the distribution of taxes in the finite horizon case. (a) When capitalists pay all the taxes ($\Omega = 1$), the workers saving function is not affected by an increase in debt, and the workers' share of capital ownership rises. (b) When workers pay all the taxes ($\Omega = 0$), capitalist saving, governed by the traditional Cambridge equation, is not affected by an increase in debt, and the workers' share of capital ownership falls.

can see that except in this case, increases in the debt burden reduce the long-run growth rate by virtue of their effects on capitalist saving.

On the other hand, the effects of debt on the distribution of capital ownership are dependent on the distribution of taxes. Evaluating the expression

$$\frac{d\phi^*}{d\sigma} = \frac{|J_2|}{|J|} = \frac{\hat{\phi}_\sigma \tilde{\phi}_g - \hat{\phi}_g \tilde{\phi}_\sigma}{|J|}$$

reveals that its sign depends critically on the value of Ω.

Figure 5.4 illustrates[16] for the extreme values, $\Omega = 1$ (capitalists pay all the taxes) and $\Omega = 0$ (workers pay all the taxes). When capitalists pay the taxes, an increase in the debt burden does not affect workers saving and $\hat{\phi}(\cdot)$ is invariant. The steady state share of capital owned by workers must clearly increase as the burden of debt inhibits capitalist saving. When workers pay all the taxes, an increase in the debt burden does not affect capitalist saving, and $\tilde{\phi}(\cdot)$ degenerates into the Cambridge equation. The steady

16. The two functions will intersect twice (not shown), illustrating that the economically relevant point is given by the dominant root, or the largest g^*.

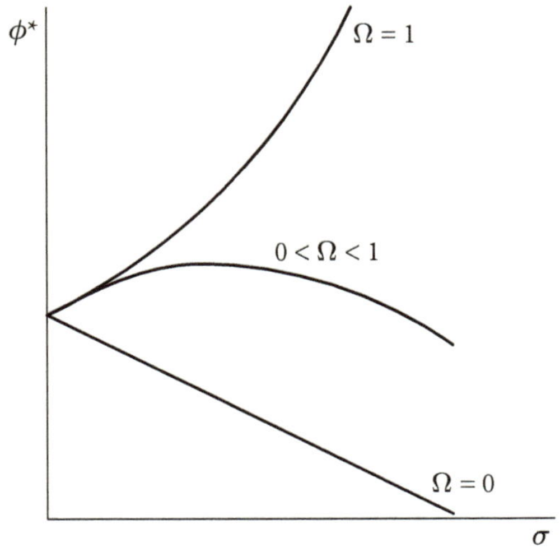

Figure 5.5 The relationship between the steady state distribution of capital wealth and the debt-capital ratio is conditioned by the distribution of taxes in the finite horizon case. For intermediate values of Ω, the relationship can be nonmonotonic.

state share of capital owned by workers must clearly decrease with the rising debt burden on workers.

Figure 5.5 illustrates the relationship in another way, by showing how the steady state distribution of capital ownership changes with a rising debt burden for different tax regimes. For intermediate values of Ω, it is possible for the debt to have first a positive and then a negative effect on the workers' share of capital wealth.

Distribution of Tax

Finally, to see the effect of changing the distribution of taxes, totally differentiating equations (5.13), setting $d\sigma = 0$, and again applying Cramer's rule yields

$$\frac{dg^*}{d\Omega} = \frac{|J_1|}{|J|} = \frac{\hat{\phi}_\Omega - \tilde{\phi}_\Omega}{|J|} < 0$$

This inequality can be established by the signs alone. Shifting the burden of taxes toward capitalists reduces growth under any conditions, even though it encourages capital formation from worker saving.

Shifting the burden of taxes toward capitalists reduces their share of capital ownership, for

$$\frac{d\phi^*}{d\Omega} = \frac{|J_2|}{|J|} = \frac{\hat{\phi}_\Omega \tilde{\phi}_g - \hat{\phi}_g \tilde{\phi}_\Omega}{|J|} > 0$$

This inequality can be established from the sign configuration alone assuming that $\hat{\phi}_g < 0$.

5.3.4 *Transitional Dynamics and Class Structure*

Once again, we can draw out the transitional dynamics of the model by specifying one of the two fiscal policy rules. The constant debt ratio again invites us to examine the boundary between the one- and two-class models.

Constant Debt Ratio

With the fiscal authorities pursuing a policy that targets the debt-capital ratio, we can compactly represent the system in the familiar form (skipping the derivation using **A**):

$$\mathbf{k}_{+1} = \mathbf{B}_3\mathbf{k} \tag{5.14}$$

(The elements of $\mathbf{B}_3$ are presented in the appendix to this chapter.)

The character of the steady state depends on which eigenvalue is dominant. Let us continue the notation that λ_1 is the root associated with the two-class solution. Consider the effects of debt on $\bar{\beta}_w$, the maximum worker saving propensity consistent with the two-class solution, which verifies $\lambda_1 > \lambda_2$. Two extreme cases illustrate how debt affects the class structure of accumulation through the function $\bar{\beta}_w(\sigma, \Omega)$. Thus,

$$\text{for } \Omega = 0 \qquad \bar{\beta}_w = \frac{\beta_c k(1+\sigma)(1+r)}{w - \sigma k(1-\beta_c)(1+r)}$$

$$\text{for } \Omega = 1 \qquad \bar{\beta}_w = \beta_c(1+r)(k/w)f(\sigma)$$

where $f(\sigma)$ is a polynomial that equals unity when $\sigma = 0$ and that has a negative derivative, $f_\sigma < 0$.

Figure 5.6 illustrates the behavior of $\bar{\beta}_w(\sigma, \Omega)$ for various values of the tax distribution parameter. We can now see that an increased debt ratio increases the ceiling on the worker saving rate, as it did in the infinite-horizon model above, when the workers pay all the taxes. But when workers pay no

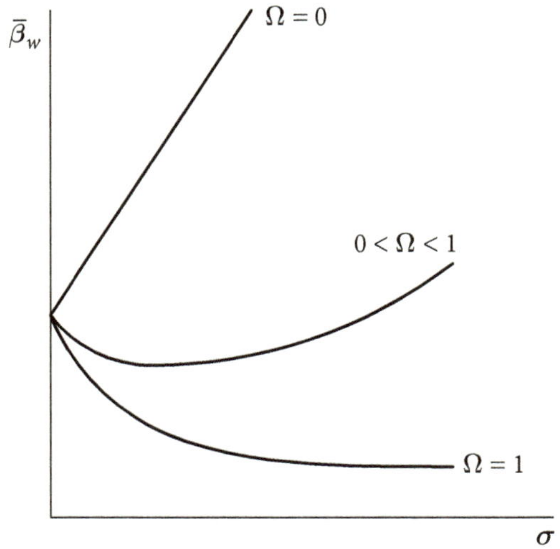

Figure 5.6 The relationship between debt and the maximum worker saving propensity consistent with a two-class model, $\bar{\beta}_w$, is conditioned by the distribution of taxes in the finite horizon case. For intermediate values of Ω, the relationship can be nonmonotonic.

taxes, an increased debt ratio lowers the ceiling on the worker saving rate because it inhibits capitalist saving. In the intermediate case, it is possible for an increased debt ratio to first decrease and then increase the ceiling on the workers saving rate.

This model can also be expressed through a single nonlinear first-order difference equation, $\phi_{+1} = f(\phi)$. This equation takes the same form as it did in the previous model, and similarly preserves the basic character of the laissez-faire model. It does not produce alternations, for example.

Constant Deficit Ratio

When the fiscal authorities pursue a target deficit-capital ratio, a, the dynamics are represented by

$$\tilde{\mathbf{k}}_{+1} = \mathbf{A}_4 \tilde{\mathbf{k}}$$

(Again, the elements of $\mathbf{A}_4$ can be found in the appendix to this chapter.)

As before, this model can be recast to describe **k** by using the permutation matrix **P**. It can then be reduced to a two-dimensional equation system along the lines of equations (5.12). The qualitative dynamics of this model are similar to those of the model with an infinite horizon; oscillations are possible. The steady state debt ratio remains $\sigma^* = a/g^*$. For the equilibrium growth rate and distribution of capital ownership, see Section 5.3.2 on the steady state. The eigenvalues of $\mathbf{A}_4$ are surprisingly difficult to recover and messy considering how little separates the matrices of the two models: $\mathbf{A}_2 - \mathbf{A}_4 = (a\Omega(1-\beta_c))[1, 1, 1]$. The latter collapses to the former when capitalists pay no taxes or when capitalists save all their end-of-period wealth.

5.4 Debt in the Endogenous Growth Models

We can now compare the properties of the model under the alternative assumptions about the capitalist planning horizon, aided by Table 5.1. The table collects the chapter's main conclusions about the effects of fiscal policy on steady state values.

Table 5.1 Debt in two endogenous growth models

	Infinite Horizon	Finite Horizon
$\frac{dg^*}{d\sigma}$	0	−
$\frac{d\phi^*}{d\sigma}$	−	$-\ (\Omega = 0)$ $\pm(0 < \Omega < 1)$ $+\ (\Omega = 1)$
$\frac{d\overline{\beta}_w}{d\sigma}$	+	$+\ (\Omega = 0)$ $\pm(0 < \Omega < 1)$ $-\ (\Omega = 1)$
$\frac{dg^*}{d\Omega}$	0	−
$\frac{d\phi^*}{d\Omega}$	+	+

Under the assumption of an infinite horizon, capitalists treat only the share of debt serviced by workers as net wealth. Fiscal policy is neutral with respect to growth (the Cambridge theorem inverted) but is not neutral with respect to distribution. From the perspective of workers, distribution is unambiguously worsened by increases in their debt burden, either from more debt itself or from a diminished share of taxes to service the debt falling on capitalists. An increase in debt is doubly punishing to workers. By temporarily slowing accumulation, it reduces the level of output and jobs in the long run (even while leaving their growth rates invariant); and by increasing each worker's tax burden, it reduces their lifetime wealth.

Under the finite horizon, capitalists treat all the debt as net wealth, and as a result, the Cambridge theorem does not go through in pure form: debt has long-run negative consequences for the rate of accumulation (not just its level) because it makes capitalists feel richer and consume more. Whether this leads to a greater concentration of capital wealth then depends on the distribution of taxes. If capitalists pay all the taxes, an increased debt ratio will reduce their share of capital wealth. But this is no boon to workers, because the growth of employment and output will be permanently lower in every case.

From a classical perspective, in both cases public debt places distinctive burdens on workers in the long run that should be considered by policy makers and economists alongside the well-established Keynesian benefits of debt-financing for stabilization purposes in the short run.

5.5 Appendix: Elements of A and B Matrices

The elements of $\mathbf{B}_1$ are

$$b_{11} = \frac{\beta_c(1+r) + (R-r)\beta_w + (1-\Omega)\bar{\sigma}(\beta_c - \beta_w)(1+r)}{1+(1-\Omega)\bar{\sigma}(1-\beta_w)}$$

$$b_{12} = \frac{-\beta(1+r)}{1+(1-\Omega)\bar{\sigma}(1-\beta_w)}$$

$$b_{21} = (R-r)\beta_w - (1-\Omega)\bar{\sigma}\beta_w(1+r) + \beta_w(1-\Omega)\bar{\sigma}b_{11}$$

$$b_{22} = b_{12}\beta_w(1-\Omega)\bar{\sigma}$$

The elements of $\mathbf{B_3}$ are

$$b_{11} = \frac{\beta_c(1+r) + (R-r)\beta_w + \bar{\sigma}(1+r)(1-\beta_w - \Omega(\beta_c - \beta_w) - (1-\beta_c))}{1+\bar{\sigma}(1-\beta_w + \Omega(\beta_c - \beta_w))}$$

$$b_{12} = \frac{-\beta(1+r)}{1+\bar{\sigma}(1-\beta_w + \Omega(\beta_c - \beta_w))}$$

$$b_{21} = (R-r)\beta_w - (1-\Omega)\bar{\sigma}\beta_w(1+r) + \beta_w(1-\Omega)\bar{\sigma}b_{11}$$

$$b_{22} = b_{12}\beta_w(1-\Omega)\bar{\sigma}$$

The $\mathbf{A_2}$ matrix is

$$\begin{pmatrix} \beta_c(1+r) - (1-\Omega)a & -(1-\Omega)a & (\beta_c + \Omega(1-\beta_c))(1+r) - (1+\Omega r) \\ (\frac{w}{k} + (1-\Omega)a)\beta_w & (\frac{w}{k} + (1-\Omega)a)\beta_w & -\beta_w(1-\Omega)r \\ a & a & 1 \end{pmatrix}$$

The $\mathbf{A_4}$ matrix is

$$\begin{pmatrix} \beta_c(1+r) - (1-\Omega\beta_c)a & -(1-\Omega\beta_c)a & \beta_c r(1-\Omega) - (1-\beta_c) \\ (\frac{w}{k} + (1-\Omega)a)\beta_w & (\frac{w}{k} + (1-\Omega)a)\beta_w & -\beta_w(1-\Omega)r \\ a & a & 1 \end{pmatrix}$$

— 6 —

Debt and Exogenous Growth

> What is being transferred here are the hard-earned tax dollars of all those admirable Americans in the form of interest payments to the Deserving Rich. Economists bloodlessly call such a transaction a "transfer payment." By any moral or ethical standard it is an outrage.
>
> MARK SHIELDS (1990)

This chapter builds on the tools developed in the first section of Chapter 5 for incorporating public debt into the growth model. In this chapter, the model is closed by the assumption of full employment of a predestined labor force with a constant natural rate of growth. As in the previous chapter, we will investigate the effects of public debt under two different assumptions about the behavior of capitalists. In the first section, we assume capitalist dynasties plan over an infinite horizon so that Ricardian equivalence prevails. In the second section, we assume capitalists plan over the finite horizon of their own life spans, so that Ricardian equivalence does not prevail. After comparing these two models, we turn to some evidence on the recent experience of the United States with debt financing. Regardless of whether one shares Mark Shields's sense of outrage over the national debt in the epigraph, it does seem useful to gain some understanding of its effects on the distribution of income and wealth under the standard assumption of exogenous growth.

6.1 Debt in the Infinite Horizon Case

The elements for constructing a model of growth with public debt have already been recorded in previous chapters. In particular, the government budget constraint, the capitalist saving function, and the worker saving function carry over from the previous chapter. The key substantive point here is that capitalists consume a constant fraction of their net wealth, which consists of capital plus the debt serviced through taxes on workers. In addition, of course, we close the model by assuming that $g_K = n$, which is necessary to ensure that full employment is maintained over time.

6.1.1 *Temporary Equilibrium*

In the most general terms, with the fiscal policy unspecified and the tax considered to be predetermined, the temporary equilibrium can be derived by recognizing that the capital stock and its distribution are themselves predetermined, having been inherited from the past. The system is compactly represented by

$$\begin{pmatrix} \frac{\beta_w}{k} & \beta_c(1-\phi)-(1-\beta')\sigma \\ 1 & k \end{pmatrix} \begin{pmatrix} w \\ r \end{pmatrix} = \begin{pmatrix} \psi_1 \\ y \end{pmatrix} \tag{6.1}$$

We will refer to the matrix on the LHS of this expression as $\mathbf{C}_1$, using subscript arabic numerals to distinguish between the various incarnations of this matrix and the consolidating term, ψ, that we encounter in this chapter.[1] The equilibrium values of w and r can be handily obtained from this system using Cramer's rule.

As in the basic laissez-faire model, the determinant of $\mathbf{C}_1$ has economic significance in terms of labor market stability since $|\mathbf{C}|/k$ equals the key derivative, dg_K/dw. We will continue to assume that

$$|\mathbf{C}_1| < 0$$

Armed with this knowledge, we can analyze the effects of fiscal policy with the help of the implicit function theorem. By differentiating equation (6.1) in the neighborhood of its equilibrium solution, and setting $d\sigma = 0$, we can solve for the flow effect of fiscal policy on distribution:

$$\frac{\partial r}{\partial \theta} = \frac{|\mathbf{C}_{12}|}{|\mathbf{C}_1|} = \frac{(1-\beta_w)(1-\Omega)}{|\mathbf{C}_1|} \leq 0$$

where we adopt the convention for implementing Cramer's rule that $\mathbf{C}_{12}$ represents the Jacobian matrix, $\mathbf{C}_1$, with the second column replaced by the vector of relevant partial derivatives, in this case $(\partial\psi_1/\partial\theta, 0)'$. Thus, we

1. In this case, $\psi_1 = 1 + n - \beta_c(1-\phi) + (1-\beta')\sigma - (1-\beta_w)(1-\Omega)\theta$.

can see that an increase in the primary fiscal surplus will reduce the rate of profit, a familiar crowding-out effect.

Similarly, we can analyze the stock effects of changes in the debt-capital ratio by differentiating equation (6.1) and setting $d\theta = 0$:

$$\frac{\partial r}{\partial \sigma} = \frac{|\mathbf{C}_{12}|}{|\mathbf{C}_1|} = \frac{-(1+r)(1-\beta_c)(1-\Omega)}{|\mathbf{C}_1|} \geq 0$$

(Recall that $\beta' = \beta_c - \beta_c\Omega + \Omega$.) Here we can see that an increase in the level of debt has a crowding-out effect on the rate of profit. Because capitalists regard the debt serviced out of taxes on workers as net wealth, they will consume more and accumulate less in response to an increase in public debt, all else equal, creating an incipient excess supply of labor that resolves itself by a collapse of the wage and a rise in the rate of profit.

Notice that both the flow and stock effects vanish when capitalists pay all the taxes ($\Omega = 1$). In this case, we are in the realm of Barro neutrality because capitalists will not regard their bondholdings as net wealth.

6.1.2 Steady State

In a steady state, the wealth of the capitalists must expand at the natural rate of growth. Recall from the previous chapter that the capitalist saving function is

$$W_{+1} = \beta(1+r)K^c + \beta'(1+r)B - \Omega T$$

By making some decisive substitutions, using $\theta = (r-n)\sigma$ and the definition of β', we obtain[2]

$$1 + g_W = \beta_c(1+r) - \frac{\Omega\sigma}{1-\phi+\sigma}(\beta_c(1+r) - (1+n))$$

Now set $g_W = n$, and remarkably, we arrive at the unalloyed Cambridge equation in its original form (with r on the LHS):

$$1 + r^* = \frac{1+n}{\beta_c}$$

This equation reads causally from right to left: the rate of profit is determined by the natural rate of growth and the capitalist saving propensity,

2. We make use of the following expressions:

$$\frac{K^c}{W} = \frac{1-\phi}{1-\phi+\sigma} \quad \frac{B}{W} = \frac{\sigma}{1-\phi+\sigma} \quad \frac{T}{W} = \frac{\theta}{1-\phi+\sigma}$$

quite independent of the worker saving propensity or technology. Once again, this verifies the finding of Pasinetti (1989) that the Cambridge theorem applies when public debt obeys Ricardian equivalence. The equilibrium wage, w^*, can be found by substitution into the wage-profit equation.

To derive the steady state distribution of capital ownership, we start with the workers' saving function, which was written

$$K_{+1}^{w} = \frac{w\beta_w}{k}K - \beta_w(1-\Omega)T$$

By dividing by $K_{+1} = (1+n)K$ and simplifying, we get the steady state distribution

$$\phi^* = \frac{\beta_w(1+R)}{1+n} - \frac{\beta_w}{\beta_c} - \beta_w\left(\frac{1-\beta_c}{\beta_c}\right)(1-\Omega)\sigma \tag{6.2}$$

As in the endogenous growth model, we see immediately that in comparison to the laissez-faire economy, the presence of public debt reduces the share of capital wealth owned by workers. From the workers' perspective, the burden of debt manifests itself in the tax required for debt service payments, which reduces their after-tax lifetime wealth and as a result diminishes their ability to save. Only in the case where the capitalists bear the full burden of taxation will the presence of public debt fail to reduce workers' capital wealth share.

From the capitalists' perspective, by contrast, the debt represents not a burden but a mechanism that redistributes wealth in a favorable direction through its (temporary) effects on the distribution of income. During the transition to the steady state, the rate of profit is increased by the stock effects of debt, permitting capitalists to accumulate more wealth than they otherwise would have. The capitalists will enjoy permanently higher consumption levels on a path with greater debt, the complement to the depressed living standards imposed upon workers by the burden of debt.

6.1.3 Comparative Dynamics

The quickest path to a comparative equilibrium analysis of the steady state is simply to differentiate the equations for ϕ^* and r^* above to obtain

$$\frac{d\phi^*}{d\sigma} = \frac{-\beta_w(1-\Omega)(1-\beta_c)}{\beta_c} \leq 0$$

$$\frac{d\phi^*}{d\Omega} = \frac{\beta_w(1-\beta_c)\sigma}{\beta_c} > 0$$

From the Cambridge equation we can see clearly that the rate of profit in the steady state is unaffected by either parameter change, sparing us the need to write down its derivatives.

Unless capitalists pay all the tax to service the debt, an increase in the debt-capital ratio depresses the share of capital owned by workers. Similarly, an increase in the share of taxes paid by capitalists will increase the share of worker capital. And in conformity with the Cambridge theorem, changes in the amount of debt or the distribution of taxation have no long-run effects on the distribution of income.

A demographic shock will clearly affect the distribution of income as it would in the laissez-faire model. The rate of profit will change in the same direction as the natural rate of growth, through the Cambridge equation, and the wage rate will change in the opposing direction along the wage-profit curve. But to ascertain the effects on the distribution of wealth, we need to specify the fiscal policy.

Under a constant debt-capital (σ) fiscal rule, we can see directly from equation (6.2) that the effects of a change in the natural rate on capital wealth distribution will be precisely the same as in the laissez-faire case. A decline in the natural rate, for example, will increase the workers' wealth share. The constant debt-capital rule (equivalently, constant debt per worker) seems to be the natural choice for studying the effect of debt on the presentation of a demographic shock.

Under a constant deficit-capital (a) fiscal rule, on the other hand, a change in the natural rate of growth will affect the debt-capital ratio since its steady state value is given by $\sigma = a/n$. This fiscal rule conflates the effects of the demographic shock and the effects of the fiscal response and therefore does not suggest itself for studying the unadulterated effect of debt on the presentation of a demographic shock.[3]

6.1.4 Transitional Dynamics and Fiscal Policy

As in the previous chapter, we will enlist two separate assumptions about fiscal policy, first taking the debt-capital ratio as the fiscal authorities' target and then taking the deficit-capital ratio as their target. In the first case, we will investigate the boundary between the one- and two-class regimes, as

3. It is possible to show that under this fiscal rule, a demographic shock can lead to a decline in the workers' share of wealth under some parameter values. In particular, if the target deficit-capital ratio is large, lower growth will raise the tax burden on workers sufficiently to diminish their capacity to save.

well as the effects of fiscal policy on the asymptotic stability of the system. In the second case, we will also inquire into the effects of fiscal policies on the labor market stability requirement.

Constant Debt Ratio

When the fiscal authorities pursue a constant debt-capital ratio, they must choose a tax in each period simultaneously with the equilibrium profit and wage rate. Nonetheless, the structure of the temporary equilibrium remains the same, described by an equation identical in form[4] to equation (6.1).

Using this system to solve for the equilibrium r, substituting into the worker saving function gives us the nonlinear first-order difference equation that governs the dynamics:

$$\phi_{+1} = z(\phi)$$

having fixed points at ϕ^* and $\phi = 1 + \bar{\sigma}(1 - \Omega)$.

As was the case in the laissez-faire model (see Chapter 3), the necessary condition for the one-class Samuelson-Modigliani regime is that the graph of the relevant branch of this function slope upward. By setting $z_\phi < 0$ and solving for the worker saving propensity, we obtain the separating condition that $\beta_w < \bar{\beta}_w$ where

$$\bar{\beta}_w = \frac{1 + n + \bar{\sigma}(1 - \Omega)(1 + n)}{1 + R + \bar{\sigma}(1 - \Omega)(1 + n)}$$

We can see immediately that the presence of debt shifts upward the separating condition in (β_c, β_w)-space and makes the one-class Samuelson-Modigliani regime more difficult to reach.

The presence of debt also changes the condition for $\phi^* < 1$. In the laissez-faire model, this condition was automatically satisfied by virtue of the two-class separating condition. But now it can become binding, particularly when workers shoulder most of the tax burden, which can be seen from equation (6.2). We must have

$$\beta_w < \frac{\beta_c(1 + n)}{\beta_c(1 + R + \sigma(1 + n)) + (1 + n)(\Omega\sigma(1 - \beta_c) - (1 + \sigma))} \tag{6.3}$$

4. The consolidating term will be $\psi_2 = 1 + n + (1 - \beta_w)(1 - \Omega)n\bar{\sigma} - \beta_c(1 - \phi) + (1 - \beta')\bar{\sigma}$ and $\mathbf{C}_2$ will be

$$\begin{pmatrix} \frac{\beta_w}{k} & \beta_c(1-\phi) + (\beta_c - \beta_w)(1-\Omega)\bar{\sigma} \\ 1 & k \end{pmatrix}$$

It is clear that this condition can dominate the previous condition, particularly if workers pay a large share of the tax.

The condition for asymptotic stability is more relevant, since it dominates the necessary condition for a two-class regime just described. By evaluating z_ϕ at the equilibrium ϕ^*, we can write the stability condition

$$\beta_w < \frac{\beta_c(1+n)(1+\bar{\sigma}(1-\Omega))}{\beta_c(1+R)+(1+n)(1+\bar{\sigma}(1+\beta_c)(1-\Omega))} \tag{6.4}$$

This expression collapses to the stability condition for the laissez-faire model in case $\sigma = 0$ (obviously) or $\Omega = 1$ (when workers pay no taxes). Thus, it is clear that the debt acts to increase the space of stable saving propensities.[5] Figure 6.1 illustrates.

Constant Deficit Ratio

As we saw in the previous chapter, if the fiscal authorities target the deficit-capital ratio, a, they will set taxes according to $T = rB - aK$. The debt-capital ratio will thus evolve, ultimately achieving a steady state value:

$$\sigma^* = \frac{a}{n}$$

The temporary equilibrium will be governed by an equation of the same form[6] as equation (6.1). The matrix $\mathbf{C}_2$ from the previous subsection continues to apply, although with $\bar{\sigma}$ replaced by a variable σ. Since the determinant of this matrix has a substantive economic interpretation as the labor market stability condition, this fact bears some significance. Evaluating $|\mathbf{C}_2| < 0$ reveals that the upper boundary for labor market stability is

$$\beta_w < \frac{(1-\phi+(1-\Omega)\sigma)\beta_c}{1+(1-\Omega)\sigma}$$

This expression collapses to the labor market stability condition for the laissez-faire model in case $\sigma = 0$ (obviously) or $\Omega = 1$. It is clear that the presence of public debt expands the space of permissable saving propensities.

5. It is interesting to observe that the stable space can contain equilibria that violate condition (6.3), i.e., having $\phi^* > 1$. In such an equilibrium, capitalists own negative capital but have positive net worth because of their bondholdings. Perhaps we might interpret this outcome as a formal representation of capitalist borrowing from worker households?

6. In this case, $\psi_3 = 1 + n + a(1-\beta_w)(1-\Omega) - \beta_c(1-\phi) + (1-\beta')\sigma$.

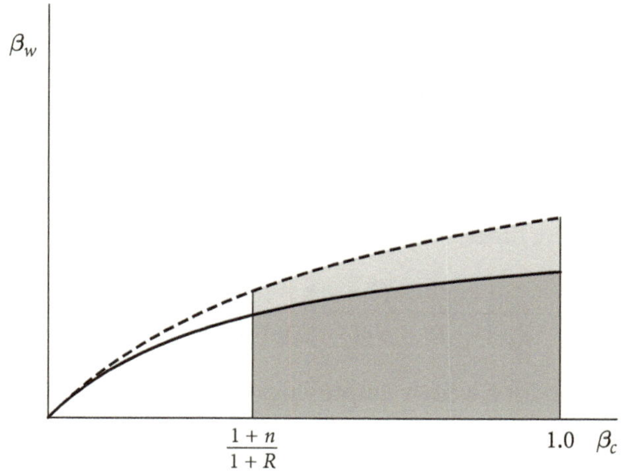

Figure 6.1 Public debt increases the space of saving propensities that generate an asymptotically stable two-class equilibrium in the infinite horizon case. The darkly shaded area represents the laissez-faire economy, while the total (light and dark combined) shaded area represents an economy with some public debt.

The dynamics of the model with a constant deficit rule will be governed by two first-order difference equations. By solving for the temporary equilibrium value of r, and substituting into the worker saving function, we obtain the difference equation for the distribution of capital ownership. By substituting the fiscal rule into the government's one-period budget constraint, we obtain the equation for the debt-capital ratio. The result is the system

$$\begin{aligned} \phi_{+1} &= z(\phi, \sigma) \\ \sigma_{+1} &= \frac{a+\sigma}{1+n} \end{aligned} \tag{6.5}$$

having fixed points at ϕ^* and $\phi = 1 + a(1-\Omega)/n$.

The asymptotic stability of equations (6.5) requires that the roots of its Jacobian matrix

$$J = \begin{pmatrix} z_\phi & z_\sigma \\ 0 & \frac{1}{1+n} \end{pmatrix}$$

are less than unity in absolute magnitude. But this system is in block triangular form (it solves recursively, starting with σ), and the roots are $1/(1+n)$ and z_ϕ. Setting $z_\phi < 1$ and rearranging gives us condition (6.4) for asymptotic stability with σ replaced by a/n. Thus, Figure 6.1 accurately describes the stabilizing effect of debt under this fiscal rule.

6.1.5 *Welfare Effect of Demographic Shock*

We saw in Chapter 3 that a demographic shock (decline in the natural rate of growth) must raise the welfare of a representative worker in the steady state. Debt does not alter that result, assuming that we stick to the benchmark case in which the debt-capital ratio remains constant.[7] Defining the indirect utility function, $V(c^w(w, \tau), c^r(w, \tau, r))$, we find that

$$\frac{dV}{dn} < 0 \Leftrightarrow \beta_w < \frac{(1+n)(1+\sigma(1-\beta_c)(1-\Omega))}{\beta_c(1+R+\sigma(1-\Omega)(1+n)) - (1+n)(1+\sigma(1-\Omega))}$$

This condition for a welfare-improving demographic shock will be dominated by condition (6.3) for the workers' wealth share to be less than unity. Thus, unless we are prepared to attribute some meaning to an equilibrium in which capitalists own negative capital, a demographic shock will benefit workers.

6.2 Debt in the Finite Horizon Case

In case the capitalists optimize over the finite horizon of their own life spans, the accumulation and saving functions from the previous chapter carry over and form the basis for an exogenous growth model with public debt. The key substantive point here is that capitalists consume a constant fraction of their after-tax disposable wealth. They effectively regard all their bond holdings as net worth, and do not mark down their portfolios to account for future tax liabilities.

6.2.1 *Temporary Equilibrium*

The temporary equilibrium for the model assuming a finite capitalist horizon will be governed by a system identical in form[8] to equation (6.1). In light of its economic significance in terms of labor market stability, we will

7. It is possible to show that if the deficit-capital ratio remains constant, a demographic shock can lower workers' utility, mainly because they value highly the return on their saving. But this result is driven by the policy of accepting an increase in debt per worker.

8. In this case, $\psi_4 = 1 + n + 1 - \beta_w + \Omega(\beta_w - \beta_c)\theta - \beta_c(1-\phi) + (1-\beta)\sigma$ and $\mathbf{C}_3$ is equal to

$$\begin{pmatrix} \frac{\beta_w}{k} & \beta_c(1-\phi) + (1-\beta_c)\sigma \\ 1 & k \end{pmatrix}$$

continue to assume that $|C_3| < 0$. Once again, this will let us sign the flow and stock fiscal policy derivatives by differentiating the system in the neighborhood of its equilibrium solution. The flow and stock effects of fiscal policy are described by

$$\frac{\partial r}{\partial \theta} = \frac{|C_{32}|}{|C_3|} = \frac{(1 - \beta_w - \Omega(\beta_c - \beta_w))}{|C_3|} < 0$$

$$\frac{\partial r}{\partial \sigma} = \frac{|C_{32}|}{|C_3|} = \frac{-(1 + r)(1 - \beta_c)}{|C_3|} > 0$$

Both the flow and stock effects of fiscal policy operate in the same way as in the model with infinite capitalist horizons, where Ricardian equivalence prevails. However, with a finite capitalist planning horizon, neither of these effects vanishes when capitalists pay all the taxes ($\Omega = 1$). Barro neutrality fails because capitalists do regard their bond holdings as net wealth.

6.2.2 *Steady State*

As was true in the endogenous growth model of the previous chapter, finding the steady state solution using the accumulation function of the capitalists and workers is slightly more involved because the Cambridge theorem does not go through in its unalloyed form. Working from the capitalist saving function, we can derive a modified form of the Cambridge equation, to wit:

$$1 + n = \beta_c \left(1 + r^* - \frac{\Omega\theta}{1 - \phi + \sigma}\right)$$

where the parenthetical term on the RHS is the after-tax rate of profit. But since ϕ remains an endogenous variable, this equation is not sufficient to determine the rate of profit unless capitalists pay no taxes.

Nonetheless, this equation makes it clear that a modified version of the Cambridge theorem prevails: the after-tax rate of profit is invariant to changes in worker or government saving (Denicolo and Matteuzzi 1990; Dalziel 1991).

The best strategy to recover the solution and analyze its properties is to once again enlist the $\tilde{\phi}$ and $\hat{\phi}$ functions that describe the steady state relationship between the distribution of capital ownership and the equilibrium rate of profit consistent with capitalist and worker behavior, respectively. The former function, relating to capitalist behavior, is

$$\tilde{\phi} = 1 + \sigma - \frac{\Omega \beta_c (r^* - n)\sigma}{\beta_c (1 + r^*) - (1 + n)}$$

We must be careful to remember that in case $\Omega = 0$, this equation degenerates to the Cambridge equation, and the denominator on the RHS vanishes.

The latter equation, relating to worker behavior, is

$$\hat{\phi} = \frac{\beta_w}{1 + n}(R + (1 - \Omega)n\sigma - (1 + (1 - \Omega)\sigma)r^*)$$

The steady state solution occurs where $\tilde{\phi}(r^*; \Omega, \sigma, n) = \hat{\phi}(r^*; \Omega, \sigma, n)$. To gain a better understanding of the steady state, we turn to a comparative equilibrium analysis of the system.

6.2.3 Comparative Dynamics

To see how changes in the debt burden and the distribution of taxes affect the equilibrium distribution of income and of capital ownership, first we will write out the equations at the steady state:

$$\begin{aligned} \hat{\phi}(r^*; \Omega, \sigma, n) - \phi &= 0 \\ \tilde{\phi}(r^*; \Omega, \sigma, n) - \phi &= 0 \end{aligned} \tag{6.6}$$

We will make use of the following signs of key partial derivatives:[9]

$$\begin{array}{ll} \hat{\phi}_\Omega > 0 & \tilde{\phi}_\Omega < 0 \\ \tilde{\phi}_\sigma < 0 & \hat{\phi}_\sigma \leq 0 \\ \hat{\phi}_r < 0 & \tilde{\phi}_r > 0 \\ \hat{\phi}_n \leq 0 & \tilde{\phi}_n < 0 \end{array}$$

The Jacobian determinant of equations (6.6) can be evaluated at the steady state equilibrium to establish that

$$|J| = \tilde{\phi}_r - \hat{\phi}_r > 0$$

This inequality reveals that the $\hat{\phi}$ function cuts the $\tilde{\phi}$ function from above.

9. We assume that $\hat{\phi}_n \leq 0$, the condition for which is

$$\sigma \leq \frac{R - r}{(1 - \Omega)(1 + r)}$$

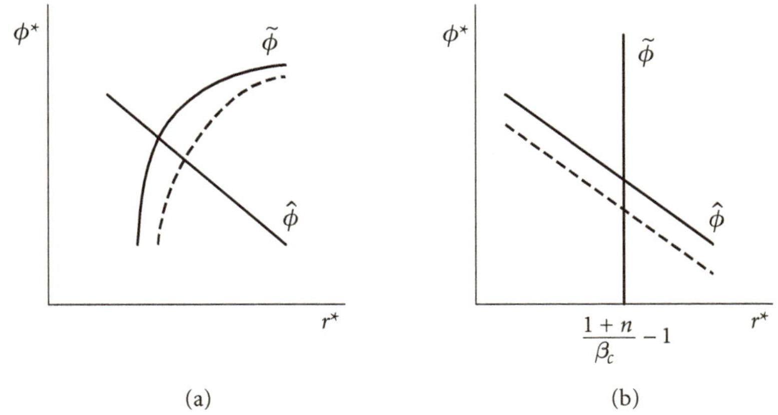

Figure 6.2 The effect of debt on the distribution of wealth in the finite horizon case is conditional on the distribution of taxes, but in all cases the effect is nonpositive. (a) When capitalists pay all the taxes ($\Omega = 1$), worker saving is unaffected by the burden of debt and the rate of profit must increase to maintain the natural rate of growth. (b) When workers pay all the taxes ($\Omega = 0$), their saving is reduced, but the rate of profit obeys the Cambridge theorem.

Debt Ratio

Totally differentiating equations (6.6), setting $d\Omega = dn = 0$, and applying Cramer's rule[10] gives us

$$\frac{dr^*}{d\sigma} = \frac{|J_1|}{|J|} = \frac{\hat{\phi}_\sigma - \tilde{\phi}_\sigma}{|J|} \geq 0$$

Evaluated at the steady state equilibrium, this derivative can be shown with some effort to be positive. On the other hand, we can establish that

$$\frac{d\phi^*}{d\sigma} = \frac{|J_2|}{|J|} = \frac{\hat{\phi}_\sigma \tilde{\phi}_r - \hat{\phi}_r \tilde{\phi}_\sigma}{|J|} < 0$$

based on the configuration of signs alone.

Figure 6.2 illustrates for the extreme values, $\Omega = 1$ (capitalists pay all the taxes) and $\Omega = 0$ (workers pay all the taxes). When capitalists pay the taxes, an increase in the debt burden does not affect worker saving and the $\hat{\phi}$ function is invariant. The steady state share of capital owned by workers must decrease as the burden of debt inhibits capitalist saving, requiring a

10. Recall the convention that J_i refers to the Jacobian matrix with the ith column replaced by the vector of relevant partial derivatives.

higher rate of profit and a lower wage, and therefore less worker saving. When workers pay all the taxes, an increase in the debt burden does not affect capitalist saving, and the $\tilde{\phi}$ function degenerates into the Cambridge equation. The steady state share of capital owned by workers must clearly decrease with the rising debt burden on workers. The effects of debt on the distribution of wealth are not conditional on the distribution of the tax burden (as they were in the endogenous growth model).

Distribution of Tax

Totally differentiating equations (6.6), setting $d\sigma = dn = 0$, and again applying Cramer's rule yields

$$\frac{dr^*}{d\Omega} = \frac{|J_1|}{|J|} = \frac{\hat{\phi}_\Omega - \tilde{\phi}_\Omega}{|J|} > 0$$

This inequality can be established by the signs alone. Shifting the burden of taxes toward capitalists requires a higher rate of profit to preserve growth at the natural rate. An alternative proof is simply to note that, with the after-tax profit rate held down by the modified version of the Cambridge theorem, any change in capitalist taxes must lead to an equal and opposite change in the profit rate before tax.

Somewhat surprisingly, shifting the burden of taxes toward capitalists increases their share of capital ownership, for the inequality

$$\frac{d\phi^*}{d\Omega} = \frac{|J_2|}{|J|} = \frac{\hat{\phi}_\Omega \tilde{\phi}_r - \hat{\phi}_r \tilde{\phi}_\Omega}{|J|} < 0$$

can be established by evaluating the numerator. The decline in the wage (before tax) dominates any reduction in the per worker tax, so that workers suffer a drop in net pay that depresses their ability to save. This result is remarkable enough to warrant an illustrative example:[11]

Ω	r	w	$w - \tau$	ϕ
0.00	2.89	767	743	0.3539
0.25	2.96	762	742	0.3532
0.50	3.06	757	740	0.3522
0.75	3.21	747	737	0.3507
1.00	3.48	731	731	0.3480

Workers would be better off paying all the tax!

11. The parameters are $n = 2.5$, $x = 1000$, $\rho = 16.6$, $\delta = 1$, $\beta_w = 0.1$, $\beta_c = 0.9$, and $\sigma = 1$.

Natural Rate of Growth

Finally, going through the same exercise, setting $d\sigma = d\Omega = 0$, applying Cramer's rule, and evaluating at the steady state gives us:

$$\frac{dr^*}{dn} = \frac{|J_1|}{|J|} = \frac{\hat{\phi}_n - \tilde{\phi}_n}{|J|} > 0$$

As in simpler models, a demographic shock shows up in a lower profit rate, as well as an increase in the workers' share of capital wealth:

$$\frac{d\phi^*}{dn} = \frac{|J_2|}{|J|} = \frac{\hat{\phi}_\Omega \tilde{\phi}_n - \hat{\phi}_n \tilde{\phi}_\Omega}{|J|} < 0$$

These results are premised on a fiscal policy rule that maintains the debt-capital ratio, which is the best framework for studying the unadulterated effects of a demographic shock.[12] Results on the welfare effects of a demographic shock, comparable to those in the infinite horizon case, involve resolving some truly barbarous expressions, but they probably are not much affected either.

6.2.4 *Transitional Dynamics and Fiscal Policy*

Let us wrap up our investigation of debt and distribution with a finite capitalist planning horizon by briefly considering the dynamics under, first, a debt target and, second, a deficit target.

Constant Debt Ratio

The temporary equilibrium when fiscal authorities target the debt-capital ratio, $\bar{\sigma}$, continues to be described by an equation of the same form[13] as equation (6.1). Matrix $\mathbf{C}_2$ remains in effect.

The dynamics of the model continue to be governed by a nonlinear first-order difference equation

$$\phi_{+1} = z(\phi)$$

having one fixed point at ϕ^* and another fixed point greater than unity.

12. Under a constant deficit-capital ratio, it can be shown that a demographic shock will reduce the profit rate but that its effect on the workers' wealth share is now ambiguous as in the infinite horizon case.

13. In this case, we put $\psi_5 = 1 + n + n\bar{\sigma}((1 - \Omega\beta_c) - \beta_w(1 - \Omega)) - \beta_c(1 - \phi) + (1 - \beta_c)\bar{\sigma}$.

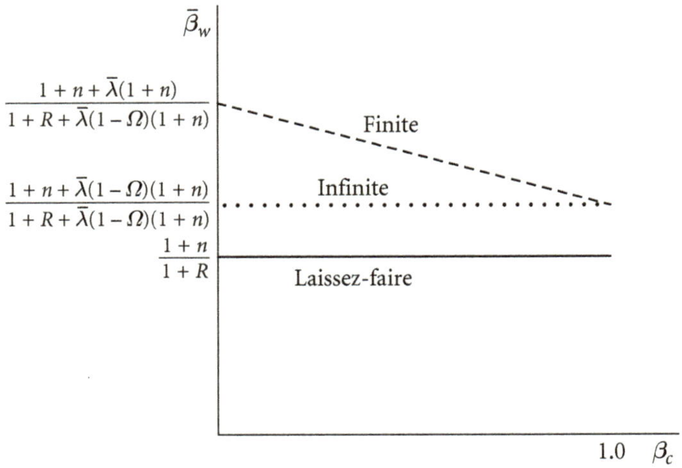

Figure 6.3 Public debt shifts the boundary between the one- and two-class models somewhat differently in the infinite and finite horizon cases.

When we investigate the condition that separates the one- and two-class regimes (ignoring the problem of keeping $\phi^* < 1$), we find that with a finite capitalist planning horizon, debt shrinks the space belonging to the one-class regime by somewhat more than in the case with an infinite horizon. The boundary is now given by

$$\bar{\beta}_w = \frac{1+n+\bar{\sigma}(1-\Omega\beta_c)(1+n)}{1+R+\bar{\sigma}(1-\Omega)(1+n)}$$

which is subtly different from the boundary in the previous section, by virtue of the presence of β_c in the numerator. (Note then that the two boundaries merge when $\beta_c = 1$.) Figure 6.3 illustrates how this boundary is shifted in (β_c, β_w) space.

Curiously, the condition for asymptotic stability that we derived in the infinite horizon case remains in place in the finite horizon case and requires no further discussion.

Constant Deficit Rule

For completeness, the temporary equilibrium with a target deficit-capital ratio, a, continues to be described by an equation of the same form[14] as

14. In this case, we put $\psi_6 = 1 + n + a((1-\Omega\beta_c) - \beta_w(1-\Omega)) - \beta_c(1-\phi) + (1-\beta_c)\sigma$.

(6.1). The matrix $\mathbf{C}_2$ (but with $\bar{\sigma}$ replaced by σ) that we first encountered in the model with infinite horizon and a constant debt target remains in effect here. The economic significance of this fact is that the discussion of the effects of either of two fiscal policies on the labor market stability requirement extends to the case of a finite capitalist planning horizon. Fiscal policy loosens up this requirement in all the cases we have considered.

With this fiscal policy, the dynamics are described by a system of two first-order difference equations, as they were in the infinite horizon case. The model has much the same character, and the main results about asymptotic stability go through here as well. The main point is that debt flattens out the $z(\phi, \sigma)$ function that governs ϕ_{+1} in the neighborhood of its relevant fixed point at ϕ^*.

6.3 Debt in the Exogenous Growth Models

Alternative assumptions about the capitalist planning horizon lead to some dramatically different results, while preserving essential features of the underlying two-class model, as summarized in Table 6.1. Increases in debt (normalized by capital) have identical effects on the wealth distribution across the two regimes. Under the infinite planning horizon, where the Cambridge theorem prevails, the rate of profit and the wage are invariant, but workers still shoulder the burden of debt through the higher taxes needed to service it. Under a finite planning horizon, the rate of profit must rise with the debt ratio, which reflects the fact that capitalists treat all the debt as net wealth, and increase their consumption as the result of a higher debt target. In order to keep growth at its natural rate, a higher profit rate is needed to offset the increased capitalist consumption. Consequently, the negative effects on workers of public debt are amplified in this case by the decline in their before-tax wage. From the capitalist perspective, of course, these redistributions represent a net gain in wealth.

A corrollary of these effects is that increased debt loosens the constraints on the class structure of the model. Preexisting debt saddles workers with a tax liability, and this attenuates the effects of their saving on their share of wealth. As a result, the system can tolerate a higher worker saving propensity before dynamic instabilities erupt or it approaches the boundary for the Samuelson-Modigliani one-class regime.

The striking differences arise when we turn to efforts to make the tax structure more equitable. Under the infinite planning horizon, the tax distribution parameter, Ω, validates the ordinary intuition that shifting the

Table 6.1 Debt in two exogenous growth models

	Infinite Horizon	Finite Horizon
$\frac{dr^*}{d\sigma}$	0	+
$\frac{d\phi^*}{d\sigma}$	−	−
$\frac{d\bar{\beta}_w}{d\sigma}$	+	+
$\frac{dr^*}{d\Omega}$	0	+
$\frac{d\phi^*}{d\Omega}$	+	−
$\frac{dr^*}{dn}$	+	+
$\frac{d\phi^*}{dn}$	−	−

tax burden to capitalists should decrease their share of private wealth. But under the finite horizon assumption, an increase in the capitalist tax share has the counterintuitive effect of raising the rate of profit and the share of capitalist wealth. The Rosetta stone for deciphering this mystery is that the Cambridge theorem now goes through in modified form with respect to the after-tax rate of profit, which will be invariant. As a result, the profit rate (before tax) must rise to maintain the natural rate of growth. What is perhaps surprising is that the attending decline in the wage will overwhelm any diminution of the workers' tax burden, so that their share of wealth winds up lower, even though they are paying for a smaller share of the debt servicing burden.

6.4 Fiscal Policy and Wealth Inequality in the United States

A core lesson of this and the previous chapter is that regardless of whether the model is capital or labor constrained (i.e., endogenous or exogenous), public debt can lead to greater concentrations of wealth in the long run. The major exception occurs when capitalists pay a large share of taxes in an endogenous setting. Debt may or may not lead to greater concentration in the short run, under more Keynesian, or demand-constrained, conditions. For example, Baldani and Michl (1987) argue in the context of a Kaleckian model with exogenous investment demand that while debt financing could stimulate demand and temporarily benefit workers, these effects would be wiped out by the subsequent tax increase on a "day of reckoning" when the tax burden of debt service is realized. In effect, a temporary, distribution-neutral tax cut followed by a return to the original fiscal surplus invokes a balanced budget theorem for interest payments, which are ultimately deflationary because they are like a regressive transfer payment. This result depends critically on the assumption of exogenous investment, as You and Dutt (1996) have argued. They point out that in the presence of a neo-Kaleckian investment function, similar to the one used in Chapter 2, a "fair" (distribution-neutral) tax cut can generate enough growth that it more or less finances itself, assuming that there is sufficient slack or unutilized capacity to support the growth. In this kind of model, the government in effect operates with no intertemporal budget constraint because it can always generate enough new saving through the multiplier process to meet its finance needs.

Whether this is an accurate depiction of fiscal policy in the United States remains debatable. We have already seen in the previous chapter that in practice the fiscal authorities behave as if they were subject to a budget constraint. Periods of debt build-up do lead to more disciplined fiscal policies. Indeed, the fiscal surplus including interest went from −2.7 percent of GDP in 1980 to −5.6 percent in 1983 (the peak year of the Reagan deficits) before returning to −2.9 percent in 1989 (Congressional Budget Office 2006b). Thus, the "day of reckoning" had arguably arrived even before Clinton's OBRA93 (Omnibus Budget Reconciliation Act of 1993) tax increase.

With these nuances in mind, we can turn to the behavior of debt and the distribution of wealth over the last four decades, as represented in Figure 6.4, using the ratio of public debt to potential GDP and the two measures of wealth concentration based on estate data (Kopczuk and Saez 2004) described in Chapter 4. The first measure is the share of total wealth possessed by the top 1 percent. One drawback to this measure is that it includes real estate, an asset that bears only a casual relationship to the capital stock (perhaps in the form of nonresidential property) as it is understood by classical economists. The second measure comes closer to the classical economist's ideal by stripping out real estate and consumer durables and

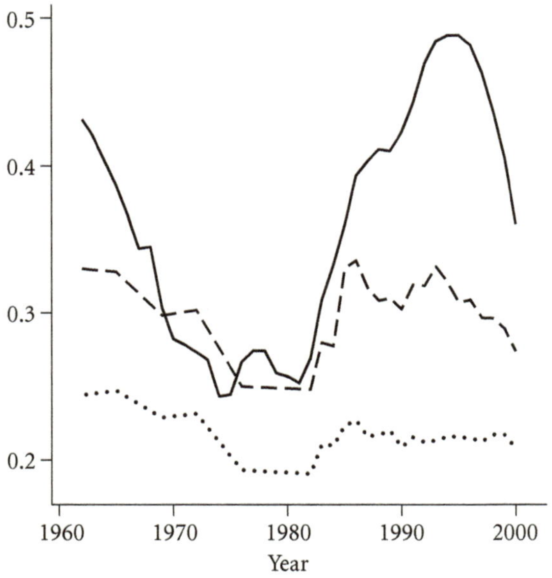

Figure 6.4 The public debt–potential GDP ratio (solid line) in the United States is shown, together with two measures of the wealth share of the top 1 percent of individuals, the top share of total wealth (dotted line) and the top share of financial wealth (dashed line) from 1962 to 2000. *Sources:* debt, Congressional Budget Office (2006a); wealth share, Kopczuk and Saez (2004) and author's calculations.

calculating the share of financial wealth (common stocks, bonds, cash, life insurance, closely held stock, and business equity) held by the top 1 percent. Whether this particular concentration ratio offers any advantage over any other as an operational definition of the capitalist wealth share is hard to judge.[15] Suffice it to say that lower and higher degrees of concentration (e.g., the top 5 or 0.5 percent) yield similar ocular impressions.

While the top share of total wealth has been remarkably constant over the last four decades (despite a quite sharp increase in the concentration of income over the last two decades), the top share of financial wealth moves obligingly with the fiscal position of the state. An increase in debt in the 1980s goes along with rising concentration. The decline in debt during the

15. Wolff (2003, Table 10.2) shows the top 1 percent wealth share rising to a plateau in the 1990s (with no decline). He uses the Federal Reserve Board's Survey of Consumer Finances. This difference is discussed in Kopczuk and Saez (2004, 475–479).

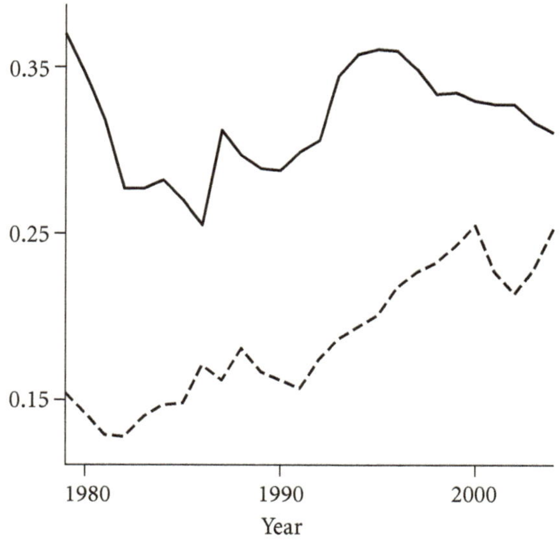

Figure 6.5 The figure shows the total effective federal tax rate (solid line) and share of federal tax liabilities (dashed line) for the top 1 percent of households in the United States from 1979 to 2004. *Source:* Congressional Budget Office (2006b).

Clinton administration accompanies a decline in concentration, made all the more remarkable by its synchronization with a stock market boom of bubble proportions, which might have been expected to disproportionately benefit equity-laden top groups.[16]

But it would be misleading to infer that these comovements represent some sort of corroboration of the theory presented here since this episodic drama is far from a natural experiment. First, the United States is a large, open economy and a substantial share of the fiscal deficits over the last three decades have been financed by foreign capital inflows. The underlying theory developed here would obviously need to be emended to deal with these issues. Second, the theory itself is ambiguous: if myopic capitalists pay a sufficient share of taxes and growth is endogenous, an increase in the debt burden could reduce their share of wealth.

Third, as Figure 6.5 makes clear, much of the action involves changes in the distribution of the federal tax burden (roughly translated as Ω). The

16. Kopczuk and Saez (2004) observe that recent changes in portfolio composition have made the top group more representative of the average, so that this effect may not be operant.

effective tax rate on the top 1 percent (*nota bene*: this time by income not wealth, and among households not individuals) has ebbed and flowed with the lunar cycle of domestic politics; one detects no hint of the theoretician's "distribution-neutral" tax changes.[17] By the end of the 1990s, the Clinton administration had, partly by design and partly by means of capital gains collections from a frenzied stock market, succeeded in restoring the *status quo ante* with respect to the effective tax rate on the incomes of the wealthy (mainly income and corporate income taxes, since the payroll tax is capped at an upper middle class level). Meanwhile, under the relentless pull of rising income inequality, the share of total federal taxes accounted for by the top group continued to rise throughout the period. Much of the movement in wealth concentration reflects these aspects of fiscal policy. As discussed in Chapter 4, the most prominent displacement over the last century was the sharp drop in wealth inequality that aligns with the Roosevelt New Deal and ascendency of the progressive income tax. The spike in war debt (over 100 percent of GDP by 1945) had no discernible effect on that great equalization. There certainly is no sign that making the tax system more progressive will actually increase the capitalist share of wealth, as it did under the hypothetical conditions of the finite horizon model in this chapter.

What we can claim, based on the models presented above, is that in principle, at least some of the increased inequality visible in Figure 6.4 can be linked to fiscal policy through the effects of rising debt ratios on the distribution of wealth. In other words, even if the tax structure were reset to the *status quo ante*, the near doubling of the debt–GDP ratio from 1980 to the present can be expected to permanently reduce the workers' wealth share. To achieve some idea of the order of magnitudes involved, Table 6.2 presents an illustrative calibration exercise in which the debt–GDP ratio rises from 0.25 to 0.50. The exercise implements the infinite horizon models; the expression for the steady state wealth share is formally identical in both the endogenous and exogenous cases. The main parameter values are fairly standard for the U.S. economy and have been taken from de la Croix and Michel (2002, 338–339). Since the workers' wealth share and the capitalist share of taxes are not directly observable, we have chosen a

17. By comparison, movements in the overall effective tax rate were attenuated over this interval. For the years 1979, 1985, 1990, 1995, and 2000, the overall rates were 22.2, 20.9, 21.5, 22.6, and 23.0 percent (Congressional Budget Office 2006b). The much larger movements in the top tax rate were indeed redistributive.

Table 6.2 Calibration of rise in the debt-capital ratio

Ω	ϕ		
		Debt/GDP=0.25	
All	0.25	0.50	0.75
		Debt/GDP=0.50	
0.3	0.244	0.489	0.733
0.5	0.246	0.492	0.738
0.7	0.247	0.495	0.743

Notes: Parameter values at annual frequency are $\rho = 0.45$, $\pi = 0.33$, $g = 0.025$, and (at generational frequency) $\delta = 1$. β_w is calibrated to give initial workers' wealth share, ϕ, as indicated. The debt-capital ratio has been calculated using $\rho\times$ debt–GDP ratio.

wide interval. The workers' wealth share spans the range under dispute by Kotlikoff and Modigliani. In each case, the initial wealth share has been standardized by the appropriate choice of the worker discount factor. The capitalist share of taxes roughly spans the range of the shares of income and corporate taxes paid by the top 1 percent and 5 percent of households (Congressional Budget Office 2006b). (The data presented in Figure 6.5 refer to total taxes, which would probably be inappropriate for this exercise because of the equalizing influence of payroll taxes, although the share of the top 5 percent in total effective taxes never drops far below 0.30.) The exercise shows that, with lifelike parameter values, the regressive effects of debt are modest but hardly subliminal. For example, taking midrange values, if the workers' wealth share were initially one-half and capitalists pay one-half the relevant tax, the rise in the debt ratio would reduce the workers' wealth share by just under one percentage point, not an inconsiderable amount in comparison with the actual variation displayed recently by the wealth shares of the top group.

The cycle of regressive tax reform, debt accumulation, and wealth concentration that these figures dramatize seems destined to repeat itself one more time in the opening decades of the twenty-first century. For the financial and economic elites who have supported the fiscal initiatives of the Reagan and Bush II administrations, regressive tax cuts must appear like a one-way bet. The government budget constraint requires that revenues eventually must be found to service any debt accumulations. If conservative political forces prevail and can make the regressive tax structure permanent, the bet pays off. On the other hand, if the pendulum swings back and the day of reckoning restores the tax structure (as it seems to have done in the Clinton administration), then the elites have little to lose. In fact, according to the models in the last two chapters, the debt accumulation will quite possibly have redistributed wealth regressively, even with no change in the distributional impact of the tax regime (although we are certainly not suggesting that this was a motivation for the policy). While the evidence neither confirms nor refutes the long-run theory of public debt presented in this and the previous chapter, it offers an opportunity to narrate the journey between the abstraction of theory and the concreteness of the statistical record.

— 7 —

Pensions and Endogenous Growth

> The beauty of social insurance is that it is actuarially unsound. Everyone who reaches retirement age is given benefit privileges that far exceed anything he has paid in. . . . How is it possible? It stems from the fact that the national product is growing at compound interest and can be expected to do so for as far ahead as the eye cannot see. . . . A growing nation is the greatest Ponzi game ever contrived.
>
> PAUL SAMUELSON (1967)

This chapter presents the basic components of an idealized public pension system similar to the U.S. Social Security system and then integrates them into an endogenous growth model. Chapter 8 weaves these components into an exogenous growth model. The central issue in the context of capital-constrained growth is to identify the effects of a public pension system on the accumulation and distribution of capital, and to show how these effects are mediated by changes in the funding level achieved by the reserve fund that is used to supplement taxes as a source of financing for retirement benefits. Most existing public pensions operate on a pay-as-you-go (PAYGO), or unfunded, basis ("actuarially unsound" in the epigraph above), but the existing public debates are often centered around whether it would make sense to achieve at least some level of funding (which is also called "advanced funding" or "prefunding" in the specialized policy literature).

The model presented in this and the following chapter is a potentially useful tool for thinking through some of the key issues in these debates.[1]

1. These chapters elaborate on models presented in Michl and Foley (2004) and Michl (2007).

In particular, we will ask whether prefunding invests fiscal policy with the power to reverse the polarizing effects that Marx found so characteristic of public debt.

7.1 Elements of a Public Pension System

The first order of business is to describe the mechanics of a stylized fiscal system for a government whose exclusive function it is to operate the public pension. The second order of business is to describe how a typical public pension plan affects the consumption and saving decisions of workers, since most plans rely mainly or entirely on taxes paid by workers, such as the payroll tax in the United States. Later, we will entertain the idea that a tax levied on capitalists could be used to prefund a public pension system when we turn to the issue of achieving an initial target level of prefunding.

It is worth pointing out right at the outset that the idealized treatment we pursue effectively prejudices the results against a public pension system. Real social security systems serve a variety of functions, including redistribution, wage insurance in an uncertain labor market, disability insurance, and spousal support. By ignoring the welfare-enhancing role of these functions, we cannot say much about why social security programs are so popular, existing as they do in every country in the world above a modest level of development.[2] The only good argument for this lopsided treatment is that it makes it possible to study the macroeconomic effects of a pension system without the encumbrance of a map at the scale of one to one. In order to emphasize our one-sided treatment of public pension systems, we will avoid the term *social security*.

7.1.1 Government

The public pension system operates a reserve fund that it invests in the capital market at the prevailing rate of profit. Government-owned capital is denoted K^G. The government finances per worker benefits, b, using its end-of-period wealth and per worker payroll taxes, τ; it saves any surplus

2. Blackburn's (2002) immaculately researched study of pensions provides a detailed history of private and public pensions and a useful Baedeker to the unfolding debates surrounding public policy toward pensions.

in the reserve fund, K^G_{+1}. We will adopt the convention that the subscript on b refers to the cohort receiving the benefit rather than the time period in which the benefit is received. The one-period budget constraint is

$$b_{-1}N_{-1} + K^G_{+1} \leq (1+r)K^G + \tau N$$

For consistency with taxes and benefits, we measure the reserve fund on a per worker basis as $f = K^G_{+1}/N$. This measure represents the reserve fund in relation to the cohort of future retirees (i.e., current workers). Clearly, the prior existence of a reserve fund necessitates a period of primitive accumulation during which taxes exceed benefits, and we return to this question after we have presented the basic growth model.

Output continues to be produced with a Leontief technology employing k units of capital per worker, so that employment given by $N = K/k$. Government saving will therefore obey

$$K^G_{+1} = \frac{f}{k}K \tag{7.1}$$

We need to specify the government's policy targets and instruments. We choose to target a constant level of benefits ($b = b_{-1}$) and a constant reserve fund ($f = f_{-1}$), using the tax as the policy instrument. Following a well-established and sensible tradition, we restrict our attention to nondistortionary lump-sum taxes and benefits. Assuming it will be satisfied as a strict equality, the budget constraint for a government adopting these targets and instruments requires that

$$\tau = \frac{b - f(r - g^K_{-1})}{1 + g^K_{-1}} \tag{7.2}$$

Having committed the government to a policy of taxes, benefits, and saving, we can turn to the effects on the worker households.

7.1.2 *Workers*

As in previous chapters, workers are assumed to plan only for their own consumption, without the implicit altruism toward future generations of the dynastic capitalists, and therefore workers do not need to take into account the government budget constraint. Assuming that a lump-sum benefit, b, is paid in the retirement period and a lump-sum tax, τ, is paid during the working period, their programming problem is

$$\max\ (1-\beta_w)\log c^w + \beta_w \log c^r$$

$$\text{subject to } c^w + \frac{c^r}{1+r_{+1}} \leq h$$

$$\text{where } h = w + \left(\frac{b}{1+r_{+1}} - \tau\right)$$

The worker's lifetime wealth is denoted (mnemonically for human capital) by h. Note that workers must formulate an expectation of the rate of profit in their retirement, r_{+1}, in order to evaluate their lifetime wealth. In the endogenous growth model with distribution predetermined, we will assume that the expected and current rate of profit are identical, or $r_{+1} = r$. The solution to the worker's consumption program, using the Lagrangian technique as in Chapter 3, is that workers will consume a constant fraction of their lifetime wealth, or

$$c^w = (1-\beta_w)h$$

and save the rest

$$s^w = \beta_w(w-\tau) - (1-\beta_w)(\frac{b}{1+r})$$

The worker's individual saving function tells a tale about the policy effects of public pensions. One can interpret the first term as saving out of take-home pay (obviously reduced by the tax), and the second term as the further reduction in saving that results from consumption out of (gross) social security wealth, that is, the present value of the retirement benefit. A central complaint about public pensions raised by (mainly conservative) neoclassical economists refers to their potential for reducing national saving when the system is unfunded or only partially funded (terms that will be defined more precisely below). But prefunding can augment workers' lifetime wealth by supporting a given benefit with lower taxes and contribute to higher saving rates on the part of workers. This can be seen by substituting the tax given by equation (7.2) into the definition of lifetime wealth:

$$h = w - b\left(\frac{1}{1+g_{-1}^K} - \frac{1}{1+r}\right) + f\left(\frac{r - g_{-1}^K}{1+g_{-1}^K}\right) \tag{7.3}$$

The worker's individual saving can also be rewritten as

$$s^w = \beta_w h - \frac{b}{1+r}$$

which makes it easy to see that by augmenting lifetime wealth, funding an existing benefit level increases worker saving in this set-up. It is also evident from these two equations that an increase in the benefit level reduces lifetime wealth and constricts worker saving. (Both these conclusions presume that the rate of profit exceeds the rate of growth, the normal state of affairs in a two-class model.) We will use this insight repeatedly below.

To derive the aggregate worker saving function, we need only be reminded that with Leontief technology, $N\ (= K/k)$ workers each contributing s^w in saving will generate total saving given by

$$K_{+1}^w = (s^w/k)K \tag{7.4}$$

$$\text{where } s^w/k = \frac{w\beta_w}{k} - \frac{b}{k}\left(\frac{\beta_w}{1+g_{-1}^K} + \frac{1-\beta_w}{1+r}\right) + \frac{\beta_w f(r - g_{-1}^K)}{k(1+g_{-1}^K)}$$

Before we put these components together in a complete growth model, it will prove useful to provide a systematic classification of the funding systems available to policy makers.

7.1.3 Money's Worth and Funding Systems

A central issue in public debates on pension systems concerns the comparison between rates of return on public and private systems. One branch of this debate focuses on whether this comparison is germane, given that real public pension systems fulfill both saving and insurance functions, while private pension systems are exclusively saving vehicles. But in the idealized world described by this model, with no risk or uncertainty, this distinction is not meaningful, and it is possible to make fairly sharp analytical statements about the relative rates of return on public versus private saving. This exercise is altogether fitting, provided that we are careful to avoid applying the results of our investigation to real pension systems without the appropriate qualifications.

A useful analytical measure of the rate of return in a public pension system is called *money's worth* in the policy literature, at least in the United States. Money's worth is defined as the internal rate of return that equates the present value of payroll taxes with the present value of expected retirement benefits. In our two-period model, we can measure money's worth very simply as

$$m = \frac{b - \tau}{\tau}$$

By substituting from the government's budget constraint, we can write out a very general expression for money's worth that conveys many of the conundrums facing policy makers:

$$m = \frac{(b - f)(1 + g^K_{-1}) - b_{-1} + f_{-1}(1 + r)}{b_{-1} + f(1 + g^K_{-1}) - f_{-1}(1 + r)}$$

Owing to the intergenerational transfer inherent in a public pension system, an increase in benefits paid to current retirees reduces the money's worth of current workers. (Formally, the partial derivative of m with respect to b_{-1} is negative, or $m_{b_{-1}} < 0$.) Current benefits must be financed, either by higher payroll taxes or by drawing on the resources of the reserve fund. By the same token, an increase in the funding level provided by the current retirees (during their working years) will increase the money's worth of the current workers since it eases the burden of paying for their parent's benefits. (Formally, $m_{f_{-1}} > 0$.) And an increase in the funding level provided by current workers for their own retirement reduces their money's worth. (Formally, $m_f < 0$.)

A slowdown on growth can impose a hardship on current workers, as is evident from

$$m_{g^K_{-1}} = \frac{b(b_{-1} - f_{-1}(1 + r))}{(b_{-1} + f(1 + g^K_{-1}) - f_{-1}(1 + r))^2}$$

Provided the numerator term on the RHS, $(b_{-1} - f_{-1}(1 + r))$, is positive, an increase in growth bestows its benefits on the next generation of workers, who being relatively numerous will have an easy time providing for their parents. Conversely, a slowdown in growth imposes a burden on the hapless generation that follows, as the cohorts following the U.S. baby boom generation are now famously discovering.

On the other hand, if the numerator term is negative, increased growth counterintuitively burdens the next generation. The secret here, of course, is that the expression above is a partial derivative that presumes a constant level of funding. The numerator term is a separatrix between a partially funded or unfunded system and a superfunded system; when this term vanishes, the system is said to be fully funded.

To make these terms more precise, let us consider a system in a steady state of balanced growth, with $b = b_{-1}$, $f = f_{-1}$, and a steady state growth rate, g. The money's worth simplifies to

$$m = \frac{bg + f(r - g)}{b - f(r - g)}$$

which is displayed in Figure 7.1 in order to bring out the relationship between money's worth and funding levels.

In an unfunded (PAYGO) system, $f = 0$, and each generation's payroll taxes finance the retirement benefits of their parents. The money's worth in such a system is plainly equal to the growth rate of capital, and more fundamentally, the labor force, as was first brought to the attention of economists by Paul Samuelson's "biological rate of interest."

In Samuelson's (1958) seminal article on social security, reliance on the steady state left him open to criticism from Abba Lerner (1959a) for unobtrusively assuming a steady state of infinite duration in his welfare theorems. Briefly, Samuelson argued that a PAYGO system calibrated to deliver the biological interest rate would maximize the well-being of everyone who ever lived. As Lerner observed, and Samuelson (1959) more or less conceded, this welfare property attributed to the biological rate of interest depends critically on the assumption that growth continues forever. As we have seen, even a decline in the growth rate reduces the return on social security (tax) contributions. If the world were to end, the last cohort would end up with a welfare loss for the same reason that the last to join a Ponzi

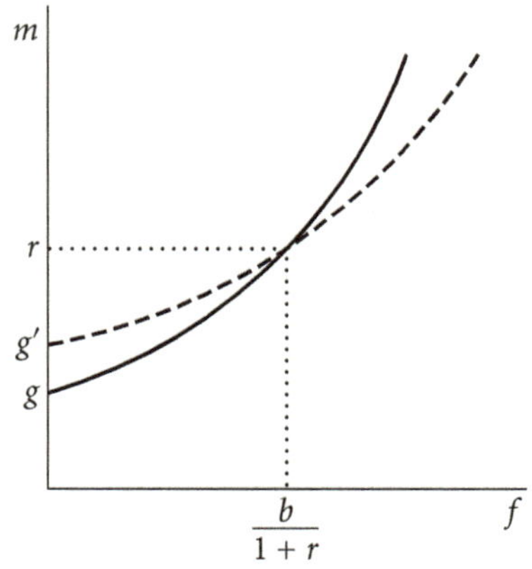

Figure 7.1 The steady state money's worth of a public pension system measuring the rate of return to payroll taxes is an increasing function of the funding level. An increase in the growth rate, from g to g', rotates the function as shown by the dashed line.

scheme lose their shirts. We will return to this issue when we take up the question of optimal policies in Chapter 9.

In a fully funded system, $f = \tau = b/(1 + r)$ and the money's worth is equal to the market rate of return, r. Payroll taxes function exactly like contributions to a private savings account. Each generation effectively finances its own retirement.

A partially funded system enjoys a money's worth between these two goalposts. A superfunded system, with $f > b/(1 + r)$, rewards participants with a premium rate above the market return. The secret is that the returns to the publicly owned capital in the reserve fund subsidize retirement benefits, permitting lower payroll taxes much like a generous college endowment permits lower tuition fees. Indeed, it may be possible to fund a public pension system generously enough that it can be operated with zero payroll tax, or even a subsidy. (We will see below that this may not be possible without violating the two-class structure of accumulation.) From this perspective, it is less mysterious why more growth should reduce the money's worth of a superfunded system, as illustrated by the dashed line in Figure 7.1. More current workers mean that a given reserve fund bequeathed from current retirees provides less public wealth per current worker, and therefore less of a subsidy to payroll taxes.

Table 7.1 Classification of public pension systems

Description	f	τ	m
Unfunded	$f = 0$	$\frac{b}{1+r} < \tau = \frac{b}{1+g}$	$m = g$
Partially funded	$0 < f < \frac{b}{1+r}$	$\frac{b}{1+r} < \tau < \frac{b}{1+g}$	$g < m < r$
Fully funded	$f = \frac{b}{1+r}$	$\tau = \frac{b}{1+r}$	$m = r$
Superfunded (a)	$\frac{b}{1+r} < f < \frac{b}{r-g}$	$0 < \tau < \frac{b}{1+r}$	$m > r$
Superfunded (b)	$f = \frac{b}{r-g}$	$\tau = 0$	undefined
Superfunded (c)	$f > \frac{b}{r-g}$	$\tau < 0$	undefined

Notes: Here we assume a steady state equilibrium with growth rate, g; constant benefit, b; and constant per-worker reserve fund, f.

The classification of public pension systems is exhaustively described in Table 7.1.

7.2 Endogenous Growth with a Public Pension

Having detailed the components of a public pension system, it remains only to put them together in a complete growth model. Since we have already specified the fiscal policy in place, we can move directly to the dynamic representation of the model.

7.2.1 Steady State

Capitalist agents are not charged with the payroll tax that finances the public pension; their saving behavior will be unchanged from the laissez-faire system; and the now familiar Cambridge equation will describe their accumulation.

$$K_{+1}^{c} = \beta_c(1+r)K^{c} \tag{7.5}$$

As in previous chapters, we will assume parameter values in the model that support a two-class equilibrium. To anticipate, the Cambridge theorem continues to apply, and the steady state growth rate of the system will be described by the Cambridge equation:

$$1 + g^* = \beta_c(1 + r)$$

This equation performs the role of the capitalist saving function, $\tilde{\phi}$, exactly as it did in Chapter 3.

To arrive at the relationship between steady state growth and the workers' share of wealth that is consistent with worker saving behavior, we need only divide equation (7.4) by K_{+1}, and using the fact that in a steady state $1 + g^* = K_{+1}/K$, obtain

$$\hat{\phi} = \frac{1}{1+g^*}\left[\frac{w\beta_w}{k} - \frac{b}{k}\left(\frac{\beta_w}{1+g^*} + \frac{1-\beta_w}{1+r}\right) + \frac{\beta_w f(r-g^*)}{k(1+g^*)}\right]$$

These two equations describe the steady state distribution of wealth, ϕ^*, and growth rate. We can visualize the steady state by referring to Figure 7.2, which shows the effects of changes in the two key policy parameters, the benefit level and funding level. The formal expressions for these effects are given by

$$\frac{d\phi^*}{db} = \frac{-(\beta_c + (1-\beta_c)\beta_w)}{\beta_c^2 k(1+r)^2} < 0$$

$$\frac{d\phi^*}{df} = \frac{\beta_w(1-\beta_c)}{\beta_c^2 k(1+r)} > 0$$

The economic intuition follows closely from the discussion above of the effects of public pensions on the lifetime wealth of workers. An increase in the benefit level (with no change in funding level) effectively reduces lifetime wealth, and reduces workers' private saving. An increase in the funding level, on the other hand, augments workers' lifetime wealth and promotes saving. Both of these effects then show up in the steady state share of capital owned by workers.

For completeness, we must also determine the government's share of capital. By dividing equation (7.1) by K_{+1} and simplifying, we obtain

$$\phi^G = \frac{f}{k(1+g^*)}$$

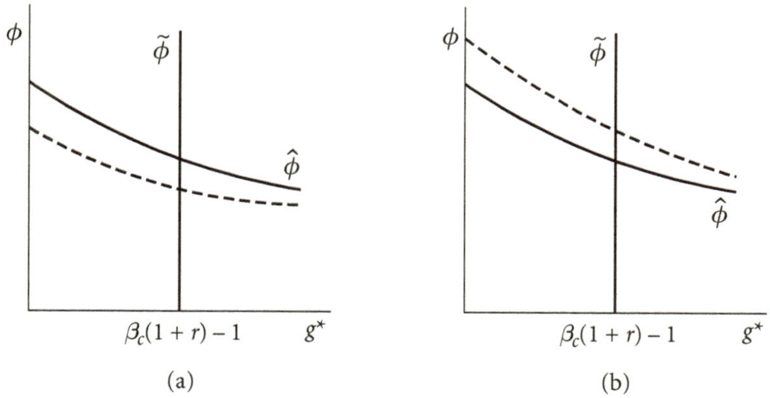

Figure 7.2 Changes in the parameters of a public pension affect the workers' share of wealth in an endogenous growth model; the steady state growth rate will be determined by the Cambridge equation. (a) An increase in the retirement benefit, b, will reduce workers' lifetime wealth, saving, and share of wealth. (b) An increase in the funding level will increase workers' lifetime wealth, saving, and share of wealth.

Thus, the public share of wealth in the steady state is a direct reflection of the fiscal target, f. Since an increase in funding contributes to a larger workers' share of capital wealth, as we have just seen, it follows that an increase in funding levels reduces the capitalist share of wealth both directly and indirectly by contributing to a larger workers' share of capital wealth. Looked at another way, an increase in funding redistributes wealth toward workers both directly by making it available to them in their role as citizens and indirectly by empowering them to save more.

7.2.2 Dynamics

The dynamical system for $\tilde{\mathbf{k}}' = (\mathbf{K}^c, \mathbf{K}^w, \mathbf{K}^G)$, the components of the capital stock, can be obtained from the Cambridge equation, (7.5); the worker saving function, equation (7.4); and the government saving function, equation (7.1). Unlike previous models in this book, the basic equation of motion is now a second-order difference equation, owing to the intergenerational nature of a public pension system:

$$\tilde{\mathbf{k}}_{+1} = \mathbf{M}_1\tilde{\mathbf{k}} + \mathbf{M}_2\tilde{\mathbf{k}}_{-1}$$

where

$$\mathbf{M_1} = \begin{pmatrix} \beta_c(1+r) & 0 & 0 \\ c_0 & c_0 & c_0 \\ f/k & f/k & f/k \end{pmatrix}$$

$$\mathbf{M_2} = \begin{pmatrix} 0 & 0 & 0 \\ c_1 & c_1 & c_1 \\ 0 & 0 & 0 \end{pmatrix}$$

and

$$c_0 = \frac{w\beta_w(1+r) - b(1-\beta_w) - f\beta_w(1+r)}{k(1+r)}$$

$$c_1 = \frac{f\beta_w(1+r) - b\beta_w}{k}$$

We will want to make two changes to this system. First, since it is more convenient to work with the vector $\mathbf{k}' = (K, K^w, K^G)$, we once again deploy the permutation matrix to define

$$\mathbf{k} = \mathbf{P}\tilde{\mathbf{k}}$$

$$\mathbf{N_i} = \mathbf{PM_iP^{-1}} \quad i \in \{1, 2\}$$

Second, for consistency with the previous chapters, we would like to express the system in a first-order difference equation. This can always be done, as is well known (Gandolfo 1997), simply by defining the vector $\mathbf{x} = \mathbf{k}_{-1}$ and using it to form an augmented vector:

$$\mathbf{k}^{\oplus} = \begin{pmatrix} \mathbf{k} \\ \mathbf{x} \end{pmatrix}$$

The equation of motion for the system can now be expressed compactly by

$$\mathbf{k}^{\oplus}_{+1} = \mathbf{D}\mathbf{k}^{\oplus} \tag{7.6}$$

$$\text{where } \mathbf{D} = \begin{pmatrix} \mathbf{N_1} & \mathbf{N_2} \\ \mathbf{I} & \mathbf{0} \end{pmatrix}$$

The eigenvalues of **D** are

$$\lambda_1 = \beta_c(1+r) \qquad \lambda_{2,3} = \frac{kc_0 + f \pm \sqrt{\Delta}}{2k}$$

where the discriminant is

$$\Delta = c_0^2k^2 + 2c_0fk + 4c_1k^2 + f$$

The eigenvector associated with the dominant eigenvalue, λ_1, assuming the two-class regime prevails, is $[1, \phi^*, \phi^G, 1/(1+g^*), \phi^*/(1+g^*), \phi^G/(1+g^*)]$.

We can see once again that the modified Cambridge theorem applies to this system. As long as λ_1 is the dominant eigenvalue, the long-run growth rate will be controlled entirely through the Cambridge equation, without any reference to the saving behavior of workers or the government.

When the discriminant is negative, the nondominant roots, λ_2 and λ_3, are complex conjugates and the system displays oscillations around its rising trend. Interestingly, expressing the discriminant as a function of β_w reveals that $\Delta(\beta_w)$ is a quadratic equation. Figure 7.3 illustrates that the relationship between workers' thrift and the sign of the discriminant is

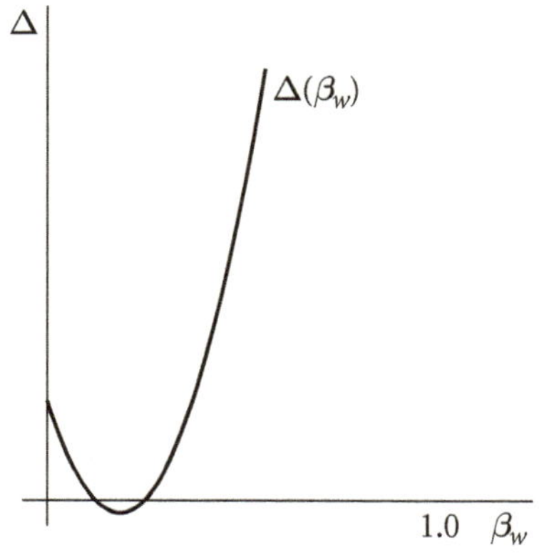

Figure 7.3 The discriminant in the nondominant eigenvalues is a quadratic function of the worker discount factor, creating the possibility of oscillating dynamics when the discount factor lies in the critical range.

subtle: it is possible for oscillations to occur over a range of values of β_w, while higher or lower values result in real roots and monotonic dynamics.[3]

7.2.3 Conditions for Two-Class Regime

A central issue raised by the endogenous growth model is whether the two-class regime will prevail. We continue to be interested in the limits on worker thrift imposed by the two-class regime. But we can also ask how the public pension system affects these limitations. In particular, at what point does the funding level promote a change from a two-class to a one-class regime?

Let us define the function $\lambda_2 = \lambda(\beta_w, b, f)$, where λ_2 is the largest of the two nondominant roots of equation (7.6). We will assume that these roots are real, and leave aside the more involved problem posed by complex roots. We can define the maximum value of the worker saving propensity consistent with the two-class solution implicitly by

$$\lambda(\bar{\beta}_w, b, f) - \lambda_1 = 0$$

The signs of the relevant partial derivatives can be obtained with some difficulty, but since the economic logic seems fairly straightforward, we skip the mathematical details. Thus,

$$\lambda_b < 0 \quad \lambda_f, \lambda_{\beta_w} > 0$$

Totally differentiating reveals that the effects of economic policy depend on the properties of the $\lambda(\cdot)$ function:

$$\frac{d\bar{\beta}_w}{db} = -\frac{\lambda_b}{\lambda_{\beta_w}} > 0$$

$$\frac{d\bar{\beta}_w}{df} = -\frac{\lambda_f}{\lambda_{\beta_w}} < 0$$

3. It is also possible to extract the single second-order difference equation describing the capital stock from equation (7.6). With initial conditions given, we obtain

$$K + a_1 K_{-1} + a_2 K_{-2} = K_0^c (1 + g^*)^t$$

where $a_1 = -(c_0 + f/k)$ and $a_2 = -c_1$. This line of attack is pursued by Michl and Foley (2004).

The economic logic recognizes that λ_2 represents the growth rate that would prevail if workers' saving dominated the system. An increase in the retirement benefit has a dampening effect on worker thrift and can thus be expected to lower this hypothetical growth rate. An increase in the funding level enhances lifetime wealth and encourages greater private thrift. This effect and the direct effect of a higher discount factor can be expected to increase the hypothetical growth rate in a worker-dominated system. In other words, increases in the retirement benefit move a given system farther from the one-class boundary, while increases in the funding level move a given system closer to this critical divide.

This then raises the question of when the funding level begins to threaten the two-class structure of accumulation. We can define the critical funding level, $\bar{f}$, by the condition that $\lambda(\bar{f}; \beta_w, b) - \lambda_1 = 0$. Making the appropriate substitutions (and continuing to restrict our attentions to real roots), we find

$$\bar{f} = \frac{b}{1+r} + \frac{\beta_c(\beta_c(1+r)k - w\beta_w)}{\beta_c + \beta_w(1-\beta_c)}$$

The first fractional term on the RHS represents full funding, and the second term shows how far beyond full funding it is possible to go before jeopardizing the class structure. Note that the parenthetical term, $(\beta_c(1+r)k - w\beta_w)$, is positive as long as the laissez-faire system is a two-class system. It follows that superfunding a public pension can, in principle, effect a change from a two-class to a one-class regime.[4]

7.3 Policy Issues

The remaining set of issues that our model is capable of illuminating concerns the initial achievement of a target level of funding, or what might be

4. One benchmark against which we might compare $\bar{f}$ is the level of superfunding at which workers do not need to pay taxes. Let us call this level $\hat{f}$. It can be shown that the condition for $\bar{f} > \hat{f}$ is that

$$\beta_w < \frac{\beta_c(k(1-\beta_c)(1+r)^2 - b)}{w(1-\beta_c)(1+r) - b}$$

Thus, it is possible that the level of superfunding that eliminates the need for payroll taxes could be unavailable without jeopardizing the class structure of accumulation.

termed the primitive accumulation of public capital. There are two analytically separate circumstances that merit our attention: the initial establishment of a pension system *de novo*, and the transition from an existing unfunded system to one with some level of funding. Feldstein (1976) and Cesaratto (2005) call these "tax design" and "tax reform," which we modify to policy design and policy reform. History has passed by the first circumstance in all the advanced economies of the world, which established public pensions in the early part of the last century. But this case offers analytical insights that are relevant to existing pension systems. The second circumstance remains topical.

We can also relax the assumption that only payroll taxes born by workers finance the public pension system, and consider the effects of a lump-sum tax born exclusively by capitalists, which might be considered the theoretical counterpart of a capital levy or steeply progressive temporary wealth tax in a real economy.

The endogenous growth model allows an increase in public saving to express itself in higher capital accumulation, at least temporarily. Orszag and Stiglitz (2001) call this broad prefunding. Narrow prefunding refers to increases in the pension reserve fund that do not necessarily result in a larger capital stock; they merely change the distribution of ownership of the existing capital stock.

7.3.1 Policy Design

Setting up an idealized public pension system offers some insights into the effects of existing systems on growth and distribution. We first consider a realistic scenario with an unfunded system before tackling funding achieved by a payroll tax or a capital levy.

Theory

In this and subsequent treatments, we will follow a scenario in which the pension system affects the cohort of workers in period 0, who will receive a given benefit, b, when they retire in period 1. The retirees in period 0 (who were workers in period -1) are not directly affected by the policy, although we will see that they are affected indirectly. Table 7.2 clarifies the timing

Table 7.2 Policy design scenario

t	b	b_{-1}	τ	τ^c	f
−1	0	0	0	0	0
0	b	0	τ_0	τ^c	f
1	b	b	τ_1	0	f
2	b	b	τ_2	0	f

of the policy for two cases, first, with any prefunding coming from payroll taxes, and second, with prefunding from a tax on capitalists, τ^c.

Recall that the retirement benefit represents the promised benefit, so that b_{-1} represents actual payment by the government.

In the first case, let us assume that any prefunding comes out of payroll taxes (so $\tau^c = 0$). The workers in period 0 pay a tax (except in the PAYGO case) that will fund the system at the level f, which will remain in effect in subsequent periods. Since all this initial tax, τ_0, is dedicated to the reserve fund, the new funding level will be equal to the tax: $\tau_0 = f$. Thus, the workers in period 1 and subsequent periods will pay the tax required by the system's parameters, (b, f).

To clarify events, we can imagine a parallel laissez-faire scenario in which no pension system has been initiated, and call this the control scenario. We can then compare the components of the capital stock in the policy or test scenario with their counterparts in the control scenario. Both scenarios are assumed to share the same initial capital stock, K_0.

Since the government owns no capital in the control scenario, it is clear that the difference (test minus control) in government-owned capital in period 1 will be the funding level times the number of workers, or (using $\text{N} = K/k$):

$$\Delta K_1^G = (f/k)K_0$$

Since capitalists are not involved in this fiscal system, their capital stock will be unaffected.

The workers in period 0 will reduce their private saving for two reasons, as can be seen from

$$s_0^w = \beta_w w - \left(\beta_w \tau_0 + (1-\beta_w)(\frac{b}{1+r})\right)$$

Both the payroll tax and the promise of a retirement benefit reduce individual worker saving. The aggregate difference in worker-owned capital will thus be

$$\Delta K_1^w = -\left(\frac{\beta_w \tau_0(1+r) + (1-\beta_w)b}{k(1+r)}\right) K_0$$

Combining these differences and recalling that $f = \tau_0$, we obtain the net effect of the policy on the capital stock in period 1:

$$\Delta K_1 = \left(\frac{(1-\beta_w)(f(1+r)-b)}{k(1+r)}\right) K_0$$

This expression neatly summarizes the effect of establishing a public pension system. Note that its sign is determined by the sign of $f(1+r) - b$, the divide between partial funding and superfunding.

If the system is unfunded, the initial beneficiaries pay no tax but receive benefits. They reduce their saving by an amount equal to their propensity to consume times the present value of the benefit, and thus the overall capital stock will be lower in the next period and, in this model, all subsequent periods. The next cohort of workers (in period 1 and beyond) will now be responsible for financing the benefits of their parent's generation. This burden is sometimes called the *legacy cost* of a PAYGO system (Diamond and Orszag 2004). Each worker in this and subsequent cohorts will reduce his or her saving because of the legacy cost, and this will further reduce the capital stock in subsequent periods.

While legacy cost is a useful concept, it is important not to lose sight of the nature of the redistribution that it measures in practice. In an economy enjoying on-going technical progress (i.e., the normal state of affairs), each cohort can expect to enjoy a higher real wage and living standard than its predecessors. The founding of a PAYGO system redistributes income from younger, richer cohorts to older, poorer cohorts. In the United States, for example, the generations that suffered through the Great Depression were the beneficiaries of an elevated money's worth (see below) on their Social Security contributions.

If the system is fully funded, the initial beneficiaries pay a tax sufficient to finance their own retirement benefits, or $\tau_0 = b/(1+r) = f$. A fully funded system is neutral with respect to capital accumulation because workers will treat their payroll tax as a form of own-saving, and adjust their private saving to compensate. The fully funded system imposes no burden on future generations, and is for that reason the benchmark against which legacy costs are measured.

There are three ways of measuring the legacy cost in this model. First, the money's worth of a PAYGO system is less than that of a fully funded system by an amount equal to $r - g$. Second, a PAYGO system requires a payroll tax that is higher than the payroll tax in a fully funded system, by an amount equal to

$$\frac{b(r-g)}{(1+g)(1+r)}$$

And third, this expression also measures the amount by which the lifetime wealth of workers in a PAYGO system is reduced as compared to workers in a fully funded system.

If the system is superfunded, the capital stock on the test path exceeds the capital stock on the control path. The initial generation of period 0 workers effectively bequeaths wealth to future generations of workers, who benefit in the form of lower taxes and a premium money's worth. In this case, the legacy takes the form of an intergenerational gift.

As a final exercise, consider the effect of funding the system by means of a tax on capitalist agents, τ^c. Since workers play no part in prefunding, $\tau_0 = 0$. (Refer to Table 7.2.) To achieve the same funding level as in previous scenarios requires setting $\tau^c = (f/k)K_0$. The tax reduces capitalist end-of-period wealth to $K_0^c(1+r) - \tau^c$. Equivalently, it acts as a capital levy or one-time wealth tax that reduces capitalist wealth by $\tau^c/(1+r)$. As a result, it is easy to show, by solving the capitalist programming problem, that the difference between the test and control capitalist wealth stock will be $-\beta_c\tau^c$. Since all the tax is saved by the government, the change in public capital will be τ^c. Workers in period 0, responding to the promise of a retirement benefit, reduce their saving as if they were entering a PAYGO system in the previous scenario. The net result will be a difference between the test and control capital stock in period 1 given by

$$\Delta K_1 = \left(\frac{(1-\beta_c)f(1+r) - (1-\beta_w)b}{k(1+r)}\right) K_0$$

Comparing this change with the previous scenario, it is clear that funding a newly established public pension by a capital levy will result in less capital formation than achieving the same funding level using payroll taxes. Indeed, unless the funding level lies above a well-defined threshold, even superfunding a new pension system will reduce accumulation absolutely. In any case, an unfunded public pension rewards the founding participants with a high rate of return on their contributions.

Measurement

Empirical estimates of the money's worth of the U.S. Social Security system are presented in Figure 7.4. These estimates are developed by calculating the internal rate of return on the benefits and taxes received by each cohort, either actually or using simulation methods for cohorts still living. The U.S. system does not conform to the theoretical ideal for two important reasons. First, rather than experiencing one start-up, the system has been repeatedly enhanced; as a result, it has effectively experienced a sequence of miniature start-ups. Second, after the 1983 reforms, the system has operated on a partially funded basis as the payroll taxes have generated a surplus and a corresponding positive balance in the trust fund. This balance is intended to be a temporary measure designed to smooth the entry of the large baby boom cohorts into retirement, and this expectation is incorporated into the simulations reported here. Both these factors prevent the system from achieving a steady state, even over the broad time interval spanned by Figure 7.4.

The most striking feature is the very high internal rate of return awarded to the early participants. This, of course, conforms to the theoretical discussion above and represents the source of the legacy costs. Although the system is not assumed to achieve its steady state in these simulations, the author reports (Leimer 1994, 22) that the long-run growth rate converges on a value slightly under 1 percent per year. Under the intermediate scenario, the internal rate of return achieves 0.94 for the 2050 cohort, which puts it very close to the theoretical steady state value. It is perhaps no accident that the intense political debate surrounding the U.S. system over the last two decades has irrupted into the public arena precisely as the system has matured, and its money's worth has declined toward its steady state value.

For cohorts whose life cycles are incomplete, the study cited uses the three scenarios suggested by the Trustees of the Social Security Administration, labeled optimistic, intermediate, and pessimistic. These scenarios segregate assumptions about future values of relevant parameters, such as mortality rates, labor force growth, and productivity growth. They are

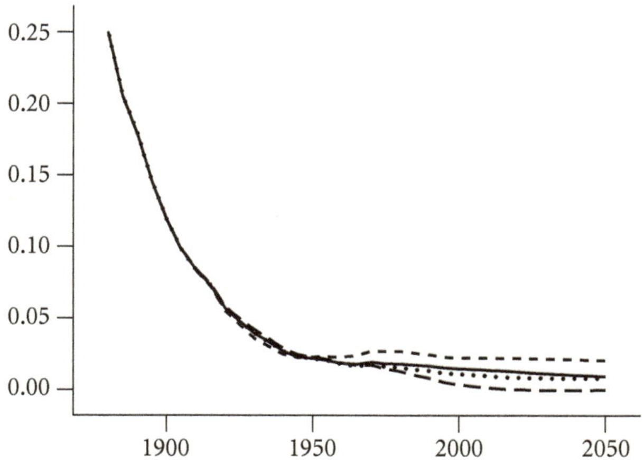

Figure 7.4 The figure shows the internal rate of return by cohort for the U.S. Social Security system from 1880 to 2050. The optimistic scenario (dashed line) and pessimistic scenario (long-dashed line) assume that tax changes maintain budget balance. The intermediate scenario assumes tax changes (solid line) or benefit cuts (dotted line) maintain balance. *Source:* Leimer (1994, tables 1, B1)

sometimes criticized for a lack of sophistication compared with an alternative methodology using variance bounds and confidence intervals, but they do provide an illustrative benchmark for our purposes. In each case, the underlying assumption is that the system will move toward a strict PAYGO funding system when the surplus currently enjoyed by Social Security either runs out (under the intermediate and pessimistic scenarios) or stabilizes (the optimistic scenario). Under the optimistic and pessimistic scenario, the assumption is that the payroll tax will adjust to maintain a balanced program budget (note that it declines in the optimistic case).

Under the intermediate scenario, this assumption is shown together with an alternative assumption that benefits will be reduced to maintain balance. In practice, when the U.S. system last encountered fiscal difficulty, the response of Congress, acting partly on the recommendations of the Greenspan Commission, was to restore solvency with a balanced approach that combined tax increases (which gave us the surplus now enjoyed) and benefit cuts (mainly an increase in the normal retirement age). Thus, the most likely scenario will probably lie somewhere between the tax and benefit cases shown.

Effects on Private Saving

The classical model can help clarify the empirical literature on the effects of social security wealth on saving. Martin Feldstein, in his seminal paper (Feldstein 1974) and subsequent work, interprets the finding that social security reduces saving from the perspective of an overlapping generations model in the tradition of Paul Samuelson (1958) and Peter Diamond (1965). Economists who dispute the size or existence of this replacement effect have traditionally appealed to alternative motives for saving, such as the bequest motive. Although it is well-known that the theoretical effect of social security on net saving is indeterminate in a life-cycle model because of the offsetting influence of social security on retirement age,[5] the accumulated empirical evidence lends some support to the argument that social security does have a net negative effect on saving.

For example, a recent survey of this literature conducted by the Congressional Budget Office (1998) reports that 12 out of 14 studies using cross-sectional household data find that each dollar of social security wealth reduces private wealth, generally by 50 cents or less. The two studies that find positive effects lend some support to the two-class hypothesis. The first (David and Menchik 1985) uses probate records, which probably selects for wealthier than average individuals. The second (Gullason et al. 1993) finds that among households in the 1983 Survey of Consumer Finances, social security wealth has an insignificant positive effect on total fungible wealth but a significant negative effect on pension wealth when that asset category is segregated from the rest. This supports the claim of Munnell (1974) that it is necessary to separate "retirement saving" from total saving because the life-cycle theory applies more precisely to the narrower category. In the two other study designs employed by researchers, time series and international cross-sectional, no clear consensus about the effects of social security on saving has emerged. This lack of concensus may be partly explained by methodological, conceptual, and measurement problems. But one might also speculate that the mixed results arise because these studies use national income accounting definitions—household, private, or national saving—which combine saving out of profits, where the bequest motive is concentrated, with saving out of labor income, where life-cycle saving predominates.

5. We abstract from this problem by assuming a fixed working life of one period. For empirical work that might be interpreted as supporting a modest role for social security in the intertemporal labor supply decisions of workers, see Krueger and Pischke (1992).

In sum, the empirical literature on the effects of social security on wealth formation points toward theoretical models recognizing the coexistence of life-cycle and bequest motives for saving, for which the classical approach would seem a natural choice.

Effects on Capital Formation

We can get some sense of the orders of magnitude implied by the basic two-class model through a numerical example that has been calibrated to the U.S. economy. Most of the parameter values have been chosen to conform to the earlier exercise on debt that used the suggestions of de la Croix and Michel (2002). The retirement benefit is computed as the future value (using the growth rate, which is the money's worth of an unfunded system) of the payroll (FICA) tax under alternative assumptions about the relevant tax. First, the statutory tax (0.124) is used. Second, in recognition of the nonpension benefits of the Social Security system, such as disability insurance, the FICA tax is reduced to two-thirds its statutory rate, which is the share of OASDI (old age, survivors, and disability insurance) paid to retirees and their families. Another reason to discount the tax is that FICA is capped, and a large fraction (10 to 15 percent) of labor compensation escapes the payroll tax altogether. The worker discount factor and share of wealth are unobservable so the calibration presents a range.

The calibration shown in Table 7.3 compares the existing pension system to a counterfactual with no pension at all. Because the path of capitalist wealth is not changed by the pension system, we can use the two predictions of the workers' share of wealth to generate estimates of the capital stock on the alternate path.[6] The fourth and sixth columns show the implied percentage effect of the pension benefit on the capital stock, calculated as a log difference to avoid having to choose which path represents the base.

Even for low values of the worker discount factor, it is clear that the effects of the unfunded pension system on capital formation are fairly substantial, although only for large values of the worker discount factor do the effects begin to reach the high levels claimed by Feldstein (1996). Yet by ignoring the role of capitalist saving, the one-class approach taken by much conventional research forces any calibration toward the very high values of the worker discount factor that generate this result, a point we return to below. In other words, critics of existing PAYGO systems probably should not

6. Using $K_w = (\phi/(1-\phi))K_c$. A similar calibration exercise appears in Michl and Foley (2004), using slightly different parameters. The results are comparable.

Table 7.3 Calibration of unfunded pension system

	Control	Unfunded Pension			
	FICA = 0	FICA = 0.124		FICA = 0.082	
β_w	ϕ	ϕ	$\Delta K/K$	ϕ	$\Delta K/K$
0.05	0.192	0.000	0.239	0.041	0.161
0.10	0.385	0.153	0.320	0.246	0.204
0.15	0.577	0.353	0.426	0.451	0.262
0.20	0.770	0.553	0.663	0.656	0.401
0.25	0.962	0.754	1.874	0.861	1.300

Notes: Parameter values at annual frequency are $\rho = 0.45$, $\pi = 0.33$, $g = 0.025$; at generational frequency of 30 years, $\delta = 1$; and $k = \$57K$. $\Delta K/K$ is the level change in capital stock under the assumed conditions, comparing an unfunded pension to the control with no pension.

feel too encouraged. This model bends the stick toward finding large effects on capital formation by ignoring any positive effects of the pension on saving and by setting the problem in a pure model of capital accumulation. It is also clear that the results are sensitive to assumptions about the extent to which the real system is a pure pension system (i.e., ignoring its insurance functions); compare columns four and six of Table 7.3.

If the model did not have the two-class structure we have assumed, the results would have been dramatically different. In this case, without the anchor of capitalist wealth, the dissaving induced by the unfunded pension benefit would have more sway over capital accumulation. This can be seen by considering the one-class model presented in Foley and Michl (1999, 245–250). With only worker saving driving accumulation, an unfunded pension benefit reduces the growth rate permanently in this model. Using the same parameter values, we can calculate[7] that the implied worker discount factor and the counterfactual growth rate in absence of a pension benefit would be

FICA	β_w	g_K
0.124	0.311	0.035
0.082	0.284	0.032

7. The computations use the result that the growth rate in the one-class model solves the quadratic equation:

$$\bar{w} = \frac{(1+g_K)k}{\beta_w} + b\left(\frac{1}{1+g_K} + \frac{1-\beta_w}{\beta_w(1+r)}\right)$$

Table 7.4 Policy reform scenario

t	b	b_{-1}	τ	τ^c	f
−1	b	b	$\dfrac{b}{1+g}$	0	0
0	b	b	τ_0	τ^c	f
1	b	b	τ_1	0	f
2	b	b	τ_2	0	f

Rather than leveling off, the percentage effect of the pension benefit on the level of capital would grow by between 70 and 100 basis points per year (recall that the actual growth rate is set at 0.025 per year). And the worker discount factors required to fit real data are very high, illustrating the point made earlier. This comparison is perhaps the most effective way to make the point that leaving capitalists out of a model of capitalism leads to overstatements of the effects of an unfunded pension system on capital formation.

7.3.2 Policy Reform

For practical purposes, the more relevant issue facing policy makers is how prefunding affects an already-existing PAYGO pension system. We can tackle this problem using the same basic set-up, with the exception that the control path consists of an unfunded system paying a benefit, b, financed by a tax equal to $b/(1+g)$. Table 7.4 clarifies the timing of the policy for two cases, prefunding through payroll taxes or through a tax on capitalists.

Payroll Tax

To prefund an existing system through the payroll tax requires that the cohort of workers in period 0 pay a tax greater than $b/(1+g)$, so that the new funding level will be $f = \tau_0 - b/(1+g)$. Each worker in this cohort will reduce his or her saving by $\beta_w f$. Since all the surplus tax is saved by the government, and since the path of capitalist saving is unchanged, the net effect on the capital stock (i.e., test minus control) will be

$$\Delta K_1 = \left(\frac{(1-\beta_w)f}{k}\right) K_0 \tag{7.7}$$

In period 1, the cohort of workers will now enjoy the benefit of the sacrifice made by the previous generation, in the form of a reduction in their payroll taxes. There will also be more workers on the test path (reflecting the additional saving generated in period 0). They will save more, both individually and collectively, contributing further to capital formation.

Figure 7.5 exhibits the results of a numerical simulation. The increase in growth persists for several periods before the system returns to its steady state rate of expansion. The sacrifice imposed on the generation that provides the initial funding is readily apparent in the diminished money's worth and lifetime wealth for this cohort. Such a pattern dramatizes the argument against this funding scheme, since there does not seem to be a good reason to ask one generation to sacrifice involuntarily in order to benefit another. In a more realistic setting with technical change increasing wages in each generation, the argument is even weaker. Why should we sacrifice for our children if they are going to be richer anyway?

The workers' share of wealth initially drops off sharply, and that is partly due to the rise of the government's share of wealth and partly due to the reduced saving of the sacrificing generation. The new steady state workers' share is only modestly larger than the old share (0.200 compared with 0.198) in this simulation.

Capital Levy

Achieving the same level of funding by means of a lump-sum tax on capitalist households will increase the government's period 1 capital by the full amount of dedicated tax, τ^c. As we have observed, capitalists will reduce their saving by $\beta_c \tau^c$. To keep this scenario comparable to the previous scenario, we assume that all of the tax on capitalist households is used to fund the system. Since workers in period 0 are providing the tax revenues to finance retirement benefits for their parent's generation, their tax will be unchanged, as will their saving.[8] The net effect on the capital stock in period 1, again comparing test to control, will be

$$\Delta K_1 = \left(\frac{(1 - \beta_c) f}{k} \right) K_0$$

8. Michl and Foley (2004) present a similar scenario in which the funding plan is structured so that some of the tax on capitalist households is used to reduce the payroll tax in period 0, resulting in a lower funding level. With this structure, the increase in capital formation comes from enhanced worker saving.

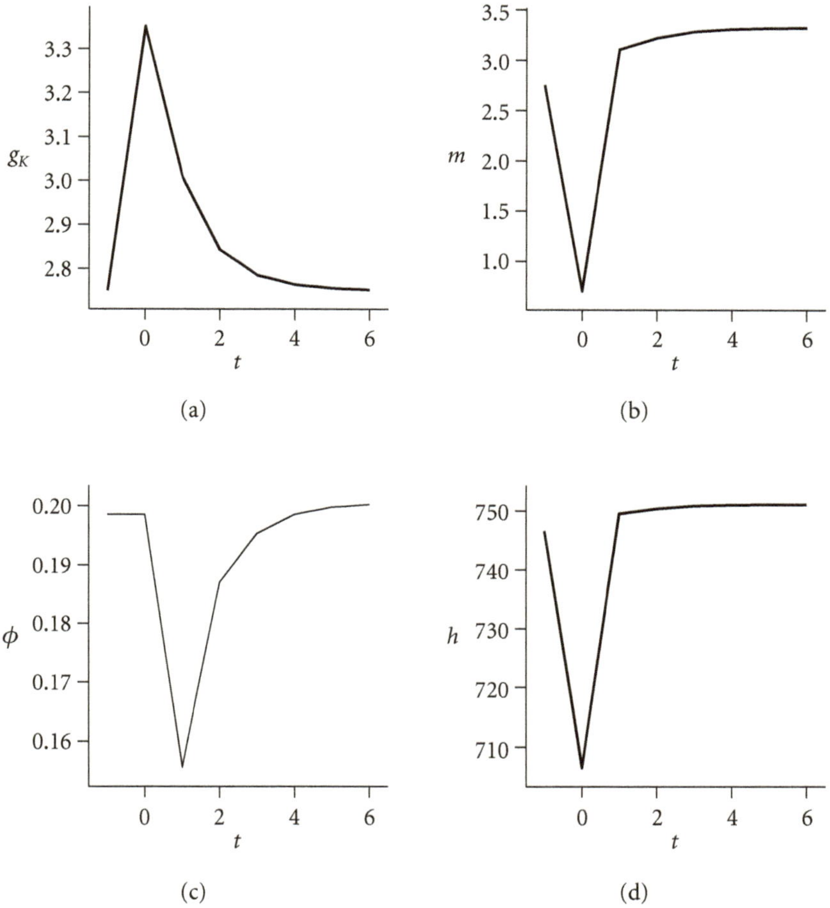

Figure 7.5 The pension system goes from PAYGO to superfunded by means of a payroll tax surplus in this simulation. Shown are the paths of (a) the rate of accumulation, g_K; (b) the money's worth of the public pension, m; (c) the workers' share of capital wealth, ϕ; and (d) the typical worker's lifetime wealth, h. The parameter values are $w = 750$, $x = 1000$, $k = 60$, $\delta = 1$, $r = 3.17$, $\beta_w = 0.1$, $\beta_c = 0.9$, $b = 100$, $f = 50$, $K_0 = 187$, $K_0^w = 37$, and $K_0^G = 0$.

It is clear in comparing these expressions (see equation 7.7) that while both approaches to prefunding increase capital formation, there will be a larger increase from a payroll tax than from a capital levy, because workers have a lower discount factor.

As before, the cohorts of workers in period 1 and beyond enjoy the benefits of funding, in the form of lower payroll taxes, and they will save more

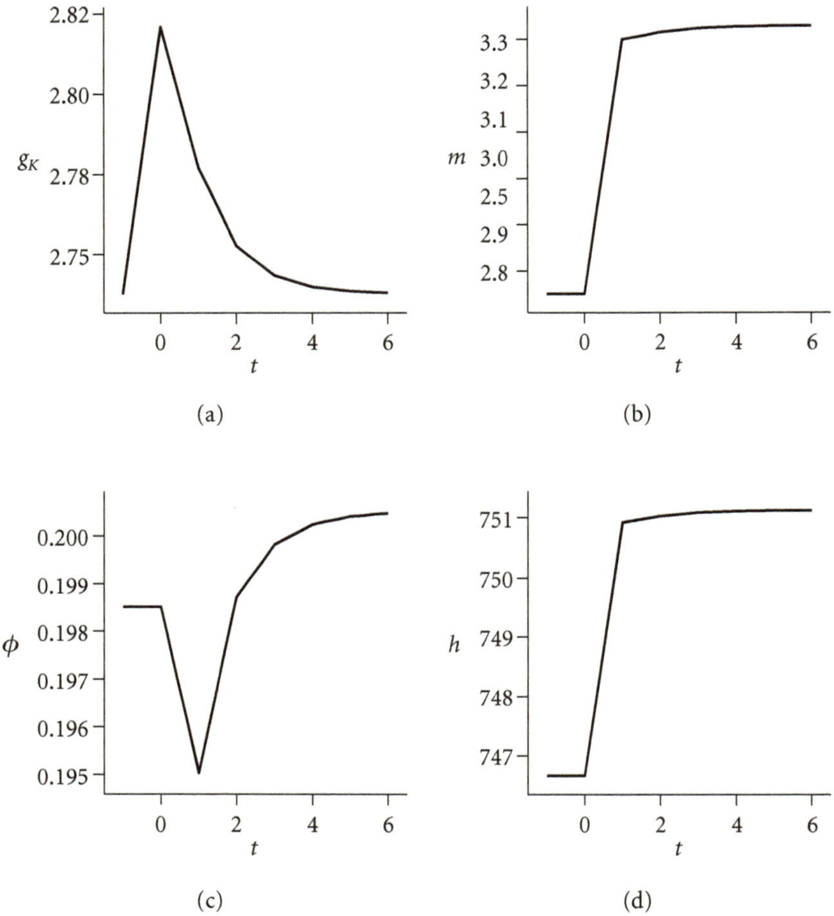

Figure 7.6 The pension system goes from PAYGO to superfunded in this simulation of a capital levy. Shown are the paths of (a) the rate of accumulation, g_K; (b) the money's worth of the public pension, m; (c) the workers' share of capital wealth, ϕ; and (d) typical worker's lifetime wealth, h. The parameter values are $w = 750$, $x = 1000$, $k = 60$, $\delta = 1$, $r = 3.17$, $\beta_w = 0.1$, $\beta_c = 0.9$, $b = 100$, $f = 50$, $K_0 = 187$, $K_0^w = 37$, and $K_0^G = 0$.

than they would have on the control path. Figure 7.6 shows the simulated effects of a capital levy on the rate of capital accumulation, the money's worth, the workers' share of capital, and the representative worker's lifetime wealth, using the same calibration as in the previous simulation with funding out of a payroll tax surplus. As expected, the impact on growth is smaller here than when the same prefunding goal is achieved out of payroll taxes (taking note of differences in scale in the two figures).

The workers' share of capital first declines before rising because the initial increase in capital formation arises from government saving, which depresses both of the private sector wealth shares. The representative worker's lifetime wealth and the money's worth of the pension system both improve immediately. Because the calibration is identical, the steady state values of the wealth share and lifetime wealth are the same in this example and the previous example. (Again, differences in scale can create the wrong impression.) Despite achieving superfunding, the changes in these measures of workers' wealth are modest in this numerical example.

Figures 7.5 and 7.6 bring out the main benefits of prefunding by means of a capital levy. The rate of accumulation rises temporarily; growth obeys the Cambridge theorem and returns to the *status quo ante* in the long run. Even though the high-saving group has been tapped by the revenue authorities, the funds raised are dedicated to public saving. Because the increased funding level increases workers' lifetime wealth, more worker saving will be forthcoming. The result of greater public and worker saving is a permanently higher level of capital, output, and employment. Because workers save more, their share of the wealth stock will increase. Because the income on the pension reserve fund subsidizes the retirement benefit, the money's worth of the system increases. This can be expected to strengthen the system politically, since the low rate of return on the PAYGO system has been a recurrent theme in the conservative campaign against public pension systems.

The main cost is born by capitalist households, some of whose wealth now resides with the public. Luxury consumption out of profits can be expected to decline. Less of the wealth that has been created by the market economy is under the private control of an economic elite, and more wealth is under the control of democratically accountable authorities. If the inequality of wealth is regarded as a problem, prefunding through progressive taxation provides an attractive pro-growth solution. Unlike the same funding level achieved by means of a temporary surplus from payroll tax revenues, the capital levy imposes no costs on any generation of workers, and in fact delivers benefits without delay.

— 8 —

Pensions and Exogenous Growth

> In principle, there is no reason why the state should not also enjoy ownership without control where management by private enterprise is considered preferable. A budget surplus . . . instead of being used to check the growth of the national debt could be used to buy industrial shares.
>
> . . . The main obstacle, all the same, to eliminating functionless wealth is lack of imagination in developing ideas and institutions appropriate to an economy that has got over the hump of heavy accumulation and needs to find a rational way of enjoying the benefit.
>
> JOAN ROBINSON (1967)

This chapter completes the set of models with a public pension system by taking up the exogenous growth closure. The final section continues the discussion from the previous chapter on the effect of prefunding the pension through a progressive tax on capitalists. Such accumulation of public capital defines Joan Robinson's vision of "the nation as rentier," to which the epigraph refers. We will also discuss the effects of a demographic shock in the presence of a pension system.

8.1 Preliminary Issues

We will let the government set a constant benefit level, so that $b = b_{-1}$. The government does have a choice about whether to use the tax, the reserve fund per worker, or some combination as its policy instrument. Generally then, the law of motion for the reserve fund is

$$f = \frac{(1+r)f_{-1} - b}{1+n} + \tau \tag{8.1}$$

and this equation can be modified to accommodate a constant reserve fund or a constant tax. We will assume a constant funding level ($f = f_{-1}$) until we turn to the issue of prefunding below.

The share of wealth owned by the government can be derived from the definition of f and is written

$$\phi^G = \frac{f_{-1}}{k(1+n)} \tag{8.2}$$

so that when $f = f_{-1}$ the aggregate saving of the government obeys

$$K^G_{+1} = \frac{f}{k}K = \phi^G(1+n)K \tag{8.3}$$

When growth is constrained by a predestined labor force under the assumption of full employment, the distribution of income functions as the equilibrating factor. From the vantage point of the capitalist agents with a log utility function, this presents no special modeling problem because their consumption plans are not affected by changes in the future path of the profit rate. But worker agents will be affected, even though they share the logarithmic form of utility function, because they must forecast the rate of profit in their retirement in order to evaluate the present value of the pension benefit, a major part of their lifetime wealth. We will find it useful to distinguish between the expected rate of profit, r^e, and the actual rate of profit, r_{+1}. Thus, we can write the typical worker's *ex ante* lifetime wealth as

$$h = w - \tau + \frac{b}{1+r^e}$$

Having committed the government to a policy of taxes, benefits, and saving, we can deduce the effects on the worker households, whose lifetime wealth can now be written

$$h = w + f\left(\frac{r-n}{1+n}\right) - b\left(\frac{r^e - n}{(1+r^e)(1+n)}\right) \tag{8.4}$$

Note that in a steady state where $r^e = r$, increases in the benefit level reduce the typical worker's lifetime wealth and increases in the reserve fund increase lifetime wealth when the rate of profit exceeds the rate of growth (the normal state in real economies, and in the two-class model). But when the rate of growth exceeds the rate of profit, benefits augment wealth and reserve funding diminishes wealth. We will return to this point in the next chapter, when we examine the issue of optimal policy in a one-class model.

Having characterized lifetime wealth more precisely, we can also limn out the aggregate saving of workers in more detail. Adopting the dynamic fiscal policy of maintaining a constant reserve funding level, f, we can write

$$K^w_{+1} = (s^w/k)K \tag{8.5}$$

$$\text{where } s^w/k = \frac{w\beta_w}{k} - \frac{b}{k}\left(\frac{\beta_w}{1+n} + \frac{1-\beta_w}{1+r^e}\right) + \frac{f\beta_w(r-n)}{k(1+n)}$$

We have now got equations for the accumulation of government and worker-owned capital wealth, to which we can add the now familiar Cambridge equation describing the capitalist agent:

$$K^c_{+1} = \beta_c(1+r)K^c \tag{8.6}$$

8.2 Exogenous Growth with a Public Pension

As with previous applications of the basic model, our expositional strategy is first to characterize the temporary equilibrium before studying the steady state and comparative dynamics in detail.

8.2.1 Temporary Equilibrium

Having specified the fiscal policy in place, the temporary equilibrium can be derived by recognizing that the capital stock and its distribution are themselves predetermined, having been inherited from the past. The system is compactly represented by

$$\begin{pmatrix} \frac{\beta_w}{k} & \beta_w\phi^G + \beta_c(1-\phi-\phi^G) \\ 1 & k \end{pmatrix}\begin{pmatrix} w \\ r \end{pmatrix} = \begin{pmatrix} \psi \\ y \end{pmatrix} \tag{8.7}$$

We will refer to the matrix on the LHS of this expression as **C** and the consolidating term[1] as ψ.

The equilibrium values of w and r can be handily obtained from this system using Cramer's rule. In particular, we will use

$$r = \frac{|\mathbf{C}_2|}{|\mathbf{C}|} \tag{8.8}$$

1. In this case, we can write $\psi = 1 + n + \frac{b}{k}\left(\frac{\beta_w}{1+n} + \frac{1-\beta_w}{1+r^e}\right) - \phi^G(\beta_w + (1-\beta_w)(1+n)) - \beta_c(1-\phi-\phi^G)$.

where $\mathbf{C}_2$ represents as usual the matrix, $\mathbf{C}$, with the second column replaced by $(\psi, y)'$.

As in the basic laissez-faire model, the determinant of $\mathbf{C}$ has economic significance in terms of labor market stability since $|\mathbf{C}|\ (1/k)$ equals the key derivative, $\partial g_K/\partial w$. We will continue to assume that

$$|\mathbf{C}| = \beta_w(1-\phi^G) - \beta_c(1-\phi-\phi^G) < 0$$

It is interesting to consider how funding the public pensions affects this condition. An increase in funding level (i.e., a greater public share of capital wealth) will reduce the ceiling on the worker saving propensity consistent with labor market stability.

Having determined the temporary equilibrium wage and profit rate, it is also possible to pin down the law of motion of the workers' share of capital wealth, conditioned by the expected rate of profit, by substitution into equation (8.5), using the fact that $K_{+1} = (1+n)K$:

$$\phi_{+1} = \frac{1}{1+n}\left[\beta_w(R-r) - \frac{b}{k}\left(\frac{\beta_w}{1+n} + \frac{1-\beta_w}{1+r^e}\right) + \frac{f\beta_w(r-n)}{k(1+n)}\right] \quad (8.9)$$

Once again we have a nonlinear first-order difference equation (since the rate of profit is a function of the current period distribution of wealth) in the same form as the basic model. However, we must now specify the process of expectations formation in order to bring it to life. We will return to this question after characterizing the steady state.

8.2.2 *Steady State*

Regardless of how workers form their expectations about the rate of profit, the steady state solution (if it exists) will require their fulfillment, or $r^e = r^*$. By substituting into the expression above, we obtain the $\hat{\phi}(r^*)$ function that describes the relationship between the steady state rate of profit and the workers' saving behavior:

$$\hat{\phi} = \frac{1}{1+n}\left[\beta_w(R-r^*) - \frac{b}{k}\left(\frac{\beta_w}{1+n} + \frac{1-\beta_w}{1+r^*}\right) + \frac{f\beta_w(r^*-n)}{k(1+n)}\right]$$

Two salient features of this relationship are immediately clear. First, as long as the rate of profit exceeds the rate of growth, which it must in the two-class model, an increase in the benefit level, b, must decrease the workers' wealth share consistent with any given steady state profit rate. Second, an increase in the funding level, f, must increase the wealth share consistent with any given profit rate. Both these features follow from the well-rehearsed effects of the public pension system on the individual worker's saving behavior.

The wealth distribution consistent with capitalist saving collapses into the Cambridge equation, as in previous models. Thus, the $\tilde{\phi}(r*)$ function will simply be

$$r^* = \frac{1+n}{\beta_c} - 1$$

Once again, we can see that the Cambridge theorem remains valid. The steady state rate of profit is determined by the natural rate of growth and the saving propensity of capitalist agents, independent of worker or government saving. The corresponding wage rate can be found using the wage-profit equation.

By equating $\hat{\phi}(r^*)$ and $\tilde{\phi}(r*)$, we obtain the following expression for the steady state workers' wealth share:

$$\phi^* = \frac{\beta_w(\beta_c(1+R) - (1+n))}{\beta_c(1+n)} - \frac{b}{k}\left(\frac{\beta_c + (1-\beta_c)\beta_w}{(1+n)^2}\right) + \frac{f}{k}\left(\frac{\beta_w(1-\beta_c)}{\beta_c(1+n)}\right) \tag{8.10}$$

From this expression, it is clear that increases in the benefit level must reduce the equilibrium workers' wealth share. By reducing the typical worker's lifetime wealth, an increase in benefits reduces individual worker saving along familiar lines. It is also clear that increases in the funding level must increase the equilibrium workers' wealth share by virtue of the augmenting effect of such increases on lifetime wealth and thus individual saving.

But it is not clear how changes in the natural rate of growth or in the capitalist saving propensity will affect the steady state solution, and we need to examine this question further.

Having determined the steady state value of the workers' wealth share, it is now possible to characterize the critical level of the worker saving rate that separates the one-class from the two-class model. By substituting ϕ^* into $|\mathbf{C}| < 0$ and solving, we obtain

$$\bar{\beta}_w = \frac{b\beta_c + (k(1+n) - f)(1+n)}{k(1+R)(1+n) - b(1-\beta_c) - f(1+n)} \tag{8.11}$$

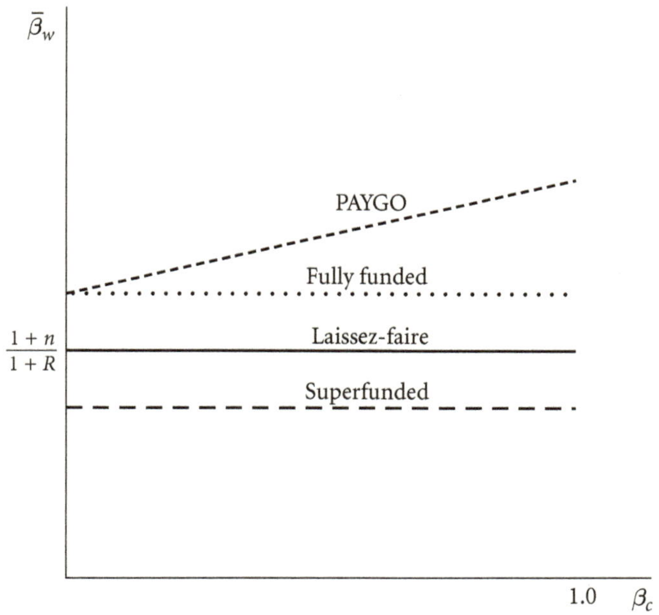

Figure 8.1 The separation between the two- and one-class regimes under alternative funding levels. (The superfunded separatrix can lie anywhere below that of the fully funded system, including as illustrated.)

It is useful to consider the effects of different funding levels on this separating condition, and to compare them to the laissez-faire benchmark. Let us normalize by setting the funding level above the full funding benchmark with a constant premium (which can be negative), ϵ, or $f = b/(1+r^*) + \epsilon$. Note that we are not holding f constant because as β_c changes, so too does the steady state rate of profit, and with it the size of the reserve needed for full funding. The separating condition will then be

$$\bar{\beta}_w = \frac{(k(1+n) - \epsilon)(1+n)}{k(1+R)(1+n) - b - \epsilon(1+n)}$$

Figure 8.1 illustrates this relationship under various funding levels and includes the laissez-faire case as a benchmark. By reducing worker saving, an unfunded PAYGO system ($f = 0$) will clearly make it harder to get into the one-class region, permitting a larger worker discount factor before the limits of a two-class system are breached.

Interestingly, a fully funded public pension ($\epsilon = 0$) will also make it harder to get into the one-class region. Despite the well-known neutrality of a fully funded system in other respects, it is not neutral with respect to the class structure of accumulation. As in the endogenous growth model of the previous chapter, full funding reduces the workers' share of wealth by increasing the government share one-for-one, leaving the capitalist share of wealth unchanged.[2] But this rearrangement reduces the importance of worker-owned wealth in the accumulation process and increases the importance of government-owned wealth. Since the government effectively functions as an engine of accumulation in managing its reserve fund, the reassignment dilutes the effects of the wage on accumulation and that explains the tolerance for a larger worker saving rate in a fully funded system.

Finally, superfunding the public pension system ($\epsilon > 0$) reduces the separating value. For a sufficiently large superfunding premium, the separating value of β_w can be depressed below its laissez-faire level, as illustrated in Figure 8.1. Superfunding a public pension beyond some critical point can, in principle at least, jeopardize the class structure of accumulation.

8.2.3 Comparative Dynamics

The three most interesting comparative equilibrium exercises involve changes in policy, changes in the capitalist saving rate, and changes in the natural rate of growth of the labor force.

Policy

We begin with the policy variables, b and f. From equation (8.10) we can see immediately that

$$\frac{d\phi^*}{db} < 0 \qquad \frac{d\phi^*}{df} > 0$$

An increase in the retirement benefit reduces the individual saving of workers. This will shift the $\hat{\phi}(r^*)$ function downward, reducing the steady state workers' share of capital wealth. Recall that the rate of profit is fully determined by the Cambridge equation and depends only on the natural rate of growth and the capitalist saving propensity. An increase in the funding

2. We substitute $f = b\beta_c/(1+n)$ into equation (8.10), solve for $\phi^* + \phi^G$, and obtain the expression for the laissez-faire value of ϕ^*.

level augments the lifetime wealth of workers and increases their individual saving. This has the effect of shifting the $\hat{\phi}(r^*)$ function upward, raising the workers' share of capital wealth. There is no ambiguity about the direction of these effects, and they follow familiar intuition, the foundations of which were laid out in the previous chapter. This is not the case, however, with changes in the capitalist saving propensity to which we now turn.

Capitalist Discount Factor

When we differentiate equation (8.10) with respect to the capitalist discount factor, we obtain

$$\frac{d\phi^*}{d\beta_c} = \frac{\beta_w}{\beta_c^2} - \frac{b(1-\beta_w}{k(1+n)^2} - \frac{f\beta_w}{\beta_c^2 k(1+n)}$$

from which it is clear that both the benefit level and the funding level reduce this expression toward zero and beyond. There is some ambiguity over the effect of changes in the capitalist discount factor on the distribution of wealth that does not appear in the laissez-faire model.

We can visualize this by using the now familiar $\hat{\phi}$-$\tilde{\phi}$ apparatus of Figure 8.2a and b, which illustrates the two possibilities. Note the peculiar hump-shape of $\hat{\phi}(r^*)$ in the figure. Evidently there is some profit rate, call it $\tilde{r}$, at which the function is maximized:

$$\tilde{r} = \arg\max \hat{\phi}(r^*) = \sqrt{\frac{b(1-\beta_w)(1+n)}{\beta_w(k(1+n)-f)}} - 1$$

This critical point is positively related to both the benefit level and the funding level. (Increases in the benefit level shift the peak downward and to the right; increases in the funding level shift the peak upward and to the right.)

When we turn to the effects of the capitalist saving rate, β_c, the non-monotonic form of $\hat{\phi}(r^*)$ assumes importance. It is evident that the sign of this effect depends on whether the rate of profit lies above or below the critical value that maximizes this function. As we can visualize in Figure 8.2, there is a region lying between n (not labeled in the figure) and $\tilde{r}$ that is potentially accessible for some permissible parameter values, where declines in the rate of profit brought about by increases in the capitalist saving rate will also reduce the workers' wealth share. (Recall that the ceiling on the rate of profit is n when capitalists save all their wealth, so that a necessary

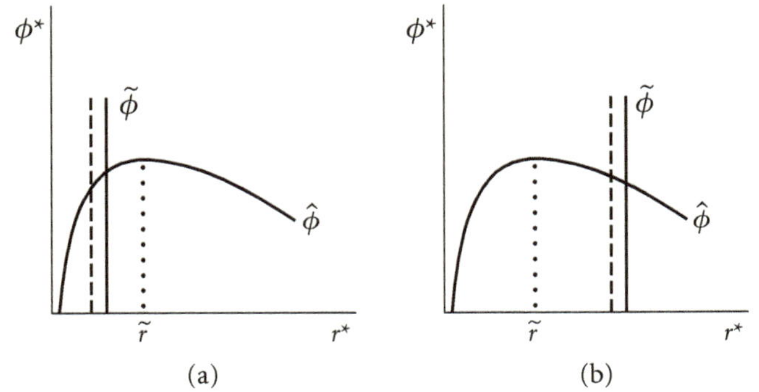

Figure 8.2 An increase in the capitalist discount factor, β_c, will shift the Cambridge equation and lower the rate of profit, but its effect on the distribution of wealth is ambiguous in the presence of a public pension system. (a) When β_c is large enough that $r^* < \tilde{r}$, the workers' share of capital wealth will decline. (b) When β_c is small enough that $r^* > \tilde{r}$, the workers' share of capital wealth will increase as it does in the laissez-faire model.

condition for this region to exist is simply that the natural rate of growth be less than $\tilde{r}$.) What is the economic rationale? Under laissez-faire conditions, a decline in the rate of profit initiated by greater capitalist thrift works through a wage increase, which in turn supports greater worker saving. The same change in the profit rate, however, interacts with the public pension system in two ways. First, the present value of the retirement benefit increases, which tends to reduce worker saving. Second, the return on the pension reserve fund (i.e., the rate of profit) declines, which requires a compensating increase in the payroll tax that also reduces worker saving. Evidently these two effects can dominate the basic mechanism of a laissez-faire economy.

Demographic Shock

As a final exercise in comparative dynamics, consider the effects of a demographic shock caused by a decline in the natural rate of growth of the labor force. Under laissez-faire conditions, as we have seen, such a change can be expected to increase the equilibrium wage rate and bring up the share of worker-owned capital through its salutary effects on worker saving. But a change in the natural rate of growth interacts with the public pension system in distinctive ways. First, a decline in the rate of growth raises the dependency rate and requires a higher payroll tax to support a given retirement benefit. A higher tax reduces the lifetime wealth of workers and cuts into their ability to save. It is possible for this effect to dominate the channel operating through the wage, and for a reduction in the natural rate of growth to result in a decline in worker-owned capital. Second, a decline in the rate of growth will reduce the part of the payroll tax required to maintain a given funding level. This effect tends to reinforce the wage channel and increase the share of worker-owned capital.

To formalize this argument, consider the derivative

$$\frac{d\phi^*}{dn} = -\frac{\beta_w(1+R)}{(1+n)^2} + \frac{2b(\beta_c + (1-\beta_c)\beta_w)}{k(1+n)^3} - \frac{f\beta_w(1-\beta_c)}{\beta_c k(1+n)^2}$$

It is possible to solve this expression for the critical level of the retirement benefit at which the sign change occurs. We will return below to the problem of a demographic shock in order to study its anatomy in greater detail.

In sum, while many of the comparative dynamic results are straightforward, we have encountered some surprises, the result of interactions between growth, distribution, and the public pension system that are reflected in the nonmonotonic form of the worker saving function, $\hat{\phi}(r^*)$.

8.3 Transitional Dynamics and Expectations

We will consider three alternative hypotheses concerning the way workers form expectations about the future rate of profit one period ahead, which they need to do to evaluate their lifetime wealth and make consumption and saving decisions. First, we will assume workers anticipate that the rate of profit will achieve its long term equilibrium value in the next period; let us call this "stable expectations" because workers will maintain their forecast during the transitional dynamics. Second, we will assume workers project the observed rate of profit into the future; let us follow convention and call this "adaptive expectations." Third, we will assume workers accurately forecast the rate of profit; convention dictates that we call this "perfect foresight." Each of these hypotheses offers some theoretical insight or practical advantage.

8.3.1 Stable Expectations

The underlying rationale behind stable expectations is that economic agents know enough about the fundamental determinants of income distribution that they can accurately forecast the long-run (steady state) equilibrium values of profit and wage rates but not enough about the dynamic structure of the world they live in to determine if the profit rate is destined to over- or undershoot the steady state value. This hypothesis does not seem too arbitrary, especially if the system is near its steady state, and it offers us the ability to make fairly straightforward comparisons with the basic laissez-faire model. Formally, we postulate that

$$r^e = r^* = \frac{1+n}{\beta_c} - 1$$

Substituting this value and the equilibrium profit rate into equation (8.9), we obtain the nonlinear first-order difference equation that governs the dynamics under stable expectations, namely,

$$\phi_{+1} = z(\phi; b, f)$$

This equation has the same monotonic form as its counterpart in the laissez-faire case.

It is clear from this equation that changes in benefit levels and funding levels affect the slope as well as the position of the difference equation at the equilibrium point, and we can examine the effect of fiscal policy on the stability condition, $|z_\phi(\phi^*)| < 1$. Since we are interested in the effects of different funding levels, let us again use the funding premium, ϵ, to define the funding level as $f = b/(1+r) + \epsilon$. Substituting into the stability condition and solving gives us

$$\beta_w < \frac{\beta_c(k(1+n) - \epsilon)(1+n)}{\beta_c(1+R)k(1+n) - 2b\beta_c - (1+n)(\epsilon(1+\beta_c) + k(1+n))}$$

We can get a clear visual picture of the effects of fiscal policy on the stable parameter space by plotting this expression for various funding levels as in Figure 8.3. Again, the benchmark case is a laissez-faire world. Increases in the retirement benefit expand the stable space, relaxing the constraints on the worker saving propensity, as can be seen by the shaded area for the PAYGO case. This follows from well-rehearsed economic intuition about the effects of an unfunded retirement benefit on life-cycle saving. Increasing the funding level of a given benefit tightens the constraints, again following from familiar economic intuition. But achieving full funding does not shrink the stable space to the laissez-faire benchmark; for that, we must

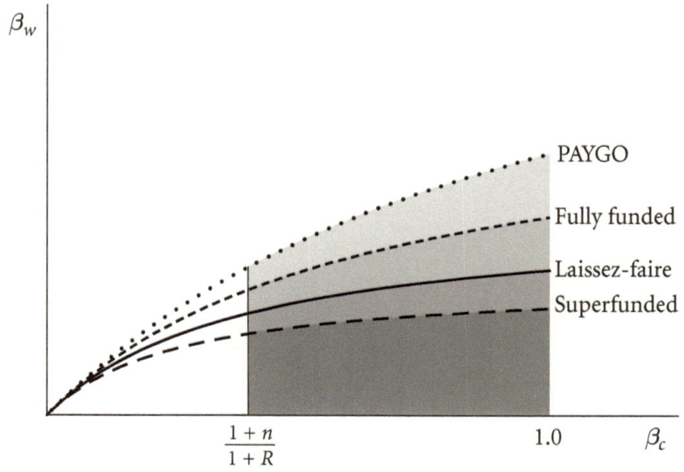

Figure 8.3 Increases in the retirement benefit expand the stable parameter space, while increases in funding level shrink the stable space. (The superfunded boundary can lie anywhere below that of the fully funded system, including as illustrated.)

increase the superfunding premium to an appropriate level.[3] Again we see that full funding is not neutral in this respect. Finally, Figure 8.3 shows a superfunded system that has a premium great enough to shrink the stable space beyond the laissez-faire benchmark. Superfunding beyond some critical point could jeopardize the stability of this model.

8.3.2 Adaptive Expectations

Economists are well acquainted with the strengths and weaknesses of the assumption that expectations are backward-looking. In the context of an overlapping generations model on a timescale of 15 to 30 years, it is standard practice to assume that agents will form expectations about their retirement years on the basis of their current experience. Formally, we will assert

$$r^e = r$$

3. In fact, the critical level of superfunding that brings the stability condition into congruence with its laissez-faire counterpart is simply $\epsilon = 2b/(R-n)$.

This assumption changes the character of the temporary equilibrium that we described above, and in fact destroys its neat linear form. The rate of profit can be obtained by substituting for r^e in equation (8.7). It will be the root of the quadratic equation

$$\mathcal{A}r^2 + \mathcal{B}r + \mathcal{D} = 0$$

where

$$\mathcal{A} = -\,|\mathbf{C}| > 0$$

$$\Psi = \psi - \beta_w R - \frac{b(1-\beta_w)}{k(1+r^e)} > 0$$

$$\mathcal{B} = \mathcal{A} - \Psi < 0$$

$$\mathcal{D} = -\left(\Psi + \frac{b(1-\beta_w)}{k(1+n)}\right) < 0$$

By Descartes's theorem, this quadratic equation will have one positive and one negative root because there is one sign change (which is the limit on the number of positive roots) and one sign continuation (which is the limit on the number of negative roots). Thus, the rate of profit will be given by the positive root, or

$$r = \frac{-\mathcal{B} + \sqrt{\mathcal{B}^2 - 4\mathcal{A}\mathcal{D}}}{2\mathcal{A}}$$

Having obtained a solution for the temporary equilibrium rate of profit in terms of the predetermined distribution of wealth represented by ϕ (recall that ϕ^G is a constant determined by the fiscal policy in place), we can substitute into equation (8.9) to obtain the first-order difference equation

$$\phi_{+1} = z(\phi; b, f)$$

The best way to see how adaptive expectations affect the dynamics of a model is to describe the model with different levels of retirement benefit and funding, again using the laissez-faire system as a benchmark case. The pure effect of a retirement benefit is to flatten out the difference equation in the neighborhood of the steady state (where it intersects a 45-degree line through the origin as in Figure 3.4b). Moreover, funding the benefit also flattens out the function, $z(\phi)$. These effects can even eliminate the function's monotonic profile. Thus, we infer that a public pension system can change the qualitative character of the transitional dynamics of the model under adaptive expectations, wiping out the alternations that prevail in the laissez-faire world.

8.3.3 Perfect Foresight

The assumption of perfect foresight implies that the worker agents know the structure of the world to the point of being able to foresee the whole path from some initial condition to the achievement of a steady state in the indefinite future. This seems a lot to demand of ordinary mortal beings, but it does have the advantage of dispensing with arbitrariness and the ad hoc. To implement this hypothesis, simply put

$$r^e = r_{+1}$$

and solve the model. Achieving anything useful by way of analytical results is difficult, but we can use this assumption to generate approximate numerical examples that provide insight when compared with examples using the alternative hypotheses about expectations.

The basic procedure (de la Croix and Michel 2002, 343–344) makes use of the fact that in each period we have two equations, (8.8) and (8.7), describing the current rate of profit and the next period's wealth distribution, each conditioned by the next period profit rate. We simply assume that at a known time in the future, T, the system achieves the steady state. If we index from $t = 0$, this gives us exactly $2T - 1$ equations to determine the $2T - 1$ unknowns, once we recognize that ϕ_0 is a given initial condition, and that r_T and ϕ_T are given terminal conditions. By choosing a value of T that is both small and plausible, it is possible to solve this system numerically using Newton's method (sometimes called the Newton-Raphson method). Fortunately, the model seems to converge quickly under the alternative expectations hypotheses over a wide range of parameter values.

This can be observed readily in Figure 8.4, which shows the qualitative properties that the three expectations hypotheses are capable of generating. Perhaps the most interesting feature is that the adaptive expectations hypothesis (historically the least favored among economists) produces the most well-behaved transitional dynamic; that is, starting from a low level of workers' wealth share, it exhibits the monotonic approach to the steady state (under these parameters, at least) that we associate with a stable node.

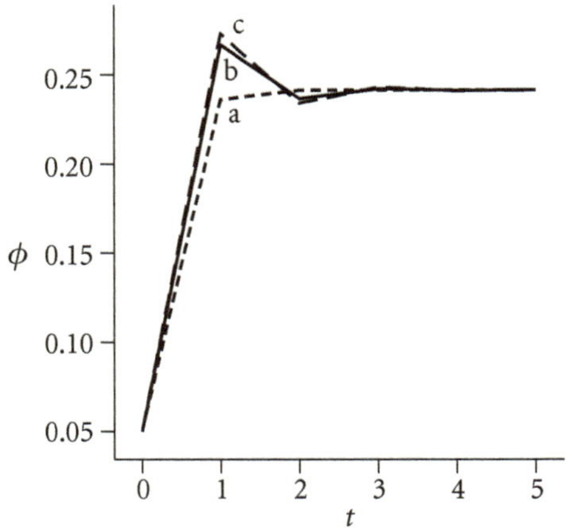

Figure 8.4 The transitional dynamics of the workers' share of capital wealth, ϕ, depend on the expectations of workers in these three simulation experiments showing: (a) adaptive expectations, (b) stable expectations, and (c) perfect foresight. The parameter values are $\beta_w = 0.1$, $\beta_c = 0.9$, $x = 1000$, $k = 60$, $\delta = 1$, $n = 2.5$, $f = 0$, $b = 100$, and $\phi_0 = 0.05$.

Because the stable expectations hypothesis can produce numerical results that closely resemble the other two hypotheses, we will use it below as a reasonable first approximation.

8.4 Demographic Shocks

This model of growth and public pensions is well suited to shine some light on the problem of a demographic shock resulting from a fertility decline that reduces the natural rate of labor force growth. We also briefly take on the question of increased longevity and the "old-age crisis."

Consider the effects of a one-time decline in the natural rate of growth, such as might be associated with a demographic transition from high to low fertility. As in the previous sections, we assume the change occurs in period $t = 0$ so that we can carefully work out the implications for each generation separately.

We have already seen in Chapter 3 that a demographic shock will increase the steady state welfare (discounted utility) of the representative worker in the two-class model under laissez-faire conditions. Will this result continue to go through with an idealized public pension system? The answer is that it depends on how large the retirement benefit is.

The crux of the problem is that a lower rate of growth requires that the payroll tax be raised, in recognition of the higher dependency ratio. The steady state tax for a given funding level (using the Cambridge equation to replace the profit rate) illustrates the mechanism:

$$\tau = \frac{b}{1+n} - f\frac{1-\beta_c}{\beta_c}$$

One notable feature of this equation is that the funding level does not affect the response of the payroll tax to a demographic shock. In other words, funding offers no protection from a demographic shock, at least in this respect.

After a demographic shock, wages do increase but the payroll tax also increases, neutralizing some of the benefit for workers. To see this, evaluate the derivative of $V(c^w(h), c^r(h, r))$, the representative worker's indirect utility function, with respect to the growth rate, n, confining all variables to their steady state values. This gives us the condition for a welfare-decreasing demographic shock, or

$$\frac{dV}{dn} > 0 \Leftrightarrow \beta_w > \beta(\beta_c, n, b, f, R)$$

It makes good sense to analyze this expression separately for the unfunded and funded cases.

8.4.1 PAYGO Case

Let us first focus on the PAYGO case ($f = 0$), where the burden of carrying a higher dependency ratio is greatest. The condition for $dV/dn > 0$ is that

$$\beta_w > \frac{k(1+n)^2 - b\beta_c(1-\beta_c)}{k(1+n)(\beta_c(1+R) - (1+n)) - b\beta_c(1-\beta_c)}$$

The question is whether this condition automatically excludes all parameter values consistent with a two-class model (as it did in the laissez-faire case), or whether it is possible to satisfy this constraint in a two-class model. By comparing this expression with the separating condition (8.11), specialized for a PAYGO system, it becomes clear that it is indeed possible for a two-class regime to support a worker discount factor that satisfies the condition above, implying that a demographic shock could be welfare-decreasing for workers.

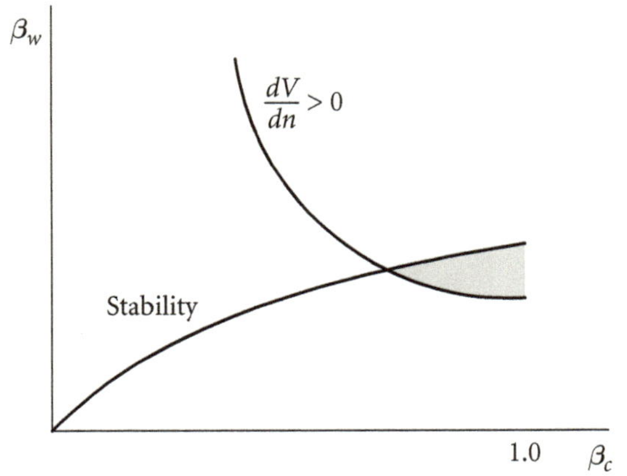

Figure 8.5 The shaded area identifies the parameter values that support a welfare-decreasing demographic shock, $dV/dn > 0$, and a stable two-class equilibrium.

Having cleared this hurdle, however, we also need to check that such a large discount factor can satisfy the stability condition. We have seen that increases in the retirement benefit in a PAYGO system relax that stability condition. It follows that there will be a critical level of retirement benefits, beyond which a demographic shock will saddle workers with lower welfare because of the burden of supporting the public pension system. Figure 8.5 illustrates by showing the boundary condition for $dV/dn > 0$ and the stability condition when the retirement benefit exceeds this critical level. Thus, the public debates about whether existing pension systems will be a burden in the event that labor force growth declines find formal expression within this model. Note that interpreted through the model, the position that the demographic shock will be welfare-decreasing for workers necessarily implies that in the absence of a public pension system, the worker discount factor is sufficiently large to support a one-class regime. Put baldly, this position requires us to believe that two-class capitalism depends on the distortions created by the public pension.

8.4.2 Funded Case

Funding is sometimes presented as a good way to prepare society for a demographic shock, but that position receives little support in this model. We have already noticed that the change in payroll tax is independent of the

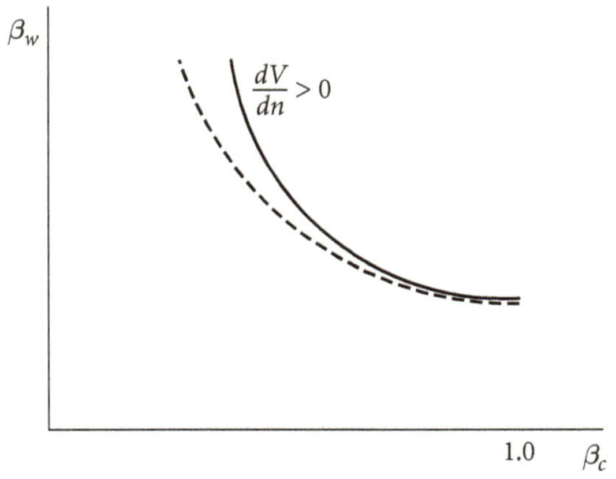

Figure 8.6 An increase in funding level will relax the parameter conditions needed for a welfare-decreasing demographic shock, by expanding the area lying above the separatrix.

funding level. What does funding do to the condition for a demographic shock to be welfare-decreasing? As Figure 8.6 illustrates, funding actually expands the relevant space. This may seem paradoxical, since funding unambiguously improves the welfare of workers in the steady state. But the reason it does so is that it reduces their tax burden. A demographic shock in a funded system will necessitate the same tax increase as in an unfunded system, but starting from a lower base, this tax increase is more likely to be welfare-decreasing.

8.4.3 *Transitional Dynamics*

The transitional path to the new steady state will impose costs and bestow benefits on successive cohorts that are most readily analyzed in the context of the stable expectations model. We will simply assume that the cohort in the impact period makes a full adjustment in expectations. The immediate effect of the decline in the natural rate of growth will be to reduce sharply the rate of profit. Thus, the cohort that retires in period $t = 0$ will experience a welfare loss because their retirement savings will earn a lower than expected rate of return. Formally, we can determine from the temporary equilibrium system described by equation (8.7) that

$$\Delta\psi = \Delta n \left(1 - \frac{b(1-\beta_w)}{k(1+n)(1+n')}\right)$$

where n' represents the new growth rate. Then the change in profit rate will be

$$\Delta r = \frac{-\Delta \psi}{|\mathbf{C}|}$$

The generation working in period $t = 0$, of course, enjoys a corresponding increase in their wage. And it will be spared the tax increase that will be shouldered by its children, whose smaller cohort requires a larger per capita contribution. Their welfare improves dramatically, their children's less so.

8.4.4 The Old-Age Crisis

Increasing life expectancy with the attendant rise in the population of older people constitutes another aspect of the demographic shock that has already begun to affect both developed and many less developed countries in the twenty-first century. While our two-period set-up is too coarse to treat this problem properly, it is possible to model the old-age crisis by treating it as an exogenous increase in the retirement benefit. Most existing public pensions operate as real annuities, the value of which rises automatically with longevity.

The effect of an increase in the mandated benefit in an unfunded pension system can be obtained by analyzing equation (8.4). Sticking to the effects on steady state lifetime wealth, we obtain

$$\frac{\partial h}{\partial b} = \frac{-(1-\beta_c)}{1+n}$$

This result is directly relevant to the PAYGO systems in place in most developed countries. Increasing the benefit level will impose a burden on workers in the steady state because it will increase the payroll tax, reducing their lifetime wealth. But we need to keep in mind that the model is too coarse to include the welfare gain from better health and longer life.

In contrast to the rather positive outlook on the demographic crisis conveyed by the effect of a lower natural rate of growth, the interaction between aging and current statutory rules presents a more pessimistic picture. Conventional studies (Auerbach et al. 1989) using calibrations of the standard overlapping generations model initially emphasized the sunny implications of higher wages associated with tight labor markets. But more recent studies (Kotlikoff et al. 2001) have stressed the negative effects of higher taxes needed to support a larger population of aged citizens.

Whether funding changes the picture materially is best studied in connection with the topic of policy design. An increase in the benefit level is in principle no different than the establishment of a public pension system. The next section takes up these issues and also uncovers some surprising features of the transitional dynamics.

8.5 Policy Issues

Many economists and political thinkers have criticized the existing PAYGO public pension system, and advocated greater funding levels. As before, we parse the question into the design of a pension system from scratch and the reform of an existing unfunded system. In these applications, we will use the assumption of stable expectations as a framework for getting to grips with the issues.

The exogenous growth model rules out any changes in the capital stock and therefore excludes the possibility of broad prefunding. Any funding that occurs involves a change in the distribution of ownership. An increase in the public pension reserve fund represents narrow prefunding.

8.5.1 Policy Design

We can investigate the establishment of a public pension system *de novo* using the same framework introduced in the previous chapter. (Readers might want to refer to Table 7.2 for reorientation.) The policy goes into effect in period $t = 0$, so that the workers in that period are promised a benefit, b, and are asked to contribute an amount, $\tau_0 = f$, toward prefunding their own retirement benefit (which could be 0 for a PAYGO system). Subsequent generations continue the benefit and funding level. We can compare the path of the model under the policy test scenario with the control path of the model under laissez-faire conditions.

The impact of this policy is felt immediately because the current generation of workers will change their saving behavior. The change will affect the temporary equilibrium system described by equation (8.7), and we can easily determine that

$$\Delta\psi = \frac{1-\beta_w}{k}\left(\frac{b}{1+r^e} - f\right)$$

If workers have stable expectations ($r^e = r^*$) and don't foresee any general equilibrium effects from this policy, clearly the sign of the change will depend on whether the newly created pension is partially, fully, or superfunded. Let us again use the superfunding premium, $\epsilon = f - b/(1+r)$, to distinguish these cases.

In this case, we can see how the change in saving behavior will affect the equilibrium distribution of income in period $t = 0$ (assuming stable expectations):

$$\Delta r = \frac{(1-\beta_w)\epsilon}{k\,|\mathbf{C}|}$$

$$\Delta w = \frac{-(1-\beta_w)\epsilon}{|\mathbf{C}|}$$

The changes in payroll tax (if any) and wages will affect the lifetime wealth of workers in period $t = 0$ by

$$\Delta h = \frac{-\epsilon(1-\beta_c(1-\phi^*))}{|\mathbf{C}|}$$

We can evaluate this expression under all of the possible funding scenarios.

PAYGO

The most relevant case is that of an unfunded PAYGO system since almost all the real public pensions established in the twentieth century have been of this type. In the PAYGO case, $f = \tau_0 = 0$ so that $\epsilon = -b/(1+r)$. It is immediately apparent that $\Delta h < 0$, recalling the negative sign on $|\mathbf{C}|$.

The explanation for this rather remarkable result is that in order to maintain full employment in the presence of the negative shock to worker saving, it is necessary that the rate of profit increase to stimulate compensatory saving from capitalist households. The founding generation scheduled to receive the first benefits experiences a collapse in its wages and *ex ante* lifetime wealth. Moreover, since we know that the model produces alternations, they will also suffer a subnormal return on their retirement savings in period $t = 1$, when they retire.

The generation that worked under the laissez-faire conditions will have retired at the right time; their savings provide them a return greater than expected, and their retirement living standard rises as an indirect effect of the new pension system even though they receive no direct benefit.

These concrete expressions depend on the maintained assumption of stable expectations. But even if workers correctly foresee that their retirement savings are going to underperform, it is difficult to see how they could escape the general equilibrium effects of lower savings on their lifetime wealth, which seems to be embedded in the structure of the accumulation process under the full employment assumption. Given the conventional wisdom that the founding generation receives a free ride, imposing a legacy cost on their children, it is surprising that in this model they actually suffer a loss in their living standards.

Their children in the $t = 1$ cohort enjoy the benefits of higher wages during their working years and a higher return on their savings during their retirement years. Their lifetime wealth increases, somewhat crazily, as the result of the dynamics of the model. And it is true that subsequent generations will eventually bear legacy costs, in the form of reduced lifetime wealth and a money's worth on their payroll taxes that falls short of the market return on savings.

Funding

Partially prefunding the retirement benefit can only ameliorate the effects on distribution and lifetime wealth. Full funding ($\epsilon = 0$), of course, will be neutral. Superfunding ($\epsilon > 0$) results in equally remarkable but opposite-signed effects to those seen with PAYGO. The founding generation experiences an increase in its lifetime wealth as the result of the higher wages it enjoys: $\Delta h > 0$. The public saving creates an incipient excess demand for labor that drives up wages and reduces the rate of profit.

The generation that worked under the laissez-faire conditions has picked a bad time to retire, and its retirement living standard falls as an indirect effect of the new pension system. The children of the founding generation suffer from the echo effects that depress wages and increase the profit rate. Even though they are the recipients of an intergenerational gift arranged socially, its benefits are neutralized by these general equilibrium effects.

We illustrate these paradoxical effects in Figure 8.7 by showing the inception of a PAYGO system and a superfunded system. The simulations assume stable expectations on the grounds that stable expectations approximate perfect foresight closely enough. This is not the source of the paradoxical effects; the perfect foresight path tends to exaggerate the distributional

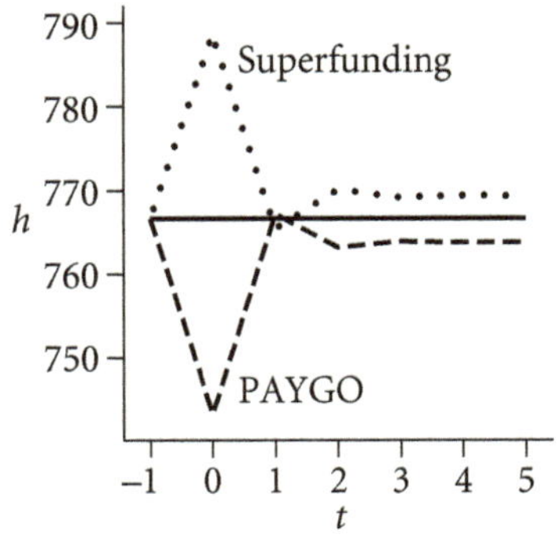

Figure 8.7 Workers' lifetime wealth under policy design in the PAYGO (dashed line) and superfunded cases (dotted line) is shown, together with the control path (solid line). Superfunding here is achieved through a payroll tax surplus. The numerical simulation assumes stable expectations. The parameter values are $n = 2.5$, $x = 1000$, $k = 60$, $\delta = 1$, $\beta_w = 0.1$, $\beta_c = 0.9$, $b = 100$, and for superfunding, $f = 50$.

changes, not attenuate them. Later we will show some perfect foresight simulations of policy reform.

If prefunding were achieved by means of a wealth tax on capitalists (a capital levy) it would have similarly paradoxical effects. The difference, as we see in the next section, is that a capital levy creates more violent changes in distribution.

8.5.2 Policy Reform

We will examine two cases of policy reform. In the first, prefunding is achieved through a surplus payroll tax. This corresponds to the approach of (mostly conservative) advocates of prefunding, such as Schieber and Shoven (1999). In the second, prefunding is achieved through a progressive tax on capitalists, an approach proposed by Michl and Foley (2004) and Blackburn (2002). (Readers may wish to refer to Table 7.4 to reorient themselves to the policy timing.)

Payroll Tax

Prefunding an existing public pension by means of the payroll tax amounts to an intergenerational bequest arranged socially. But in an exogenous growth model, it creates general equilibrium effects on the distribution of income that complicate the picture by changing the cast of givers and receivers.

We can see this most clearly in the case of stable expectations discussed above, and it turns out that this case provides a good prelude to more complex stories involving forward-looking expectations. As in the previous chapter, we assume the system is in a steady state prior to the target date at $t = 0$ when policy makers make their move by raising the payroll tax above its PAYGO level by an amount just equal to the new target funding level, f. Working with the temporary equilibrium system described by equation (8.7), we can determine that $\Delta\psi = -(1 - \beta_w)(f/k)$, where (as previously) we measure the discrete change in a variable by the difference between its test level (with the fiscal change) and the control level (with continuation of steady state conditions). The changes in distribution are then

$$\Delta r = \frac{(1 - \beta_w)f}{k\,|\mathbf{C}|}$$

$$\Delta w = \frac{-(1 - \beta_w)f}{|\mathbf{C}|}$$

Recalling the negative sign on the determinate of **C**, it is clear that the impact of prefunding (in period $t = 0$) will lower the rate of profit and raise the wage. The economic intuition is that the increased saving from the government's budget surplus creates an incipient excess demand for labor. Retired workers in the $t = -1$ cohort are innocent bystanders who experience a reduction in the rate of return on their retirement saving.

On the other hand, the cohort that has been called upon to sacrifice enjoys a wage increase. Moreover, the wage increase will dominate their payroll tax increase, raising their *ex ante* lifetime wealth by

$$\Delta h = \Delta w - \Delta\tau = \frac{f(1 - \beta_c(1 - \phi))}{\beta_c(1 - \phi) - \beta_w}$$

where ϕ equals the old steady state value. Thus, an unexpected and paradoxical consequence is that the "sacrificing" generation will be enriched. Of course, the actual lifetime wealth, evaluated *ex post* as $(w_0 - \tau_0)(1 + r_1) + b$, will not correspond to the anticipated lifetime wealth, since expectations will not be realized. But we know that this model produces alternations, so it is certain that the rate of profit will spring back toward and beyond its steady state level. As a result, the sacrificing generation is doubly blessed; their savings will earn a premium return in their twilight years.

In order to get some appreciation for the dynamic response to prefunding, Figure 8.8 presents a numerical example using the perfect foresight model, estimated by the Newton-Raphson method. The rate of profit quickly returns to its steady state value in this example. The money's worth rises from the natural rate of growth to a level exceeding the rate of profit; we have achieved superfunding. The effect on the workers' share of wealth is modest; most of the action lies in the drop in the capitalists' share (from 0.76 to 0.52) and the rise in the government's share of wealth (from 0 to 0.24). The *ex ante* lifetime wealth of workers illustrates the pattern of transfers. The $t = -1$ cohort suffers a loss on their wealth *ex post* that is not shown; they did not have perfect foresight of the policy reform and receive a subpar return on their savings. The $t = 0$ cohort that pays the surplus taxes enjoys an increase in lifetime wealth due to the wage increase and subsequent profit increase in periods 0 and 1. Finally, the $t = 1$ cohort, who were presumably the target recipients of prefunding, do enjoy the benefit of lower taxes (see Figure 8.8b) but that is neutralized by the wage cut they experience. The gains, which are modest, are enjoyed by subsequent cohorts.

Capital Levy

At the other extreme, let us consider a similar prefunding plan that uses a lump-sum tax directed at capitalist households, or a capital levy, for its source of finance. We will follow the precedent set in the previous chapter and assume that the workers in period $t = 0$, when the policy is implemented, receive no direct benefit in the form of a tax cut. Workers in period $t = 1$ are the first beneficiaries of prefunding. Our findings in the previous section should alert us to the possibility of indirect, general equilibrium effects that change the disposition of benefits.

To achieve the same level of funding as in the previous section, the lump-sum tax on capitalist households will be $\tau^c = (f/k)K_0$. Tackling the impact problem as before in terms of the temporary equilibrium system in equation (8.7), we find that $\Delta\psi = -f/k$, which lets us calculate the change (test minus control) in distribution as

$$\Delta r = \frac{f}{k\,|\mathbf{C}|}$$

$$\Delta w = \frac{-f}{|\mathbf{C}|}$$

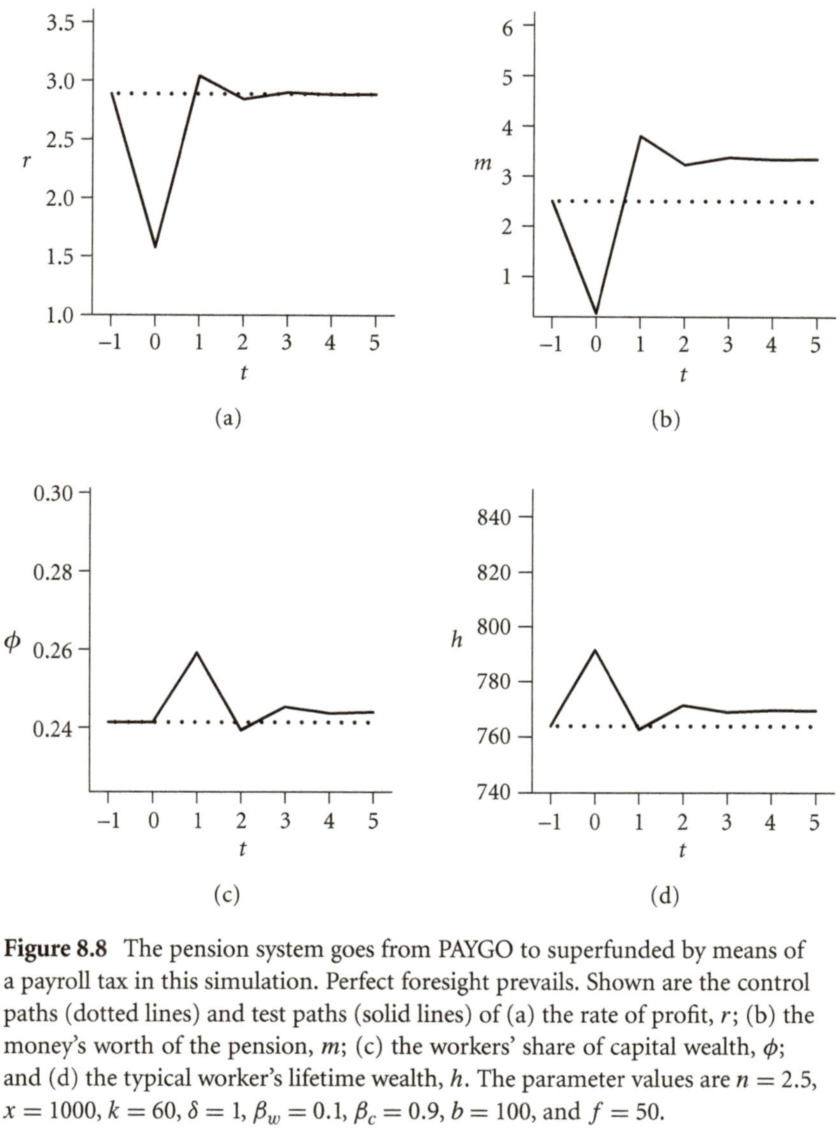

Figure 8.8 The pension system goes from PAYGO to superfunded by means of a payroll tax in this simulation. Perfect foresight prevails. Shown are the control paths (dotted lines) and test paths (solid lines) of (a) the rate of profit, r; (b) the money's worth of the pension, m; (c) the workers' share of capital wealth, ϕ; and (d) the typical worker's lifetime wealth, h. The parameter values are $n = 2.5$, $x = 1000$, $k = 60$, $\delta = 1$, $\beta_w = 0.1$, $\beta_c = 0.9$, $b = 100$, and $f = 50$.

The impact effect of a capital levy will be in the same direction as, and somewhat larger than, the same funding level achieved through a payroll tax. The generation of workers active during the capital levy receives an unintended boon, in the form of a wage hike that increases its lifetime wealth (both *ex ante* and *ex post*), undiluted by any tax increase.

The echo effect in period $t = 1$ will reward the generation of workers active during the capital levy and punish its children, for the rate of profit will rebound above its steady state level (rewarding retirees) and the wage rate will collapse below its steady state level. The children are the first generation to receive the blessing of prefunding, which takes the form of a lighter tax burden. But somewhat surprisingly, this turns out to be a mixed blessing that may not be sufficient to overcome the effects of the wage cut that the children's generation experiences.

One might suspect that at least some of the paradoxical effects observed in this case might be attenuated or reversed under the perfect foresight assumption. To allay such suspicions, Figure 8.9 shows the effects of a simulated capital levy in a perfect foresight model, using the same parameters as the previous example of prefunding through a payroll tax for comparison purposes. The capital levy generates larger swings in the distributional variables. As a result, the effects on lifetime wealth are also larger in magnitude. The $t = 0$ cohort experiences a sharp improvement in their wealth brought about by the general equilibrium effects. The $t = 1$ cohort, presumably the intended beneficiaries of prefunding, do enjoy higher returns on their pension contributions but these are not large enough to compensate for the decline in their wage and retirement income; their lifetime wealth drops visibly below the control benchmark. Once again the (modest) benefits are experienced by subsequent cohorts. Lifetime wealth increases from \$764 to \$769 in the long run.

The effects in the long run on the wealth shares and on lifetime wealth are identical to those in the previous example. Most of the decline in the capitalists' share of wealth is accounted for by the increase in the government's share; the workers' wealth share has increased modestly from 0.241 to 0.244.

The moral presented by these stylized examples is that policy makers need to pay attention to the dynamic general equilibrium effects of a prefunding plan. It is difficult to know how seriously to take the paradoxes that in both cases the intended beneficiaries were transformed into victims, that innocent bystanders saw losses or gains, and that prefunding through payroll taxes bootstrapped the sacrificing generation to higher lifetime wealth. Some responsibility can be assigned to the volatility that perfect foresight introduces, or to other model-specific sources of unrealism that might reduce these paradoxes to mere curiosities. Nonetheless, it does not seem unreasonable to believe that in a labor-scarce environment, an increase in

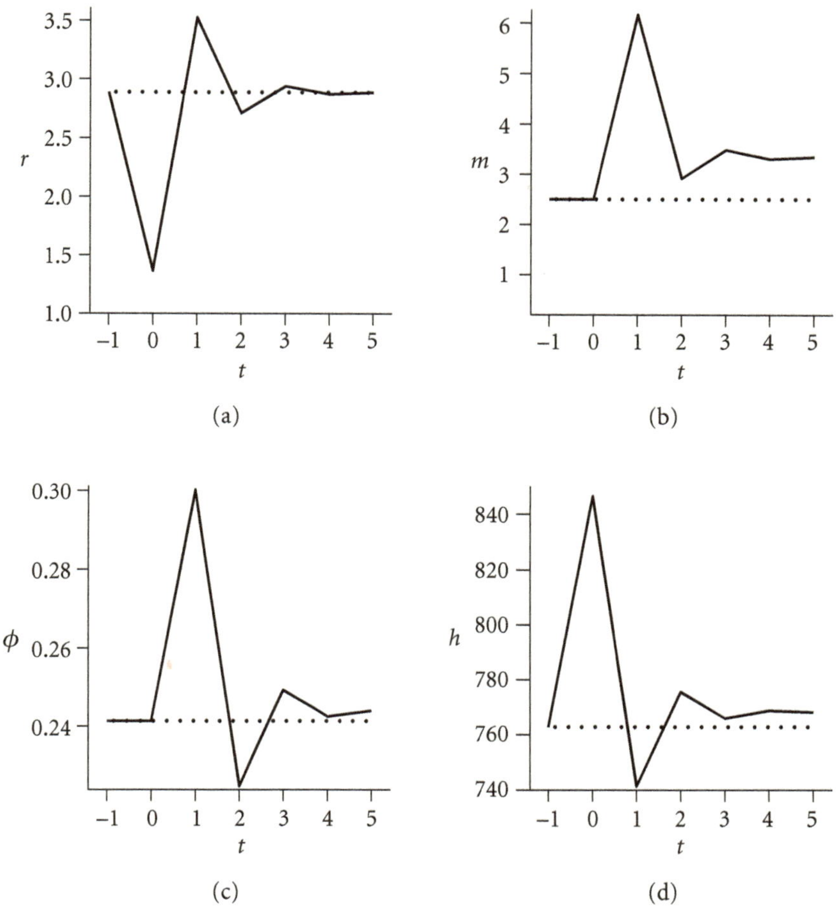

Figure 8.9 The pension system goes from PAYGO to superfunded in this simulation of a capital levy with perfect foresight. Shown are the control paths (dotted lines) and test paths (solid lines) of (a) the rate of profit, r; (b) the money's worth of the pension, m; (c) the workers' share of capital wealth, ϕ; and (d) the representative worker's lifetime wealth, h. The parameter values are $n = 2.5$, $x = 1000$, $k = 60$, $\delta = 1$, $\beta_w = 0.1$, $\beta_c = 0.9$, $b = 100$, and $f = 50$.

public saving that encourages investment spending will put upward pressure on wages through the employment growth it stimulates. The associated downward pressure on profits will hurt retirees counting on capital income unless the policy is designed to prevent this unintended consequence.

The full-employment assumption in particular demands careful handling. In order to maintain capital stock growth at the natural rate, the wage and profit rates must change in the current period to avoid an imbalance between employment and labor supply in the next period; how that is supposed to happen has been left unspecified. This kind of model needs to be interpreted as a description of what must happen in order to maintain balanced growth rather than as a behavioral theory of real capitalist economies. Real economies rarely come close to satisfying these demanding preconditions, but the models can help identify the fault lines along which conflicts over the accumulation process are likely to erupt.

The argument in favor of prefunding through a capital levy is not as sharp in the exogenous growth model as it was in the endogenous model. The effects on growth are, by assumption, nonexistent. And, paradoxically it seems, in the stylized models presented here, the same redistributive goals could be achieved using a payroll tax because the general equilibrium effects of public saving work in a progressive direction. The long-run redistributive effects remain significant in either case. By transferring wealth from private capitalists to public control, narrow prefunding raises the lifetime wealth of workers. With higher lifetime wealth supporting more worker saving, the share of wealth owned by workers also increases. The public pension reserve fund subsidizes the benefits of the retirement system and increases its implicit rate of return. This improvement in the money's worth of the public pension can be expected to strengthen the system politically. If the inequality of wealth or the democratic deficit associated with concentrations of private ownership are perceived as a problem, prefunding through a capital levy can be a practicable solution, even when it is restricted to narrow prefunding.

Ultimately, whether the primitive accumulation of public capital is achieved by means of a payroll tax or a capital levy, future generations of workers experience an unambiguous improvement in their lifetime wealth. In traditional economic terms, they enjoy an outward shift in their budget constraint that will enhance their welfare by supporting more consumption in their working and retirement years. Chapter 9 examines this point in greater detail.

— 9 —

Optimal Policy

> Samuelson's mathematics, however, indicate a "solution" in which the rate of interest is equal to the biological rate of growth of population. What this "solution" indicates is that the authorities can pretend that "social security" is not a "socialistic" tax and give-away program by the government but a "saving" by each worker out of his current income to provide for his old age.
>
> Abba Lerner (1959a)

> The tax-and-pension is nothing but a device by which today's pensioners are maintained out of today's social product, which is, of course, produced by today's workers.
>
> Abba Lerner (1959b)

This chapter takes up two topics related to the pursuit of an optimal policy in connection with our simple two-class model. What is the optimal rate of growth? What is the optimal pension? Since the concept of a social optimum is not well defined with such heterogeneous agents, we concentrate on the more restricted (and somewhat iconoclastic) objective of maximizing the welfare of workers in a steady state. One might rationalize this exercise as an attempt to provide political guidance to an idealized trade union leadership in a hypothetical country with centralized bargaining and rather complete union coverage (e.g., Robert Heilbroner's "slightly imaginary Sweden"). Since most advanced countries are projected to experience slower rates of labor force growth under current policies, the issues raised here are bound to resonate in real economies.

9.1 Natural Rate of Growth

While most growth modeling exercises take population or labor force growth to be parametric (witness the "natural" rate of growth), public policies can and do influence the rate of growth of labor supply. For example, immigration policies, child subsidies and other pro-natalist measures, education policies, and policies to encourage or discourage labor force participation all affect the size of the labor force. If we also consider technical change as part of the broadly defined natural rate, research and development subsidies and other technology policies can influence growth, in this case of the effective labor force. A *locus classicus* for the study of optimal growth of population is Samuelson (1975a), and we will follow closely his pathbreaking analysis.

9.1.1 One-Class Regime

We begin in the one-class regime in an otherwise laissez-faire world and commission the social planner with the task of finding the natural rate of growth that maximizes the welfare of a representative worker in a steady state. We assume the economy can achieve this rate of growth forever. (Below, we take up Lerner's objections to this assumption.) Since we are interested in a sustainable solution, we will impose a nonnegativity restriction on n to rule out the decumulation of capital and people. Recall from Chapter 3 that the parameter space of a basic laissez-faire model is confined by a feasibility condition (the economy must be productive enough to pay the steady state wage) and a stability condition. The feasibility condition requires that $n \leq \beta_w \rho - 1$, which rules out $\beta_w < 1/\rho$ since that would require negative growth. The stability condition turns out to be nonbinding so we ignore it until after we have achieved the solution.

The social planner's most general problem is to choose the consumption plan of a representative worker subject to the requirements that full employment is maintained.[1] An alternative way to approach this problem is through the related problem of choosing the growth rate that maximizes the worker's indirect utility function, $V(c^w, c^r)$, by allowing the equilib-

1. Stated formally, the planner chooses $\{c^w, c^r, n\}$ to maximize the worker's utility, $U(c^w, c^r)$, subject to the constraint that $c^w + c^r/(1+n) + c^c + nk \leq x - \delta k$, where c^c represents capitalist consumption per worker (obviously $= 0$ in the special one-class case).

rium distribution of income to emerge naturally and letting workers solve their own consumption plan. Formally, the planner seeks

$$\max_{n} V[c^{w}(w(n)), c^{r}(r(w), w(n))] \quad \text{where } n \geq 0$$

and where $V[\,\cdot\,]$ represents the worker's discounted logarithmic utility function, $c^{w}(\,\cdot\,)$ and $c^{r}(\,\cdot\,)$ represent the worker's consumption functions, and $r(w)$ is just the wage-profit curve. This problem is solvable because in any particular regime, it is possible to specify $w = w(n)$ for the steady state equilibrium. For example, in the two-class regime discussed in the next section, the Cambridge equation and the wage-profit curve make $w(n)$ a monotonically decreasing function, while in the one-class regime, it is an increasing function.

The Kuhn-Tucker conditions for this problem in the one-class regime are[2]

$$V_n \leq 0 \qquad n \geq 0 \qquad nV_n = 0$$

There are two possible types of solution for the workers' optimal growth rate, n^*. First, when $n^* = 0$, $V_n \leq 0$, and the first-order condition is either unavailable or is just satisfied at $n = 0$, we have a corner solution. Second, when $n^* > 0$, we need to examine the first-order condition to find the interior solution.

Totally differentiating $V[\,\cdot\,]$ gives the first-order condition that

$$\frac{dw}{dn}[V_{c^w}c^{w}_{w} + V_{c^r}(c^{r}_{r}r_w + c^{r}_{w})] = 0$$

Since this first-order condition also appears in the two-class problem, it is remarkable that the term in brackets vanishes no matter what the sign of dw/dn. In a one-class model, of course, dw/dn is positive since all saving comes out of wages, while in the two-class model, dw/dn is negative since the Cambridge equation controls the dynamics of accumulation. Solving for the term in brackets gives us

$$w = \frac{(1+r)k}{\beta_w} \tag{9.1}$$

2. For guidance on the techniques of nonlinear programming used here, see Chiang (1974, ch. 20).

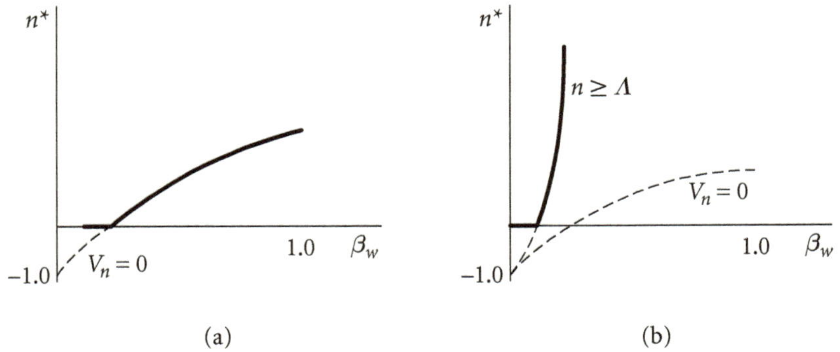

Figure 9.1 The bold lines identify the workers' optimal growth rate in the exogenous growth model. (a) In the one-class regime, the social planner will choose either an interior solution or a boundary solution with zero growth. (Very small worker discount factors will not support any nonnegative growth.) (b) In the two-class regime, the social planner will choose a boundary solution, constrained either by the stability condition or the nonnegativity of growth.

In the one-class model, all saving comes out of wages and the equation governing accumulation with full employment simplifies to

$$w = \frac{(1+n)k}{\beta_w}$$

It is immediately obvious by inspection that optimal growth involves a golden rule equilibrium with $r = n$. By substituting into the wage-profit curve, we obtain the optimal rate of growth.[3] This rate of growth, appropriately dubbed the *goldenest golden rule* by Samuelson (1975a), is written

$$n^* = \max\left[0, \frac{\beta_w R - 1}{1+\beta_w}\right]$$

Figure 9.1a illustrates the relationship between the optimal growth rate and the worker discount factor. Recall that very low discount factors ($< 1/\rho$) are not feasible.

One final loose end that needs to be tied up is satisfying ourselves that stability concerns will not interfere with the planner. We know from Chapter 3 that when $\beta_c < (1+n)/(1+R)$, stability obtains for any feasible

3. Alternatively, we could solve the planners' program directly as described in the previous footnote, since the social budget constraint takes the form $c^w + c^r/(1+n) + nk \leq x - \delta k$. The solution for n^* emerges directly from the first-order conditions on the Lagrangian.

worker discount factor that satisfies the condition for a one-class regime. But when $\beta_c > (1+n)/(1+R)$, $\beta_w < \beta_c(1+n)/(\beta_c(1+R)-(1+n))$ must be satisfied for stability.[4] Solving this inequality for n and comparing the result to n^* proves that the optimal growth rate will also be stable.

9.1.2 Two-Class Regime

Working through a similar analysis in the two-class regime reveals the deep qualitative change effected by incorporating the class structure of accumulation in a growth model. It also provides a more realistic setting in which to analyze the complications introduced by a public pension.

Laissez-faire

In the two-class regime, we first need to ask if the planner must accept the limitations of the two-class solution, for it is possible to imagine a decline in the natural rate of growth sufficient to effect a regime-change. Let us accept this limitation, which requires that the feasible set includes only stable, two-class solutions. In this case, it turns out that the stability restrictions will be potentially binding so we include them in the statement of the planner's problem, which is to choose n in order to

$$\text{Max } V[c^w, c^r]$$
$$\text{subject to } n \geq \Lambda$$

where $n \geq \Lambda(\beta_c, \beta_w, R)$ restates the stability condition[5] from Chapter 3. As before, we will require a nonnegative growth rate. Thus, writing the Lagrangian for this problem, $\mathcal{L} = V(n) + \mu(n - \Lambda)$, we have the following Kuhn-Tucker conditions:[6]

$$\mathcal{L}_n \leq 0 \qquad n \geq 0 \qquad n\mathcal{L}_n = 0$$
$$n - \Lambda \geq 0 \qquad \mu \geq 0 \qquad \mu(n - \Lambda) = 0$$

4. And it must be a strict inequality to rule out the nonhyperbolic equilibrium, which would be unstable.

5. The stability condition rearranges to give

$$\Lambda = \frac{\beta_c \beta_w (1+R)}{\beta_c - \beta_w} - 1$$

6. Since the objective function is concave and the constraint is linear, the Kuhn-Tucker conditions are necessary and sufficient for an optimum (Chiang 1974, 723).

Two types of solution are possible, though a third type, not obtainable, is, as they say regarding crime suspects, "of interest." First, when $n^* = 0$, the shadow price vanishes ($\mu = 0$) because the stability constraint is not binding; only the nonnegativity constraint is binding. Second, when $n^* > 0$, $\mathcal{L}_n = 0$. If the stability condition binds, then $\mu = -V_n$, and $V_n < 0$ is satisfied strictly so that $n^* = \Lambda$.

The third type is an interior solution, with $n > 0$ and $V_n = \mu = 0$. This solution is not achievable. To demonstrate this fact, we solve equation (9.1) for the two-class steady state ($r = (1 + n)/\beta_c - 1$) and obtain

$$n = \frac{\beta_c \beta_w (1 + R)}{1 + \beta_w} - 1$$

But this value will always be less than the stability threshold, Λ. Therefore, in any feasible two-class equilibrium, workers will find it in their interest to achieve a lower natural rate of growth than that prevailing. We saw this already when we discovered that a demographic shock is unambiguously welfare enhancing in the laissez-faire regime.

Figure 9.1b illustrates the two-class optimal growth rate, in relation to the worker discount factor. Also shown is the (unobtainable) interior solution involving the first-order condition on $V[\,\cdot\,]$. The figure dramatizes the antagonistic relations of production in a capitalist economy, showing that the interests of workers conflict with the constraints imposed by the class structure of accumulation. Interestingly, even when capitalists consume nothing ($\beta_c = 1$), so that the system is always in a golden rule equilibrium, this conflict will remain. In this case, the first-order condition collapses to the goldenest golden rule for a one-class regime, but it will still be unobtainable without violating the class structure.

With a Public Pension

As a practical matter, workers and their political representatives face the problem of judging policy proposals that affect the natural rate of growth in the presence of well-established public pension systems. The existence of a public pension system changes the structure of the social planner's problem and creates the possibility for an interior solution. The obvious reason is that the cost to workers of supporting an unfunded or partially funded retirement benefit will be reduced by growth.

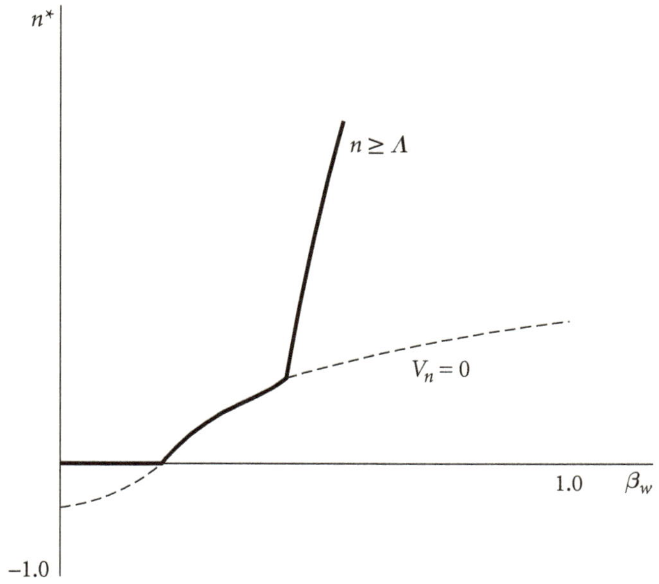

Figure 9.2 In the two-class model with a public pension system, the workers' optimal growth rate (bold line) can be an interior solution for some parameter values.

In this case, the planner's problem has the same structure but the objective function needs emending so that consumption is related to lifetime wealth, $h(n)$. More important, the stability condition changes to accommodate the public pension, and as we saw in Chapter 8, the existence of an unfunded benefit generally relaxes this limitation on the parameter space. (As in that chapter, we will stick to the most tractable expectations hypothesis, which we called stable expectations.) As Figure 9.2 illustrates, it now becomes possible to achieve an interior solution, at least for some parameter values. We have already seen in Chapter 8 that it is possible for a demographic shock to be welfare-reducing, and this rephrases that possibility.

The practical significance of this result is clearly that as long as the limitations imposed by the narrative are accepted, including the existence of a public pension system and the class structure of accumulation, workers may not always desire slower population or labor force growth, even though they increase wages. There is an argument in favor of maintaining the growth of the wage base that supports the public pension (e.g., through immigration), even though that may also prevent wages from rising. However, as we saw in Chapter 8, the parametric restrictions underlying this case are dubious. We conclude that a lower natural rate tends to favor workers in the two-class model of exogenous growth.

9.2 Optimal Public Pension

Despite misgivings about the relevance of the one-class model expressed above, we can benefit from this case as a heuristic device that helps clarify some outstanding issues in the theory of public pensions before turning to the complications arising in the two-class model.

9.2.1 One-Class Case

We begin with the optimal consumption plan under laissez-faire conditions to highlight the logic of the golden rule.

Laissez-faire

A benevolent social planner intent upon maximizing the welfare of each generation could achieve this objective by commandeering the allocation between consumption during working and retirement years. In the two-class regime, however, there is no clear way of aggregating over the heterogeneous agents, capitalists and workers, unless we assume some kind of Benthamite utility that can be measured and added. There does not seem to be much point in pursuing the social planner's problem here.

Despite the fact that stability considerations render nugatory the one-class version of this model, as we have seen, it does provide a good heuristic platform from which to launch an exposition of the social planner's problem. This problem has been studied extensively in precisely this context, where it is well defined since workers are homogeneous. We begin with the approach associated with Samuelson before turning to an alternative proposed by Lerner. Pick a representative generation and choose c^w and c^r to

$$\max\ (1-\beta_w)\log c^w + \beta_w \log c^r$$

$$\text{subject to } c^w + \frac{c^r}{1+n} \leq c$$

$$\text{where } c = x - (n+\delta)k$$

The last equation is the consumption-growth equation, and c represents consumption per active worker (not per person). Since the social planner recognizes the constraint imposed by technology and the full employment requirement, he or she would optimize subject to the social budget constraint, represented by the second equation above. Since this solution would be identical to that chosen by workers in the chance event that the rate of profit happens to equal the rate of growth, it is clear that the social, optimum allocation consumption plan implies the golden rule that the rate of profit equal the rate of growth. In this case, the private budget constraint and the social budget constraint are equivalent.

But in the one-class regime the rate of profit will not equal the rate of growth, unless by some fluke the appropriate worker saving propensity happens to obtain. In general, the private budget constraint created by the steady state distribution of income between wages and profits (assuming we can overcome the stability issues raised above) will lead agents to either consume too heavily during their working years and too little during retirement, or vice versa. The relationship between the private and social budget constraints can be visualized in Figure 9.3, which shows the golden rule and a laissez-faire equilibrium with $r > n$. In the equilibrium shown at point A, workers consume too little (save too much) during their active years relative to the golden rule at point G. (In the interest of simplicity, we omit the other possible type of equilibrium to the southeast of point G, in which workers consume too much during their active years and $r < n$.)

In the two-class regime, the golden rule is achievable but only if capitalists are so thrifty that they resist the temptation to consume any of Keynes's proverbial cake,[7] to which they have been granted the property rights. Any capitalist consumption at all results in a deviation from the golden rule optimum from the perspective of workers.

Public Pensions: Samuelson's Approach

The benevolent planner, a purely fictive device of the theorist, is useful for establishing a benchmark against which to evaluate realistic policies like social security that can decentralize the allocation chosen by the central

7. "On the one hand the laboring classes accepted . . . a situation in which they could call their own very little of the cake that they and Nature and the capitalists were co-operating to produce. And on the other hand the capitalist classes were allowed to call the best part of the cake theirs and were theoretically free to consume it, on the tacit underlying condition that they consumed very little of it in practice."(Keynes 1920, 18)

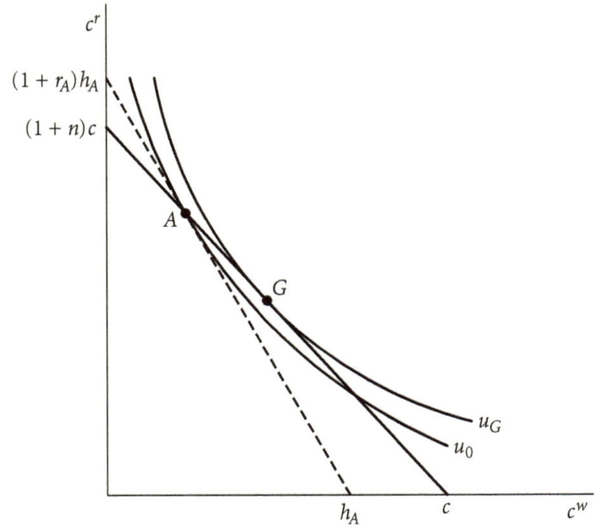

Figure 9.3 The private budget constraint (dashed line) and the social budget constraint (solid line) are shown for the one-class model. The laissez-faire equilibrium (where $h = w$) of the one-class model will only reach the golden rule (G) by chance. In the equilibrium at A, $r > n$. The social planner can use a public pension and exploit general equilibrium effects that rotate the private budget constraint (in this case counterclockwise) to achieve a golden rule.

planner. We will consider an idealized social security system in the one-class regime as a kind of prologue to the two-class regime. Following Samuelson (1975b), we take the benchmark to be the golden rule state.

By assuming that capitalists do not exist, we can continue the discussion of optimal social security policy where Samuelson left off. The full employment condition requires that social saving, the sum of private and public saving, just meet the needs of population growth, or

$$s^w + f = (1 + n)k$$

Substituting for worker and government saving yields the equation describing the wage required to maintain full employment:

$$w = \frac{(1+n)k}{\beta_w} + b\left(\frac{1}{1+n} + \frac{1-\beta_w}{\beta_w(1+r_{+1})}\right) - f\left(\frac{\beta_w(r-n)+1+n}{\beta_w(1+n)}\right) \tag{9.2}$$

The required-wage function, equation (9.2), and the wage-profit curve determine the steady state wage and profit rate in the one-class regime. In a steady state with correct foresight ($r_{+1} = r$), the rate of profit will be the largest root of the quadratic equation that solves this system, assuming it has an economically meaningful value.

The social planner can manipulate equation (9.2) in order to achieve welfare improvements for workers. If the laissez-faire rate of profit exceeds the rate of growth, workers consulting only their private interests are led to consume too little during their active years, as we saw in the previous section. An unfunded social security benefit will increase the required wage, and correspondingly reduce the rate of profit. The equilibrium in Figure 9.3 will thus move from point A in the direction of the golden rule at point G. The planner could combine equation (9.2) and the social budget constraint, $c = x - (n + \delta)k$, to calculate directly the optimal unfunded benefit, since in a golden rule state it must be true that $w = c$.

In fact, as Samuelson noted, once funding is considered, there is an infinite number of combinations of funding levels and benefit levels that would achieve the golden rule.

On the other hand, if the laissez-faire equilibrium rate of profit were to fall short of the rate of growth (not shown in Figure 9.3), it would be necessary to diminish the required wage function to effect a welfare improvement, and this can only be done by a social security system that is superfunded.

It is important to be clear on why these welfare improvements occur. For example, an unfunded social security benefit, in and of itself, reduces lifetime wealth. But it has general equilibrium effects on the wage rate that overcome these partial equilibrium effects, so that in the laissez-faire state represented by point A in Figure 9.3, an unfunded benefit rotates the private budget constraint, ultimately, in the case of the optimal (golden rule) policy, into perfect alignment with the social budget constraint.

Samuelson's pathbreaking analysis took the existence of a well-behaved neoclassical production function for granted, and as a result, wound up conflating two quite separate welfare issues: first, the issue of the allocation of consumption over the life cycle, and second, the issue of productive efficiency or optimal choice of technique. Unfortunately, it is the latter effect that has attracted the most attention. Samuelson describes an equilibrium with $r > n$ as one of "underaccumulation" because the putative "marginal product of capital" exceeds its golden rule optimum. The policy implication, which has been seized upon by advocates of prefunding, is that public saving moves the system toward its golden rule. In Samuelson's neoclassical model, only when $r < n$ does an unfunded system improve welfare. A prominent neoclassical text summarizes neatly:

> . . . if there is a steady state in the competitive economy larger than the golden rule (over-accumulation), the optimal transfer is a positive transfer to the old household. Interpreting this transfer as a pension, Samuelson's paper can be viewed as a positive theory of pensions. However, the empirical evidence in favor of the existence of over-accumulation is rather weak and controversial, which gives Samuelson's argument little weight. This explains why many economists now argue against existing pay-as-you-go pension schemes and in favor of a transition towards fully funded pensions. (de la Croix and Michel 2002, 141)

We can now see that if Samuelson wanted to put forward a "positive theory of pensions," he would have stood on firmer ground by discarding the neoclassical production function. Operating with a given technique exposes the underlying allocational issue clearly, free from the mischief done by neoclassical capital theory.[8] Since the rate of profit exceeds the rate of growth in most real economies (at least at low frequencies), there might be a strong case for an unfunded social security system in the one-class model. But if, as averred throughout this book, the one-class model falls short of the mark, then we need to extend this analysis to see how much of Samuelson's theory of pensions survives in the two-class setting.

Public Pensions: Lerner's Approach

The definition of an optimum that we have adopted descends from Samuelson's (1958) classic paper. It was criticized by Lerner (1959a), who proposed an alternative definition: maximize the utility of the current population (retirement and working age alike).[9] To recreate this debate, let us adopt the

8. As a point of logic, it is interesting that the condition that neoclassical economists habitually consider to be underaccumulation ($r > n$) actually is revealed by our analysis to result from an incipient tendency toward excessive saving or insufficient consumption during the active years.

9. In other words, the planner's objective function under Lerner's criterion is written

$$(1 - \beta_w) \log c^w + \frac{1}{1+n} \beta_w \log c^r$$

following assumptions. First, there is no mechanism for saving, so that any retirement consumption depends on a coercive mechanism such as a public pension. In the laissez-faire economy, workers would consume all that they produced. Second, for simplicity, the worker discount factor is exactly 0.5, so that equal weight is given in the (log) utility function to consumption over the two stages of a life cycle.

Lerner questions the method deployed by the planner of maximizing the utility of the representative agent in a steady state on the grounds that the natural rate of growth is destined to decline at some point in the finite future. In other words, the fiction of an everlasting golden age obscures the costs that must be imposed on future generations when the day of reckoning is reached at which growth slows, or for purposes of argument, the Earth dramatically ends. At this point, the current generation who restricted their working-age consumption in hopes of receiving the biological rate of interest, $r = n$, would be disappointed. Being dead, they have no chance of enjoying the consumption in retirement that they had planned. They would have been better off had the social planner followed Lerner's optimality criterion.[10]

Under the simplifying assumption of no systematic time preference, Lerner's optimal consumption plan is

$$c^w = c^r = \frac{1+n}{2+n}c$$

while Samuelson's optimal consumption plan is

$$c^w = \frac{1}{2}c \qquad c^r = \frac{(1+n)c}{2}$$

It is evident that the two are only identical in the stationary state where $n = 0$. In a growing economy, Samuelson's plan offers workers a reward, in the form of higher retirement consumption, for consuming less during

where we have normalized the current population of workers to unity. Lerner implements a Benthamite social utility function, while Samuelson relies on a representative worker's utility function.

10. As Samuelson (1959, 522) observes, Lerner's criterion is equivalent to maximizing the social utility function for everyone who has ever lived up to the present, and this set-up gives present workers a decisive influence.

their working years.[11] It is precisely this premium that Lerner questions in the event of a collapse in the natural rate of growth: "the Samuelson plan has the same flaw as a chain letter" (Lerner 1959b, 524).

This realization led Lerner to the sentiments expressed in this chapter's epigraph. In particular, he rejects the idea of a "biological" rate of interest as an illusion created by the fiction of an everlasting steady state. In its place, he offers the commonsense view that public policy should concentrate on the problem of distributing today's product in a fair and socially acceptable fashion. Indeed, such a sensible view of distribution can and should be generalized to include the nature of wages and profits themselves, which are in the end only "devices" for allocating today's output between social groups.

The Samuelson-Lerner exchange, one of the truly splendid tournaments of twentieth-century economic theory, clarifies the limitations of the steady state analysis. Samuelson's response that he has solved a different problem and that both approaches teach us something about the policy dilemmas can only take us so far.[12] As we have seen in recent public debates, the impending demographic shock has promoted this dispute from an academic controversy to a pressing practical issue. What ultimately separates these two intellectual giants is infinity. Samuelson's conceptualization turns out to depend critically on the maintained fiction that the world will last forever. Ironically (for a neoclassical theorist), his optimum presupposes an infinite supply of resources. Lerner turns out to be the true intellectual conservator by insisting that we live in a finite world with scarce resources. Nonetheless, Samuelson's conceptualization dominates the neoclassical conversations about optimality. In a world where some kind of growth appears to be sustainable for the indefinite future, this does not seem unreasonable and we have accepted the orthodox approach in this book for that reason. But by the same token, with ecological constraints of uncertain nature looming on the horizon, Lerner's message has resurfaced.[13]

11. More precisely, Samuelson's plan reduces c^w by $cn/(2(2+n))$ compared to Lerner's and increases c^r by $cn(1+n)/(2(2+n))$. It may also help to see that the Lerner plan is isomorphic with a laissez-faire economy having a zero rate of interest or profit.

12. For an extensive elaboration of Lerner's position in the context of current debates about public pension systems, see Cesaratto (2005).

13. See in particular the discussion over the *Stern Review* (Stern 2007) on global warming commissioned by the U.K. Treasury Department. This report renews the ethical arguments against pure time discounting but concedes the need for a modest discount rate to represent the risk of a random calamity.

9.2.2 *Policy Dilemmas in the Two-Class Model*

Since it is possible to imagine a funding system that jeopardizes the class structure of accumulation, we begin by restricting the social planner to a public pension that remains within the constraints of a two-class model.

Two-Class Case

A benevolent planner might try to avoid the mare's nest of defining a social welfare function in a two-class society by attempting to improve life for the working class by means of lump-sum transfers through a social security system. After all, it worked in the one-class case. But in the two-class case, the steady state rate of profit is determined by the Cambridge equation to be $\frac{1+n}{\beta_c} - 1$ as we have seen, and the wage follows from the wage-profit curve. The general equilibrium effects that operate through the distribution of income are unavailable to the social planner in a two-class world. Thus does Samuelson's positive theory of pensions founder on Pasinetti's paradox. What looked like a promising case for an unfunded pension fails in the transition to a two-class world because the capitalist class occupies the commanding heights through its control over the accumulation process, preventing the planner from manipulating the distribution of income.

What remains manipulable to the planner is the distribution of wealth. The share of wealth owned by government is a potential policy instrument. This is the only avenue open to the planner who seeks to increase the welfare of workers.

The best way to see the planner's dilemma is to consider her optimizing problem. Define c^c to be capitalist consumption per active worker. The social budget constraint is now written

$$c^w + \frac{c^r}{1+n} \leq c - c^c$$

The consumption by capitalists represents a kind of levy on workers that reduces the resources available for worker consumption (Figure 9.4). The social planner can change the position of the social budget constraint relevant to workers' lifetime consumption plans only by means of policies that change the distribution of wealth. We can see this more clearly by parsing capitalist consumption:

$$c^c = \frac{1-\beta_c}{\beta_c}(1+n)(1-\phi-\phi^G)k$$

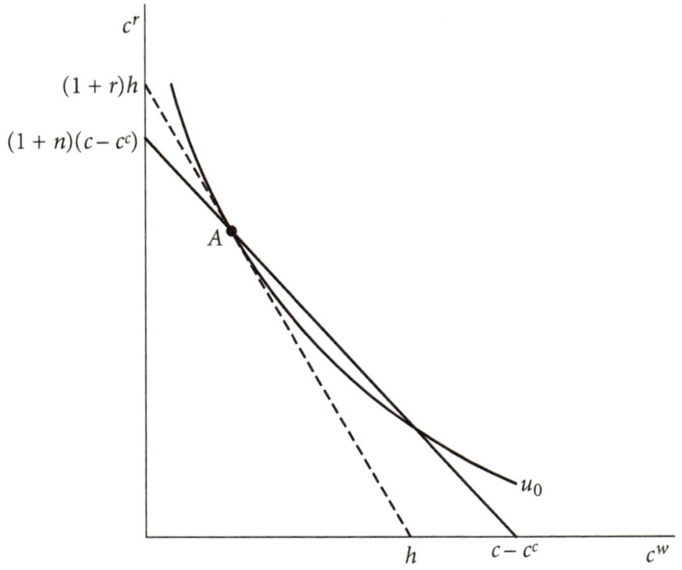

Figure 9.4 The solid line represents the social budget constraint in the two-class model; the dashed line represents the private budget constraint. The option of exploiting general equilibrium effects (changes in slope of the private budget constraint) is no longer available to the planner. An unfunded benefit will shift the social budget constraint inward; reserve funding will shift the social budget constraint outward.

It is now clear that in the case relevant to the two-class model, $r > n$, the option of unfunded social security can not increase worker welfare as it did in the one-class model. It fails on two counts. First, this policy (or any policy) will not change the slope of the workers' private budget constraint. Second, by reducing lifetime wealth, the policy moves workers farther away from the golden rule rather than closer to it. From the planner's empyrean perspective, an unfunded benefit actually constricts the social budget constraint relevant to workers by increasing the share of wealth owned by capitalists, and raising the levy imposed by their consumption.

Funding social security rescues the social planner by offering the option of relaxing the social budget constraint (as it applies to workers). Changes in funding affect lifetime wealth, h, and move workers out along the expansion path $(c^w(h), c^r(h))$. The log utility function is homothetic, so as Figure 9.5 illustrates, the expansion path is a linear segment along the ray $(1+r)\beta_w/(1-\beta_w)$. As long as the social planner is restricted to preserving

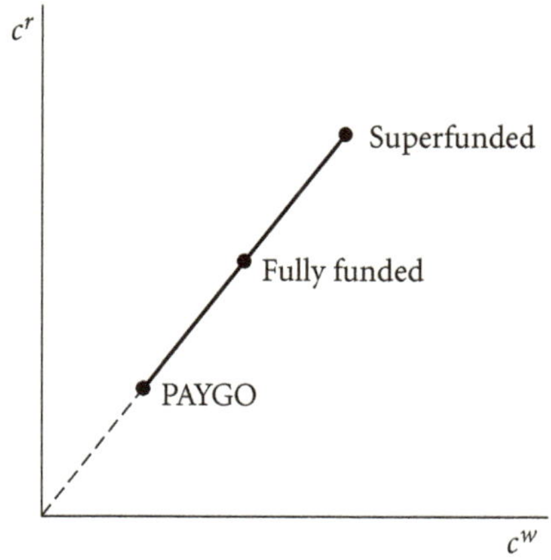

Figure 9.5 The expansion path locates along the ray $(1+r)\beta_w/(1-\beta_w)$. Superfunding is limited by the stability condition.

the two-class structure of accumulation, he or she must respect the limitations imposed by the stability condition. It is clear from the discussion surrounding Figure 8.3 in the previous chapter that superfunding will eventually impinge on the stability condition at some critical level of f.

It can readily be seen that if we take the baseline case to be the laissez-faire equilibrium, the social security system must be superfunded in order to effect any welfare improvement on the part of future workers. The welfare improvement derives from the increase in lifetime wealth. If we take the baseline case to be an unfunded or partially funded system (such as in real public pension systems), it is clear that any increase in funding levels raises the welfare of future workers. The highest welfare level the planner can achieve without violating the two-class structure is given by the funding limit set by the stability condition.

This conclusion remains valid whether we adopt the Samuelson or the Lerner approach toward optimal policy. In either case, the social planner must respect the social budget constraint.

Euthanasia of the Rentier

If the planner is willing to violate the two-class structure of accumulation, he or she will have accomplished Keynes's euthanasia of the rentier: the elimination of capitalist agents as a social type. We have seen that even prefunding from the payroll tax can reduce the capitalist wealth share, and in principle nothing prevents the planner from driving it to zero, either through a payroll tax or an outright capital levy. By turning the capitalist wealth over to the public authority, the planner can achieve a welfare level for workers that exceeds the best position in the two-class system.

A government pension system so generously funded that it has effectively replaced the capitalist class requires no payroll revenue at all if it can finance the retirement benefit out of its end-of-period wealth, and simply save any surplus:

$$K^G_{+1} = (1+r)K^G - \frac{bK}{k(1+n)}$$

With this fiscal rule in place, the model can be characterized using the tools developed in Chapter 8.[14] The steady state workers' share of wealth will be the (smaller) root of the quadratic equation

$$\phi^2 - \mathcal{A}\phi - \mathcal{B} = 0$$

where

$$\mathcal{A} = (1-\beta_w) + \frac{\beta_w(1+R)}{1+n}$$

$$\mathcal{B} = \frac{\beta_w(n - R + b/k(1+n))}{1+n}$$

The steady state distribution of income can be obtained from the workers' saving equation:

$$w^* = \frac{k(1+n)}{\beta_w}\phi^*$$

The rate of profit can be obtained from the wage-profit schedule, $r^* = (x - w^*)/k - \delta$. It is interesting to note that the steady state does not in any way depend on how much wealth the capitalist sector had before it was euthanized.

Stability depends on the nonlinear first-order difference equation $\phi_{+1} = z(\phi)$. Setting $|z_\phi| < 1$, we obtain

$$\beta_w < \frac{1+n}{(1+R)+(1+n)}$$

14. In particular, the consolidating term will be $\psi = n + \phi + b/k(1+n)$ and **C** will be

$$\begin{pmatrix} \frac{\beta_w}{k} & (1-\phi) \\ 1 & k \end{pmatrix}$$

This stability condition is identical to the stability condition for the two-class model, with Λ specialized for $\beta_c = 1$, and that makes good sense because the government sector acts like a capitalist class that does no consuming at the margin. The fixed pension benefit does not affect stability.

Although the government does not consume at the margin, it does originate a transfer payment that begets consumption by retirees. For that reason, the rate of profit will exceed the rate of growth, and the wage will exceed the golden age wage. However, if the benefit is set at zero, the rate of profit will equal the rate of growth and the system will be in a golden age. The workers' wealth share can be obtained by substituting $b = 0$ and is given by

$$\phi^* = \frac{\beta_w(R - n)}{1 + n}$$

which is identical to the wealth share in the two-class model specialized for $\beta_c = 1$.

A government operating along these lines can improve worker welfare by choosing the appropriate pension benefit, and it is apparent that the optimal benefit is no benefit at all, $b = 0$. (Recall that we have abstracted from other functions of a social security system.) That puts the system in a golden rule equilibrium, which we have already seen is the workers' optimum given the natural rate of growth.

If the planner endeavors to choose the optimal growth rate as well (with $b = 0$), she will face the same problem that we addressed above in the two-class case, specialized for $\beta_c = 1$. As we saw there, the optimal choice will be constrained by the stability condition or the nonnegativity of growth. The planner will be unable to achieve an interior solution without violating the social structure of accumulation. In this case, the social structure involves a public sector that functions as a hypercapitalist agent, accumulating for its own sake.

This result makes some sense because we began by assuming a two-class equilibrium that we dissolved through superfunding. In other words, the worker saving propensity was initially insufficient to support a self-sustaining growth equilibrium. If we want to achieve the complete euthanasia of the rentier, we have to establish a surrogate rentier.

Funding Sources

There remains the issue of who will make the sacrifices required in order to create the reserve fund in the first place. As we saw in Chapter 8, this model presents paradoxical features that make it possible for prefunding, by means of a payroll tax, to transfer wealth almost painlessly from capitalists to workers. It seems prudent to regard this as a curiosity, and to recognize that in less abstract settings, this mode of prefunding is likely to amount to an intergenerational transfer among workers orchestrated by the state. Most proposals to prefund social security in the United States, such as Schieber and Shoven (1999), fall into this category. The future generations benefit at the expense of the current generation. In a more realistic setting, the existence of technical progress makes these transfers even less appealing. Why should current generations of workers sacrifice for future generations who will have a higher standard of living anyway?

We also need to confront our ignorance of the constraints on growth. The paradox of prefunding occurs only in an exogenous growth model, where an effort to increase social saving expresses itself through changes in income distribution. The case for prefunding by means of a progressive wealth tax is stronger to the extent that growth is not tightly confined by labor supplies.

The other obvious source of primitive accumulation would be some kind of tax or capital levy on the capitalists. It has not gone unnoticed in this book that the social security reserve fund represents an ideal vehicle for effecting a progressive redistribution of wealth. A socialist or populist government could achieve one of the historic goals of socialism—social control over the economic surplus—with minimum disruption of the underlying capitalist property relations by encouraging the prefunding of pensions through progressive taxation on capitalist wealth. As we have seen, the case is even more attractive in a classical endogenous setting (capital-constrained growth); here it is possible to design a wealth redistribution from capitalists to the reserve fund that increases the level of the social capital stock, creating "jobs and justice" together. This approach might also be extended to socialize corporate governance by giving a greater activist role to pension funds, as in the proposal of Blackburn (2002) for a share levy invested in regional and national retirement funds.

9.2.3 Conclusion

Traditional neoclassical treatments of optimal pensions rely on the well-behaved aggregate production function. We have argued that the production function misleads economists into exaggerating the importance of productive efficiency, and misclassifying the symptoms of overaccumulation. Freed from these distortions, the one-class framework does make it possible to construct a positive theory of pensions, but it lacks relevance and plausibility. The two-class structure that defines classical political economy robs the social planner of the general equilibrium effects that give him or her purchase over the optimizing problem in the one-class case. In this more relevant and plausible setting, improvements in workers' welfare brought about through pension design demand prefunding, and exceeding the laissez-faire welfare benchmark requires superfunding. Only by introducing the public sector into the structure of accumulation can the social planner achieve his or her objectives. Taxes that directly attack the distribution of wealth are good candidates for this task, particularly because the extent to which labor supply constrains real economies remains an open question—one that we return to in Part III, which elaborates an alternative to the neoclassical production function.

— III —

Technical Change and the Production Function

— 10 —

Fossil Production Function

Theory

> Moreover, the production function has been a powerful instrument of miseducation. The student of economic theory is taught to write [X=F(K,L)] . . . and then he is hurried on to the next question, in the hope that he will forget to ask in what units [K] is measured. Before ever he does ask, he has become a professor and so sloppy habits of thought are handed on from one generation to the next.
>
> JOAN ROBINSON (1953)

In the neoclassical literature on the two key issues in fiscal policy, public debt and pensions, the production function plays a central role, while in the classical models presented in this book, technology has played a subsidiary part in a drama dominated by the class structure of accumulation. The purpose of this chapter is to outline a classically inspired theory[1] of technology that can provide an alternative explanation for some of the same stylized facts as the neoclassical production function and a justification for the use of the fixed-coefficient assumption in the previous chapters. To quote once again from Joan Robinson's unforgettable landmark essay: "We cannot abandon the production function without an effort to rescue the element of common-sense that has been entangled in it" (Robinson 1953, 83). The central argument is that what we experience as capital-labor

1. The inspiration actually comes from Okishio (1961). The Okishio theorem establishes that a capital-using, labor-saving technical change must raise the rate of profit in a multicommodity model if the real wage remains constant, thus disputing one interpretation of Marx's Law of the Tendency for the Rate of Profit to Fall. The fossil production function simply explores the implication of ongoing biased technical changes.

substitution is typically the expression of biased technical change rather than movement along a well-behaved neoclassical production function.[2]

Early in the 1990s, for example, the refuse haulers in my town switched over from trucks with a crew of one driver and two handlers to trucks with a crew of one driver who operated a hydraulic handling device to empty the trash receptacles. This was not a period notable for rising real wages among the less-skilled workers who perform this kind of labor, yet the private companies in this industry chose to substitute a more mechanized process, mainly because of technical innovations by the producers of refuse-handling equipment. This chapter argues that this anecdote describes a kind of holotype for the biased (capital-using, labor-saving) technical change[3] that forms the basis for the fossil production function, and that the fossil production function justifies our use of the Leontief production function in the growth models above.

We embed the fossil production function in a pair of simplified growth models in order to illustrate its properties before examining some relevant empirical evidence. Given the limited purpose of the chapter, we make two major deviations from the growth models presented previously, both of which are designed to facilitate the task of showcasing the fossil production function. First, we assume that workers perform no saving as a class. In the context of the overlapping generations approach, this assumption might be viewed as a first approximation that abstracts from the saving contributed by active workers, after the dissaving of retirees has been netted out. Second, we work in continuous time, abandoning the period analysis. Differential calculus is a lot more transparent in this context than difference calculus.

10.1 Theory of Production

We begin by assuming that technical change takes what Foley and Michl (1999) call a Marx-biased form, meaning that it is labor saving but capi-

2. This chapter and the next elaborate on the presentations of the fossil production function in Foley and Michl (1999), Michl (1999), Michl (2002), and Michl and Foley (2003).

3. There should be nothing controversial about hypothesizing bias. Neoclassical economists (Berman et al. 1998) show no reluctance to accept the existence of biased technical change when it helps them solve prominent riddles, such as the rise of the skills premium in the United States during a period of increasing relative skill supply.

tal using. Each generation of "machine" is inscribed by a more mechanized production process. If we were to enter a well-stocked museum of science and industry, we could imagine visiting the history of mechanization much like a geologist observing the stratigraphy of a sedimentary formation. For example, the textile industry has over several centuries progressed from hand-spinning on the legendary spinning wheel, to machine-assisted spinning on the spinning mule of the nineteenth century (Lazonick 1990), to modern, computer-assisted automated processes. The formal, mathematical representation of that progression, we will call the "fossil production function" in deference to the geological analogy.

We model technical change as exogenous, exponential growth in the technical coefficients. Capital goods are treated like "putty-putty," meaning that it is possible to retrofit the existing capital stock to new engineering specifications without cost. In other words, technical change is taken to be disembodied; an investment in the latest vintage of machine is not required in order to enjoy its effects.[4]

Because we are in a one-commodity environment, it makes sense to think that an individual technique can be represented by its unique technical coefficients. It is well known that in a multicommodity environment, no such simple relationship exists in general between the technique and the aggregate analytical ratios, x, k, and ρ, because changes in distribution beget changes in the vector of prices that must be used in order to calculate the aggregates. Indeed, these Wicksellian price effects generate the reswitching and reverse switching phenomena that invalidate the neoclassical production function, according to the Cambridge critique (Harcourt 1972). This same critique could be applied to the fossil production function, and our special plea here is that in practice the wage-profit curves of real economies are not obtrusively nonlinear. And the critique does not seem to carry such devastating force, since the fossil production function makes fewer claims than the neoclassical theory of production. In this sense, the fossil production function underwrites an *a fortiori* argument against the neoclassical theory, by conceding the validity of the one-commodity fiction and proposing to confront the neoclassical theory on its own chosen level of abstraction.

4. For a vintage model of the fossil production function that treats technical change as embodied in the machines themselves, see Michl (2002).

10.1.1 Biased Technical Change

Let us represent technical change as a continuous process taking the form of the following *parametric equations* of exponential growth in the three key parameters (using the hacek symbol to indicate best-practice technical coefficients).

$$\begin{aligned} \check{x} &= x_0 e^{\gamma t} \\ \check{\rho} &= \rho_0 e^{\chi t} \\ \check{k} &= k_0 e^{(\gamma - \chi)t} \end{aligned} \tag{10.1}$$

Note that the most recent, best-practice technique takes the Leontief form, but the whole set of techniques, comprising what Joan Robinson (1953) called the "book of blueprints," includes all past techniques that are available to current entrepreneurs. Technical change takes the form of a new page added to the book of blueprints in every moment.

This set-up may feel unorthodox to many neoclassical economists who are used to thinking of technical change as a more or less uniform displacement of the entire production function. Ironically, however, we are staying quite close to the original and pioneering approach of Cobb and Douglas (1928), who estimated the production function from historical data without allowances for technical change. As we will see, the fossil production function is a kind of creation myth that answers the question: How did the production function get its Cobb-Douglas form?[5]

The assumption of exogenous technical change, however, should be familiar. We justify this by an admission that not enough is reliably known about the economics of technical change to incorporate it into the model, exactly as does Solow (1994).

Marx-biased technical change is the hypothesis that $\gamma > 0$ and $\chi < 0$. Harrod-neutral technical change is the hypothesis that $\chi = 0$. There is no obvious way in which the fossil metaphor underwrites the assumption that technical change is Marx-biased. Mechanization, in itself, amounts to the

5. By the fundamental theorem of calculus, it should be possible to recover other functional forms using the same approach. For example, if the growth rates of labor and capital productivity obey a Verhulst logistic equation (found by differentiating the constant elasticity of substitution, or CES, function), the fossil production function will take a CES form.

presumption that the capital-labor ratio is increasing over time. It does not include the auxiliary presumption that these increases do not bring sufficient proportional improvements in the productivity of labor so as to prevent the output-capital ratio (loosely termed the "productivity of capital") from remaining constant. Indeed, there are many economists who, following Kaldor's (1965) famous list of stylized facts of economic growth, believe that constancy of the productivity of capital has the status of an established fact. But, as we can see from the data presented in Table 10.1, the historical and statistical record does not support such an unequivocal interpretation.

First, the process of capitalist development seems to involve a fairly large decline in the output-capital ratio, according to the historical data assembled by Angus Maddison (1995). Among countries that have achieved a high level of industrial and economic development for which historical data exist going back a century or more (United States, United Kingdom, and Japan), we find that capital productivity declines sharply in the early stages of development, from values well over one to the range of 0.3 to 0.6 typical of industrialized economies. Second, once these countries achieve a high level of development, we see a pattern of long periods of declining capital productivity punctuated by shorter periods of capital-saving technical change that keep the overall trend fairly flat. Kaldor's stylized fact was partly the result of his temporal vantage point, closely following the recovery in capital productivity surrounding WWII that Duménil et al. (1993) have called the "great leap forward." While the Golden Age of Capital Accumulation from 1950 to 1973 was generally a period of rising capital productivity, the Great Slowdown that followed the oil crisis of 1973 has been witness to almost universally declining capital productivity among the most developed nations.

Labor productivity, on the other hand, has shown a persistent upward trend, with only a few episodes of decline that have fairly obvious explanations (such as the effect of WWII on Germany and Japan). The movements in capital intensity (the capital-labor ratio) can be inferred from Table 10.1 through the identity $g_k = g_x - g_\rho$. Like labor productivity, capital intensity displays an almost unbroken rising profile. For our purposes, then, substantial parts of the historical and statistical record are qualitatively consistent with the standard treatment of the Solow-Swan growth model, in which economic development is conceived as a process of movement along

Table 10.1 Capital and labor productivity in selected countries, 1820–1992

	United States	France	Germany	The Netherlands	United Kingdom	Japan
Year	Labor Productivity Level (1990$ per worker-hour)					
1820	1331				1477	0441
1870	2297	1362	1577	2330	2643	0464
1913	5122	2855	3500	4012	4281	1034
1929	7533	4152	4366	6323	5544	1777
1938	8651	5352	4841	6256	6021	2194
1950	12,676	5767	4365	6504	7863	2025
1973	23,604	17,766	16,637	19,020	15,925	11,148
1992	29,101	29,622	27,550	28,803	23,978	20,025
End Year	Labor Productivity Growth (% per year)					
1870	2.05				2.19	0.19
1913	3.51	3.23	3.49	2.38	2.11	3.51
1929	4.53	4.40	2.60	5.35	3.04	6.36
1938	2.89	5.30	2.16	−0.22	1.73	4.40
1950	5.98	1.17	−1.62	0.61	4.18	−1.25
1973	5.08	9.20	10.94	8.77	5.77	13.94
1992	2.07	5.06	4.99	4.11	4.05	5.80
Year	Capital Productivity Level (per year)					
1820	1.055				1.462	
1870	0.584				1.109	
1913	0.303				1.192	1.130
1929	0.316				1.105	0.857
1938	0.277		0.499		1.102	0.855
1950	0.409	0.613	0.552	0.486	1.237	0.566
1973	0.473	0.645	0.516	0.506	0.759	0.574
1992	0.412	0.440	0.423	0.438	0.551	0.331
End Year	Capital Productivity Growth (% per year)					
1870	−1.18				−0.55	
1913	−1.52				0.17	
1929	0.27				−0.48	−1.73
1938	−1.47				−0.02	−0.03
1950	3.24		0.85		0.96	−3.44
1973	0.63	0.22	−0.30	0.18	−2.12	0.06
1992	−0.73	−2.01	−1.04	−0.76	−1.69	−2.89

Sources: Maddison (1995) and author's calculations.

an existing production function impelled by the accumulation of capital on a per capita basis. This, together with the obvious fact that mechanization has been an ambient feature of commercial and industrial life since the Industrial Revolution, may account for some of the acceptance of the neoclassical production function among economists. The aim here is to show that the fossil production parsimoniously accommodates these same facts.

For notational clarity, we use the unadorned symbols (no hacek) to indicate the actual technical coefficient, and we use g_x, g_k, and g_ρ to refer to the actual growth rates. The actual growth rates can differ from γ, $\gamma - \chi$, and χ, for example when the best-practice technique is adopted with a lag.

10.1.2 Fossil Production Function

To derive the fossil production function in rectangular form, let us assume time-invariant Marx-biased technical changes. Taking time derivatives of the first and last equations in (10.1), and forming their quotient in order to eliminate dt, we have

$$\frac{d\check{x}}{d\check{k}} = \frac{\gamma}{\gamma - \chi}$$

Now let us define the parameter α, which for reasons made evident below, will be called the *viability threshold parameter*:

$$\alpha = \frac{\gamma}{\gamma - \chi}$$

Rearranging and taking definite integrals from some initial time to the current time, t, we have

$$\int_0^t \frac{1}{\check{x}} d\check{x} = \alpha \int_0^t \frac{1}{\check{k}} d\check{k}$$

which resolves to an equation familiar to economists,

$$\check{x} = \mathcal{A}\check{k}^\alpha$$

In dynamics, this equation would be called the integral curve (Gandolfo 1997, 347) of the system (see equations (10.1)). As mentioned earlier, we will call it the fossil production function. The parameter $\mathcal{A}$, of course, represents the consolidated constant of integration; it can be definitized from the initial conditions. Combining this with the fact that the most recent technique forms a ceiling on labor productivity, we can write the following expression for the fossil production function as it presents itself to entrepreneurs:

$$x = \min[\mathcal{A}k^{\alpha}, \check{x}_t] \quad k \geq \check{k}_0$$

Figure 10.1 illustrates the fossil production function in logarithmic form. The sequence of past techniques forms the linear segment with slope equal to α. The most recent technique available sets the limit on labor productivity. It is possible to increase the capital-labor ratio above $\check{k}_t$, but that just means giving the same number of workers more machines and has no effect on their output, as is represented by the horizontal segment. On the other hand, going back to an old technique by reassembling the stock of putty-capital does make it technically possible to employ more workers.[6] It is possible to make production more labor intensive. But it is not possible to increase labor productivity beyond $\check{x}_t$ since more mechanized techniques have not yet been invented.

This relationship stands in dramatic contrast to the standard neoclassical production function in its Cobb-Douglas form, which predicts that it is possible for one worker to produce the entire GDP with a finite amount of capital. For the other main functional form used by neoclassical theorists, the constant elasticity of substitution, or CES, production function, there is a limit on output per worker if the elasticity of substitution is less than unity (de la Croix and Michel 2002, 9). This gives the neoclassical economists some refuge from the absurdity of an economy run, as in Sismondi's unforgettable metaphor, by "a king, remaining alone on the island, [who] by constantly turning a crank, might produce, through automata, all the output of England" (de Sismondi [1819] 1991, 563). But not much, for the standard explanation in these precincts (Gollin 2002) of the profit share's constancy is precisely that the elasticity of substitution is roughly 1.

10.1.3 Viable Technical Changes

It remains to demonstrate under what conditions technical changes will be adopted by profit-maximizing entrepreneurs. Since we are assuming that the rate of depreciation is time invariant, we can work entirely in

6. For completeness, we should note that the possibility also exists under Leontief technology of employing superfluous workers. This would be represented by a ray from the origin to the point on a figure in level form (not logs) representing the coefficients of the technique in question. Any point along that ray would be feasible because the same number of machines would be operated to capacity by an excess number of workers.

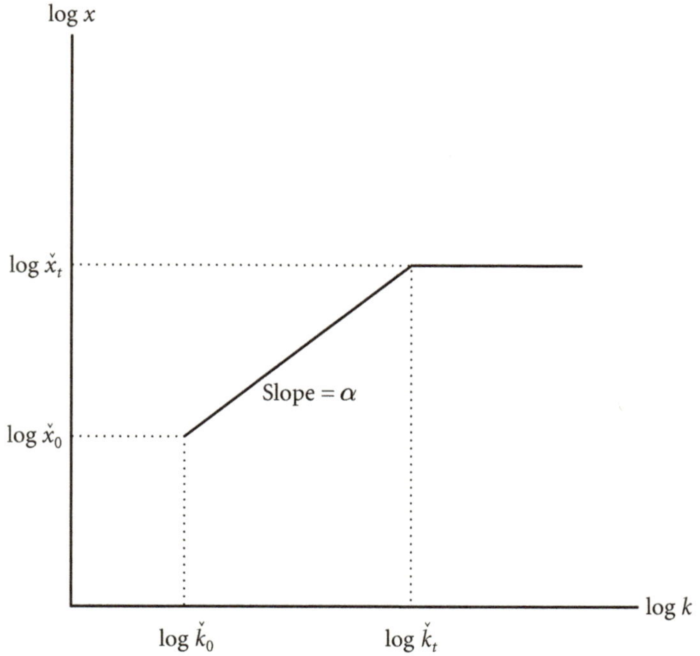

Figure 10.1 The fossil production function has a Cobb-Douglas form (note logarithms) for past techniques. The best-practice technique ($\check{k}_t$, $\check{x}_t$) is the most mechanized invented.

terms of the gross rate of profit, $v = r + \delta$. Let us write the profit share $\pi = 1 - w/x$. Then the gross rate of profit is $v = \pi\rho$. When a Marx-biased technical change offers capitalist entrepreneurs a higher rate of profit than the unimproved technique, we will say it is *viable*.

To make the analysis as general as possible, let us simply assume that the wage is growing at a constant rate, g_w (which could be negative), and that capitalists have perfect foresight. Then we can write the (instantaneous) change in the wage as $dw = g_w w dt$; a similar expression for the changes in the technical coefficients under consideration can be obtained from equations (10.1).

The new rate of profit associated with adoption of the technical change is found by differentiating. Using the grave accent (`) to identify the new technical coefficients, wage, and profit rate, we write

$$\grave{v}(\grave{x}, \grave{\rho}, \grave{w}) = v + dv = v + \pi d\rho + \rho d\pi$$

The benchmark of comparison is the expected rate of profit using the existing (unimproved) technique, identified by the acute accent (´). Since the wage rate still increases, this will be given by

$$\acute{v}(x, \rho, \grave{w}) = v + dv = v + \rho d\pi$$

where we should note that $d\pi = -dw/x$.

The technical change will be viable when the profitability of the new technique exceeds that of the unimproved technique, or

$$\grave{v}(\grave{x}, \grave{\rho}, \grave{w}) > \acute{v}(x, \rho, \grave{w})$$

Making the appropriate substitutions and recalling that $\chi < 0$ by assumption, this inequality can be reduced to the (necessary and sufficient) viability condition

$$\pi < \frac{\gamma}{\gamma - \chi} \tag{10.2}$$

or simply $\pi < \alpha$, which justifies the soubriquet attached to the viability threshold parameter, α.

In the neoclassical theory of production, this parameter is called the "output elasticity of capital" and is interpreted as the proportional increase in output that can be obtained from a unit percent increase in the capital stock, holding the labor force constant. In the fossil theory of production, the viability parameter regulates first and foremost the adoption of new techniques. In an economy undergoing a process of viable technical change, the best-practice technique in use conforms to a single Leontief function, for which the output elasticity of machines (under the neoclassical definition) is zero.

We can achieve a fuller understanding of the fossil production function by means of the wage-profit schedule, or

$$w = x - vk \tag{10.3}$$

Note that the wage-profit schedule has intercepts at x and ρ. Marx-biased technical change thus presents itself as a clockwise rotation of the wage-profit schedule around a pivot point that we will call the *switch point*, as is illustrated in Figure 10.2. There are four points around which the narrative revolves: (1) the switch point itself; we call the switch point profit rate ς and the switch point wage rate ω. (2) the original position at (v, w). (3) the new position under adoption of the new technique, $(\grave{v}, \grave{w})$. (4) the new position using the unimproved technique, $(\acute{v}, \grave{w})$.

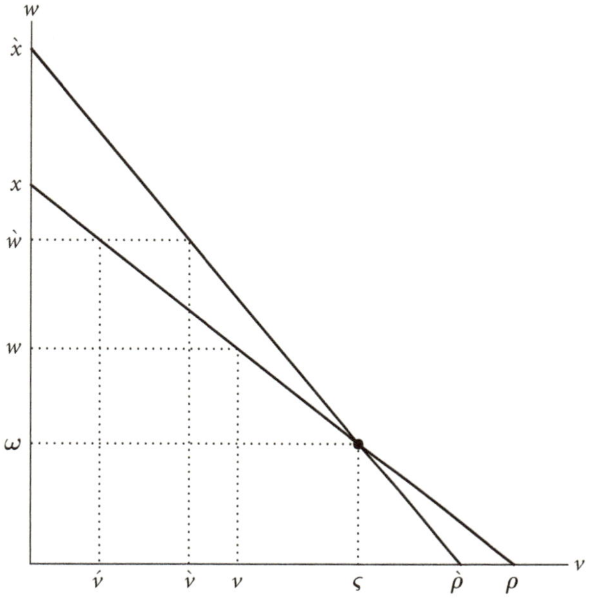

Figure 10.2 The wage-profit schedules for two techniques adjacent in time illustrate a viable Marx-biased technical change. In this example, the rate of profit decreases after adoption but that is contingent on the proportional increase in the wage.

Figure 10.2 describes a viable technical change, and it is clear that the defining feature of the geometry of the viability condition is that the original position lies *above* the switch point. Alternatively, the wage is greater than the switch point wage, $w > \omega$, and the profit rate is less than the switch point profit rate, $v < \varsigma$. The figure shows a switch that reduces the rate of profit, under the assumption that the proportional increase in the real wage has been sufficiently large.

These inequalities facilitate comparison between the fossil and neoclassical production functions. As Samuelson (1962) showed, if there is an infinite number of techniques in a one-commodity world such as ours,[7] ranked

7. Actually, Samuelson worked with a special multicommodity model and assumed that each industry had the same machine-labor ratios so that the wage-profit schedules remained linear, as they must be in a one-commodity world. This turned out be a losing gambit in the defense of marginal productivity theory precisely because the wage-profit schedules of a more general multicommodity world are not linear, creating all sorts of behavior considered anomalous from the neoclassical perspective. See Harcourt (1972) for a complete account of the Cambridge debates around this point.

by capital-intensity, they form an envelope in profit rate–wage rate space that is the dual to the aggregate function he called the *surrogate production function*. In neoclassical theory, this envelope in profit-wage space is usually referred to as the *factor price frontier*. An ongoing process of Marx-biased technical change will leave behind a section of the surrogate production function, or a section of the factor price frontier formed by the locus of switch points. Samuelson, of course, was trying to justify the neoclassical production function by reconstructing it from an activity analysis foundation. The switch point wage (profit rate) would be interpreted as the marginal product of labor (capital) in the neoclassical theory.

The fossil production function considers the mechanization process to be relatively independent of the wage. In Figure 10.2, it is clear that even if the wage were constant, the new technique would be adopted.[8] This contrasts with the neoclassical theory in which substitutions of capital for labor occur as a response to increases in the wage. The fossil production function does admit the possibility of neoclassical substitutions, however. For example, these could occur if the wage were low enough to make old, fossil techniques viable. Some might think that this makes the fossil production function observationally equivalent to the neoclassical production function, in the sense that both predict wage cuts will induce firms to employ more labor per unit of output. But this is not true. In the fossil production function, it will take a proportional wage cut of $(\alpha - \pi)/(1 - \pi)$ before the most recently rejected techniques become profitable.[9] Calibrating to typical estimates of these observable parameters discussed below, wages would have to be cut in half before inducing substitutions of labor for capital.

Alternatively, we could calculate the length of time before the technical changes cease to be viable presuming that the wage abruptly stops growing. Under this scenario, the profit share will rise until it equals the viability threshhold parameter after a time interval given by $T = (1/\gamma)\log(1 - \pi_t)/(1 - \alpha)$, where π_t is the profit share when the wage stops growing. For typical values of the observable parameters, T will be around 35 years. In this way, we see that while rising wages are not an immediate cause of tech-

8. In this case, clearly, the profit rate would increase, this being the essence of the Okishio theorem (Okishio 1961).

9. Matters are slightly more complicated under embodied technical change because a wage cut can push back the inframarginal vintage. But in terms of the intensive margin, the basic point goes through. See (Michl 2002) for further discussion.

nical changes, they constitute an ultimate condition for sustained technical dynamism.

Moreover, the fossil theory of production suggests a test that would identify which kind of substitutions prevail: the "classical" substitutions that are independent of the wage, or the neoclassical substitutions that are not.[10] If the viability condition is satisfied as a strict inequality, the former prevail. If the viability condition is satisfied as an equality, the latter prevail (and in fact, the fossil and neoclassical theories become observationally equivalent). Before turning to empirical evidence, it is worth embedding the fossil production function in a pair of growth models to sharpen the discussion.

10.2 Biased Technical Change and Growth

We will embed the fossil production function in an endogenous or capital-constrained model and in an exogenous or labor-constrained model. In both cases, let us impose the restrictive assumption that workers do no saving as a class so that we can showcase the issues raised by biased technical change.

Capitalist saving will be governed by a continuous-time version of the Cambridge equation. We can dispense with identifying sub/superscripts since only capitalists save. In continuous time (using the dot notation to indicate a time derivative, or $\dot{Z} = dZ/dt$, and $Z(t)$ to date variables), the capitalist dynasty's programming problem is

$$\begin{aligned}
&\text{choose } C(t) \\
&\max \int_0^{\infty} (\log C) e^{-\beta t} dt \\
&\text{subject to } C = rK - \dot{K} \\
&\text{given } r(t),\ K(0)
\end{aligned}$$

This problem can be solved using optimal control theory (see the Appendix to this chapter) and has a well-known and by now familiar form. The capitalist consumption function is written

$$C = \beta K$$

10. In a vintage model with technical changes embodied in machines, there is a third possibility in which the substitutions are conditioned by growth of the wage, and the viability condition is merely sufficient to ensure a higher rate of return on new machines; for more details, consult (Michl 2002).

Substituting into the budget constraint gives us the capitalist saving function. In both models, growth of capital will be governed by the continuous-time version of the Cambridge equation, or

$$g_K = r - \beta \tag{10.4}$$

With equations (10.1) and (10.4), we are one equation shy of a system that can determine the unknowns, w, r, and g_K.

10.2.1 Endogenous Growth

To close this model under the assumption of endogenous growth, we replace the conventional real wage with a conventional wage share, as in Foley and Michl (1999). The conventional wage share will be identified by $(1 - \bar{\pi})$. In this way, the model will be consistent by construction with the well-established stylized fact (Gollin 2002) that the wage share remains remarkably constant, both over time and across countries, including countries at rather different levels of development. We will thus assume that

$$\begin{aligned} w &= (1 - \bar{\pi})x \\ v &= \bar{\pi}\rho \end{aligned} \tag{10.5}$$

Over time, the wage grows with labor productivity, so that $dw = \gamma w dt$. Similarly, the profit rate grows (negatively) with capital productivity, so that $dv = \chi v dt$. Forming the quotient dw/dv to eliminate dt, rearranging and integrating from some initial time period to the current period, we have

$$\int_0^t \frac{1}{w} dw = \frac{\gamma}{\chi} \int_0^t \frac{1}{v} dv$$

which resolves to the integral curve or trajectory for the distribution point, (v, w):

$$\log w = \mathcal{B} - \frac{\alpha}{1 - \alpha} \log v$$

where $\mathcal{B}$ is a constant of integration that can be definitized by the initial conditions. (Note that we have replaced γ/χ with $\alpha/(\alpha - 1)$ to draw out the connections between this structure and the neoclassical factor price frontier.)

For purposes of comparison, it is useful to derive the integral curve of the switch points. Recall that they evolve according to the parametric equations

$$\begin{aligned} \omega &= (1-\alpha)x \\ \varsigma &= \alpha\rho \end{aligned} \tag{10.6}$$

Submitting this system to the same treatment in order to reexpress it in rectangular form, we obtain the integral curve for the switch point, (ς, ω):

$$\log \omega = \mathcal{C} - \frac{\alpha}{1-\alpha} \log \varsigma$$

where $\mathcal{C}$ is a constant of integration obtained from the initial conditions. This equation describes a structure that corresponds very closely to the factor price frontier attached to the neoclassical production function.

With viable Marx-biased technical change, we have an example of unbalanced growth. Over time the wage rate will be rising while the profit rate declines, and the economy will be moving along the integral curve, as shown in Figure 10.3. Because the technical change is viable, we know that $\pi < \alpha$, and thus the integral curve of the switch points will be the displaced

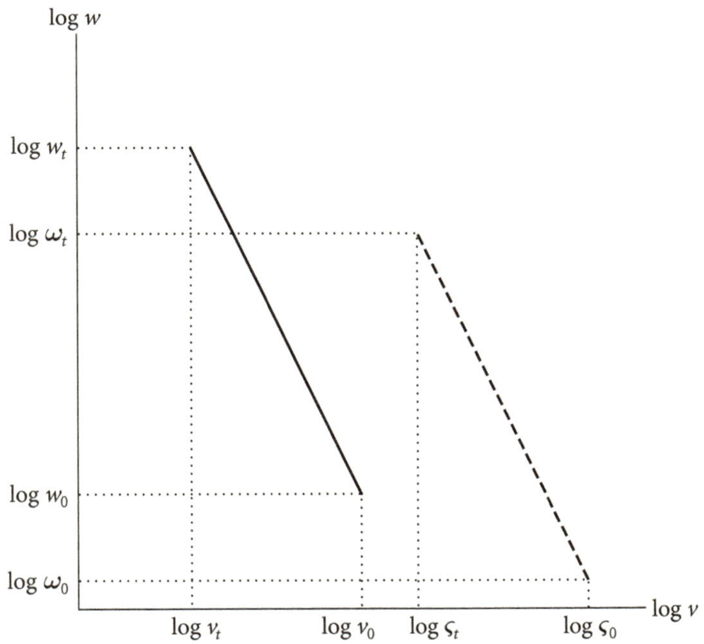

Figure 10.3 In the endogenous growth model with a constant wage share, the integral curve (solid line) or trajectory of the distribution point (v, w) lies to the northwest of the integral curve (dashed line) of the switch points, (ς, ω). The integral curve of the switch points is the dual of the Cobb-Douglas segment of the fossil production function.

image of the integral curve of the distribution points, or the observable trajectory of the economy.[11] An unwary observer might confuse them. A neoclassical economist, for example, presented with declining capital productivity and increasing labor productivity, together with a declining profit trend, might be inclined to describe a Solow-Swan economy undergoing its transitional dynamics.

This kind of growth is clearly unsustainable because the rate of capital accumulation is falling continuously. Eventually, capital *de*cumulation will set in. But based on Maddison's (1995) data, it is clear that this process has prevailed in some fairly prominent historical episodes.

10.2.2 Exogenous Growth

At the other extreme, let us assume that growth is constrained by the available labor force that grows (exponentially) at the natural rate, n. Full employment is maintained by change in the distribution of income and/or modulation in the rate of adoption of technical changes that allow the growth of labor demand to keep abreast of the growth of labor supply, or

$$g_K - g_k = n \tag{10.7}$$

Obviously, we need also to specify that the initial capital stock provides jobs for the initial labor force.[12]

Viable Technical Change

Let us assume without loss of generality that the economy begins with an equilibrium profit share that satisfies the viability condition. In this case, technical changes will be adopted without delay, and $g_k = \gamma - \chi$. Changes in the distribution of income are required to satisfy continuously equation (10.7), so that the net rate of profit will be

$$r = n + \beta + (\gamma - \chi)$$

Now we can see that since the net and gross rates of profit must remain constant during a period of viable, Marx-biased technical change, which

11. The displacement could be measured as the norm of the vector difference $(v, w) - (\varsigma, \omega)$, which remains constant over time.

12. One alternative is to consider an economy that starts out with a labor surplus but then makes a transition to a labor-constrained growth regime when the reserves of labor are depleted, as in Michl and Foley (2004).

is characterized by declining capital productivity, the profit share must be rising in order to compensate for the decline in capital productivity. In fact, the growth rate of the profit share will be $g_\pi = -\chi$. Thus, the conditions that initiate this process of accumulation with viable technical change are subverted by the process itself. The profit share must clearly rise until it achieves equality with the viability threshold parameter, α. At that point, call it T_1, the system changes qualitatively.

Time Delays

Once the profit share achieves equality with the viability threshold parameter, the new techniques will be adopted with a time lag, if they are adopted at all. The trajectory of the economy's distribution point has now joined the integral curve of the switch points; the model behaves as would a model with a well-behaved neoclassical production function of Cobb-Douglas form. The profit share from now on must remain equal to α.

This means that going forward the full employment condition expressed in equation (10.7) will be sustained by modulation in the pace at which techniques are adopted. The best-practice frontier will now part company with the technique in use at any given time, and capitalist entrepreneurs will have a locally rich spectrum of techniques from which to choose, more or less as the neoclassical production theory envisages them to have under all conditions. With the gross profit rate now given by $\alpha\rho$, and the Cobb-Douglas segment of the fossil production available (so that $\rho = Ak^{\alpha-1}$), the full employment condition can be solved for the fundamental equation using the Cambridge equation (10.4):

$$\dot{k} = \alpha A k^{\alpha} - (n + \delta + \beta)k$$

We are now ensconced in the world described by the Solow-Swan growth model (with the now-minor difference being the class structure of saving we have imposed). The economy evolves according to the transitional dynamics of a neoclassical growth model, and it even achieves a steady state, beyond which no technical changes will ever get adopted without a change in the fundamental or primitive parameters. Using an asterisk to identify steady state solutions, this milestone arrives at $t = T^*$, where the steady state technology will be

$$\rho^* = \frac{n + \delta + \beta}{\alpha}$$

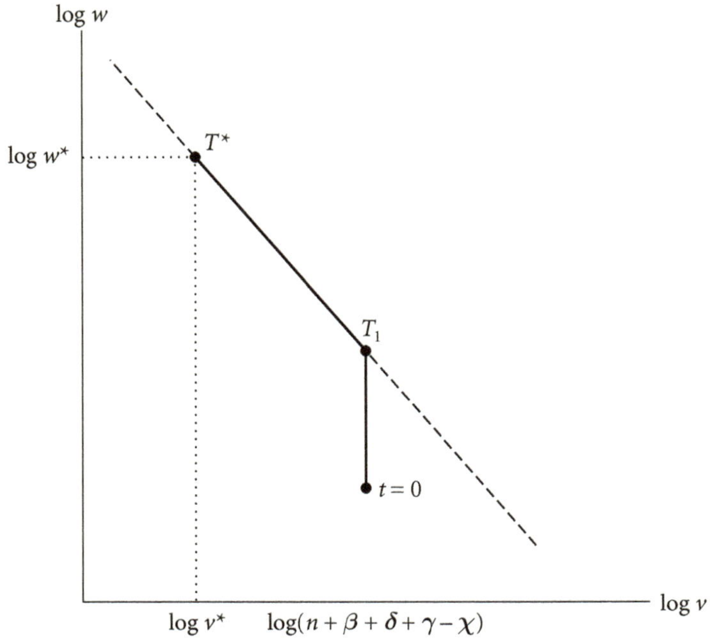

Figure 10.4 In the exogenous growth model the integral curve (solid line) or trajectory of the distribution point $(v,\ w)$ joins the integral curve (dashed line) of the switch points $(\varsigma,\ \omega)$ at T_1. In the steady state achieved at T^*, technical changes are no longer adopted.

and the other steady state solutions can easily be derived from this expression; for example, $v^* = \alpha\rho^*$.

We can visualize the whole drama, starting at $t = 0$ and ending at T^*, as it plays itself out on the phase plane in Figure 10.4. For convenience the figure includes the integral curve of the switch points, shown as a dashed line. This helps remind us that along the first leg of the journey, from $t = 0$ to T_1, the profit share lies below the viability threshold parameter. Only after T_1, when the system joins up with the integral curve of the switch points, does the profit share equal the viability parameter. This is significant because both the profit share and the viability threshold parameter are observable variables. We now have enough theoretical structure built up to make some sense of the historical and statistical record.

One final point concerns neutral technical change. If we replace the assumption of biased change with one of Harrod-neutral change, these two basic models still work. Under both the conventional wage-share assumption and the full employment assumption, the integral curve of the distribution point would be a vertical line headed due north. The viability parameter would trivially equal unity: technical changes would be viable at all wage levels. Thus, the two models would be observationally equivalent. In fact, a Solow-Swan model with neutral technical change in its steady state would also be indistinguishable empirically.

10.2.3 Total Factor Productivity?

In addition to the marginal productivity theory of income distribution, another casualty of the fossil production function is the doctrine of total factor productivity usually associated with Solow (1957). The fossil production function moots the distinction between capital accumulation and technical change, and treats them as aspects of the same dynamic process of transformation and development. It takes seriously Kaldor's injunction that "any sharp or clear-cut distinction between the movement *along* a 'production function' with a given state of knowledge and a *shift* in the 'production function' caused by a change in the state of knowledge is arbitrary and artificial" (Kaldor 1957, 596). The Solow decomposition is an effort to rescue the neoclassical theory of growth from the data, since as is well known, in the absence of the external stimulus of technical change, it predicts the ultimate cessation of per capita growth under the influence of diminishing returns.

In terms of the fossil production function, the Solow decomposition can be shown to be equivalent to a change of variables that eliminates any gap between the actual wage and the switch point wage (that is, the apparent marginal product of labor) through the magic of accounting. First, define total factor productivity growth, g_{TFP}, under Harrod-neutral technical change[13] using the standard decomposition:

$$g_x = \pi g_k + (1 - \pi) g_{TFP}$$

Second, assume that the economy is on a trajectory with viable Marx-biased technical changes, as in Figure 10.3, well away from the integral

13. The argument goes through under Hicks-neutral technical change as well; see (Foley and Michl 1999). Yet there seems to be no theoretical argument for assuming neutral technical change.

curve of the switch points. Thus, the rate of growth of labor productivity and capital intensity will mirror the technical change, or $g_x = \gamma$ and $g_k = \gamma - \chi$. That makes

$$g_{TFP} = \gamma + \frac{\pi}{1-\pi}\chi$$

Third, the Solow decomposition interprets the difference, $g_x - g_{TFP}$, as the measure of the effect of capital deepening or movement along the production function; in this case, we can replace γ with $\gamma - g_{TFP}$. If we recalculate the viability threshold parameter using this redefinition of productivity growth to filter out the effects of pure total factor productivity growth, renaming it $\breve{\alpha}$, we get

$$\breve{\alpha} = \pi$$

Thus, the Solow decomposition reduces to an accounting device that eliminates any apparent discrepancy between the observed marginal product of labor (capital) and the observed wage (profit rate) by redefining the former.

The irony here is that the original formulation of Cobb and Douglas (1928), before Solow's "improvement," turns out to be closer to the truth (or what Joan Robinson (1953) called the "common sense" of the production function) from the vantage point of the fossil theory.

The question that now confronts us is whether the evidence points towards a trajectory along the integral curve of the switch points as in the later stages in Figure 10.4, in which case the prediction of marginal productivity theory would be supported, or towards a trajectory well away from the integral curve, as in Figure 10.3 or in the earlier stages in Figure 10.4. The next chapter attacks this question in a data set that contains enough observations with Marx-biased technical change to support a detailed empirical investigation.

10.3 Appendix: Control Theory

The solution to the continuous-time capitalist programming problem using optimal control theory makes a companion piece to the solution presented in the Appendix to Chapter 3 using dynamic programming and discrete time. We restate the capitalist problem:

$$
\begin{aligned}
&\text{choose } C(t)\\
&\max \int_0^{\infty} (\log C)e^{-\beta t}dt\\
&\text{subject to } C = rK - \dot{K}\\
&\text{given } r(t),\ K(0)
\end{aligned}
$$

The solution to this problem using control theory requires writing out the Hamiltonian and applying the maximum principle. The current-value Hamiltonian is

$$H = \log C + \mu(rK - C)$$

where μ is the co-state variable or shadow price of wealth.

From the first-order condition on the Hamiltonian, H_C=0, we immediately deduce that

$$\mu = \frac{1}{C}$$

We can easily determine that the capitalists will consume a constant fraction of their wealth.[14] From the necessary condition on the co-state variable,

$$\dot{\mu} = -\frac{\partial H}{\partial K} + \beta\mu = (\beta - r)\mu$$

we can see that optimal consumption grows instantaneously at the rate

$$\frac{\dot{C}}{C} = r - \beta$$

From the necessary condition on the state variable, K, which is just the equation of motion $\dot{K} = rK - C$, it is clear that

$$\frac{\dot{K}}{K} = r - \frac{C}{K}$$

14. Weitzman (2003) provides an introduction to the maximum principle, a handbook on how to apply it, and a good example of how neoclassical economists interpret this principle and apply it to income accounting.

The easiest way to solve this system is to guess the form of the solution and then verify that it works. Based on our experience with the discrete-time version of the problem, let us try a proportional solution in the form $C = \mathcal{A}K$, where $\mathcal{A}$ is an undetermined coefficient. The only coefficient that satisfies these two differential equations is $\mathcal{A} = \beta$, so that the consumption function is[15]

$$C = \beta K$$

The capitalist saving function follows from simple substitution.

15. A more rigorous solution first solves for consumption, $C = C(0)\exp(\int (r - \beta)dt)$, and the co-state variable, $\mu = \mu(0)\exp(\int (\beta - r)dt)$. Recall that r is a sequence of known quantities. To find $C(0)$, substitute into the equation of motion for wealth, which becomes a differential equation with an integrating factor, $\exp(\int(-rdt))$. We can solve this equation for K up to a constant of integration. To definitize the constant of integration, substitute into the transversality condition,

$$\lim_{t \to \infty} \mu K e^{-\beta t} = 0$$

The constant turns out to equal zero, allowing us to recover $C(0) = \beta K(0)$, and since the problem remains the same, we can drop the time subscript and obtain the time-invariant consumption function in the text.

— 11 —

Fossil Production Function

Evidence

The striking agreement between the actual production series and the one generated by the Cobb-Douglas function is at the basis of the success of this production function.

DAVID DE LA CROIX AND PHILIPPE MICHEL (2002)

I have never thought of the macroeconomic production function as a rigorously justifiable concept. In my mind it is either an illuminating parable, or else a mere device for handling data, to be used so long as it gives good empirical results, and to be abandoned as soon as it doesn't, or as soon as something better comes along.

ROBERT M. SOLOW (1966)

Chapter 10 showed that when technical change is Marx-biased, it should be possible to estimate the parameters of the fossil production function and interpret the results in two aspects. First, the theory describes the conditions under which the standard neoclassical or marginalist theory would be reasonably accurate, and when it fails. Second, the theory suggests that the behavior of the distribution point, (v, w) where v is the gross profit rate and w is the wage, will differ depending on how growth is constrained. When technical change is Harrod-neutral, however, it is not possible to make any distinctions along either facet.

Based on the two growth models elaborated in Chapter 10, an empirical strategy implementing the fossil production function takes the form of a nested interrogation of the data:

1. What is the relationship between the profit share, π, and the viability threshold parameter, α? If we find "striking agreement" that $\pi \approx \alpha$,

some version of the neoclassical theory applies, in the usual sense that the choice of technique is mediated by the wage. If we find that $\pi < \alpha$, either the endogenous model or the first stage of the exogenous model could be valid, so we can move on to the second question.[1]

2. Does the trajectory of the distribution point seem to move along a vertical path,[2] as in Figure 10.4, or a negatively sloped path, as in Figure 10.3? The former path signifies exogenous growth, while the latter path signifies endogenous growth.

The question of the parameters of the fossil production function has been addressed (Michl 1999; Foley and Michl 1999; Michl 2002) using less statistical firepower than we deploy below. In every case, the data speak clearly: where we find Marx-biased technical change, we find it to be viable. Translated into a statement about the neoclassical production function, the wage almost universally exceeds the apparent marginal product of labor and the profit rate falls short of the apparent marginal product of capital. These results find their counterparts in the neoclassical literature on the speed of convergence and the output elasticity of capital, which is frequently found to be too large for the observed distribution of income.

Because these studies take the individual country as the unit of analysis, they are vulnerable to the defense that they ignore "total factor productivity" as discussed in the previous chapter. This chapter imposes enough structure on the problem to be able to overcome this potential defense of marginalist theory.

The question of constraints on growth has received surprisingly little attention. Thirwall argues that an asymmetry in Okun's law provides evidence that growth is not constrained by labor. At the height of the business cycle, the rate of growth at which the unemployment rate stabilizes (which can be recovered from estimates of Okun's law) appears to increase, which Thirlwall (2002, 90) adduces as evidence that high growth "must have been pulling more workers into the labor force and inducing productivity growth." On the other hand, Sedgley and Elmslie (2004) interpret their finding that labor productivity and per capita income are cointegrated

1. If we find that $\pi > \alpha$, we are in pathological territory where we should probably regroup and rethink the whole question. Fortunately, there is not much evidence for this pattern.

2. This trajectory attends capital-using technical change, so it implies a continuous decline in the profit share, making it less plausible than it might seem.

as evidence in favor of the full employment closure. It is certainly inconsistent with a simplistic version of the endogenous growth model in which all accommodation to variations in growth arise through fluctuation in the size of an internal reserve of labor.

11.1 The Aggregate Data

We follow a well-beaten path and utilize the Penn World Tables (Summers and Heston 1991). The Extended Penn World Tables (EPWT) include estimates of capital stock compiled by Adalmir Marquetti using perpetual inventory methods, thus permitting measurement of capital productivity.

11.1.1 Adjustments

In order to measure the rate of profit, we also need estimates of the profit share, or one minus the wage share. The EPWT estimate uses United Nations National Accounts and follows the standard practice of dividing employee compensation by GDP to measure the wage share. Douglas Gollin (2002) points out that the United Nations (UN) data include in GDP the income of the self-employed but that employee compensation is based on the wages paid by business enterprises. Thus, countries with large self-employed or informal sectors will seem to have low (unadjusted) wage shares. He proposes several adjustments to correct or attenuate this measurement error. The most persuasive adjustment exploits the UN System of National Accounts category operating surplus of private, unincorporated enterprises, or OSPUE. Since the income of the self-employed will fall into this category, Gollin proposes to remove OSPUE from GDP and then to proceed as before in calculating the wage share.[3] Let us call this the Gollin adjustment. If the PUE's are in fact made up entirely of the self-employed, then this procedure is equivalent to calculating the wage share among incorporated business firms where recognizable capitalist social relations prevail, which makes good sense from a classical point of view. On the other hand, if the PUE's pay wages (think of a corner bodega run by a

3. Here GDP is measured at factor cost by first subtracting out indirect taxes net of subsidies from GDP at market prices. Gollin also proposes two other adjustments that are less attractive. One treats all OSPUE as employee compensation. The other imputes the average wage to the self-employed, and treats the residual of their income as a return to capital.

family that employs the neighborhood teens) that are recorded by the national accountants in employee compensation, this procedure can overstate the wage share among the incorporated sector where larger firms and full-blown capitalist relations of production prevail.[4] We will operate on the presumption that the former statement lies closer to the truth and treat the adjusted wage share data as the most precise available.

A second adjustment, which is really a modification of the Gollin adjustment, has been proposed by Bernanke and Gürkaynak (2001) in order to increase the number of countries in the data sample. They impute the magnitude of OSPUE using data on the share of the labor force employed in the corporate sector. This imputation assumes that the share of corporate employment is the same as the share of corporate income in GDP, an assumption they find gives reasonable results for countries that have reached a threshold share of corporate employment. Call this the Bernanke-Gürkaynak adjustment. This adjustment extends Gollin's methodology to countries that do not report OSPUE.

In order to maximize the sample size, we have defined the wage share using the best data available in each case, according to the following ranking: Gollin adjustment (27 cases), Bernanke-Gürkaynak adjustment (29 cases). We then merge the wage share data with the EPWT data set, giving us a sample of 56 countries with fairly complete coverage of the macroeconomic aggregates.[5]

The wage share data in our sample cover the period 1963 to 1998 incompletely; for some countries we have data for only a few years. Most of the other macroeconomic aggregates taken from the EPWT give complete

4. Gollin himself seems to recognize this problem in footnote 14, but perhaps has underestimated its potential significance. His motivation for the adjustment is that it assumes that the self-employed earn capital and labor income in the same mix as the rest of the economy. True to neoclassical form, this justification treats capital and labor as "factors of production" independent of social relations of production, and this conceptualization lies at the heart of the differences between the classical and neoclassical traditions.

5. Most of the wage share data is taken from unpublished files provided to us by Gürkaynak. From these data, we have included one country, Turkey, which they excluded in their data analysis on the grounds that its corporate employment share is too low for the Bernanke-Gürkaynak adjustment to produce reasonable results. In addition, we have added two countries, India and Hungary, using unpublished files provided to us by Gollin. From these two sources, we have constructed a sample with as many countries over as many years as possible. We are grateful to Refet Gürkaynak and Douglas Gollin for generously sharing their unpublished worksheets.

Table 11.1 Macroeconomic variables from a cross section of selected countries, 1963–1998

Variable	Mean	Median	Standard Deviation	Observations
		Full Sample		
π	0.3325	0.3218	0.0773	56
Naive π	0.5971	0.5990	0.1250	91
x (\$, 000/yr/N)	15.1570	12.3410	12.4950	118
ρ (/yr)	1.3638	1.0354	1.2132	118
γ (/yr)	0.0134	0.0151	0.0193	118
χ (/yr)	−0.0045	−0.0032	0.0200	118
α	0.7337	0.7135	7.4635	118
	Subsample with Profit Share Data			
π	0.3325	0.3218	0.0773	56
Naive π	0.5527	0.5275	0.1078	54
x (\$, 000/yr/N)	21.9300	20.5630	12.297-	56
ρ (/yr)	0.9101	0.6960	0.5218	56
γ (/yr)	0.0184	0.0171	0.0152	56
χ (/yr)	−0.0036	−0.0030	0.0134	56
α	1.1400	0.7752	1.9648	56
	Subsample with Biased Technical Change			
π	0.3285	0.3201	0.0826	32
Naive π	0.5369	0.5130	0.1077	30
x (\$, 000/yr/N)	23.2180	21.6780	12.4960	32
ρ (/yr)	0.9303	0.7444	0.4909	32
γ (/yr)	0.0232	0.0211	0.0128	32
χ (/yr)	−0.0107	−0.0085	0.0086	32
α	0.6802	0.7160	0.1841	32

coverage. Table 11.1 reports the main variables for the full sample, the subsample with adjusted profit share coverage, and the subsample of these that exhibit Marx-biased technical change. This last subsample will be the focus of subsequent investigation. The measurements are taken over the whole sample period.

The adjusted profit share data in the first line of each panel compare with the naive profit share taken from the EPWT. The adjusted wage share is, as expected, higher on average than its unadjusted counterpart, and its distribution is more compact as well. The structure of the relationship has been examined thoroughly by Gollin (2002), and there is no need to plow the same field twice. In all samples, a large disparity between the two is apparent. In the full sample, the naive share is nearly twice as large as the corrected share. This difference attenuates somewhat in the subsample because, as Gollin points out, the underlying measurement error is more severe in less developed countries, but it remains disturbingly large. We will limit investigation to observations that are covered by the adjusted profit share data.

11.1.2 Technical Change

In the full sample, we first observe the prevalence on average of Marx-biased technical change, namely, that it is capital-using ($\chi < 0$) and labor-saving ($\gamma > 0$).[6] In fact, there is considerable heterogeneity of technical change as is shown by a simple count of the sign patterns:

γ	χ	Full Sample	Profit Coverage
+	−	53	32
−	+	14	6
+	+	36	17
−	−	15	1

The subsample with adjusted profit coverage does not differ too much from the full sample, although a slightly larger proportion (57 percent compared to 45 percent) of the observations displays Marx-biased technical change.

Table 11.1 shows that the implied average value of the viability threshold parameter, α, is less than unity in the full sample and in the subsample with biased technical change.[7] A crude comparison with the profit share shows the viability parameter to be around twice as large, both in the full sample and in the restricted subsample. We need to examine this finding carefully before drawing any substantive conclusions.

6. Careful readers of Chapter 10 will notice that we have jumped the gun a bit by using Greek letters rather than g_ρ and g_x. Since we do not find much evidence that techniques are adopted with a lag, this expositional liberty seems harmless.

7. The standard errors for α are not typographical mistakes. If the technical changes have the same sign, α can take large absolute values just by the laws of arithmetic.

The countries in the subsample with share data appear to be slightly richer than the average, as indicated by output per worker, which is measured in real purchasing power parity dollars. The level of capital productivity is lower in this subsample and that is consistent with the stylized fact that capital productivity declines with economic development, at least up to a point. In all the subsamples, the distribution of capital productivity is skewed toward large values (compare mean and median). The distributions of other variables are fairly symmetric (with the exceptions involving α mentioned above). We need to be sensitive to outliers and nonnormal distributions of any variables that involve capital productivity such as the profit rate.

As indicated by the theory presented in the previous chapter, we concentrate on the subsample with Marx-biased technical change in the remainder of this chapter.

11.1.3 Profit Share

Our first task is to probe the behavior of the profit share in the subsample with biased technical change in order to identify any possible patterns. In particular, is there evidence that economic development under biased technical change forces the profit share to rise? Figure 11.1 plots the profit share against output per worker, and fits a curve to the data using a nonparametric technique called loess that was developed by Cleveland (1993), where a detailed explanation can be found.

We make extensive use of loess so let us describe its main features briefly. Loess uses weighted local regressions of polynomials having degree = 1 (locally linear fitting) or = 2 (locally quadratic fitting), estimated at each data point over a bandwith that is controlled by the smoothing parameter. The smoothing parameter selects the proportion (which can exceed 1) of the full sample that is used at each point. The weights descend following a tricube weight function. By choosing these two parameters, the degree of polynomials and the smoothing parameter, it is possible for researchers to strike a balance between a lack of fit and a surplus of fit by visually examining the residuals or, more formally, by optimizing over some objective measure, such as the Akaike information criterion (AIC).[8]

8. To be more precise, we seek the minimum of a bias-corrected AIC, following Hurvich et al. (1998). The AIC alone tends to oversmooth and is overly sensitive to changes in data.

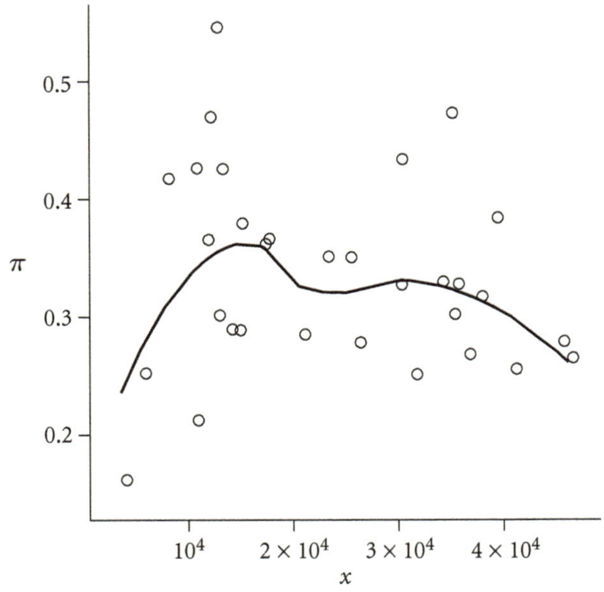

Figure 11.1 The profit share is plotted (∘) against output per worker. The solid line represents a loess fit of these data. The smoothing parameter is 0.9, and the degree of local polynomials is 2.

In Figure 11.1, this procedure led to use of locally quadratic fitting, which is appropriate when the data seem to imply local extrema. The pattern that emerges is an inverted U-shape reminiscent of Kuznet's law. The initial rising segment might be evidence that development begins on a vertical path in the distribution space, (v, w), and the subsequent flat or declining segment might be evidence of positions along the integral curve of the switchpoints, all consistent with the exogenous closure detailed in Chapter 10. But we need to be sensitive to the presence of outliers before we draw any conclusions.

Despite the suggestive form of the inverted Kuznet's curve, it does not capture very much of the underlying variation in the data. Figure 11.2 plots the fitted values minus their means and the residuals against the quantile, or f-value, of the observations. This tool, called an r-f spread plot (Cleveland 1993, 40–41) facilitates visual appreciation of the relative amount of variation captured by the fitted function (more or less a visual R^2). The profit share exhibits a substantial amount of random variation across countries.

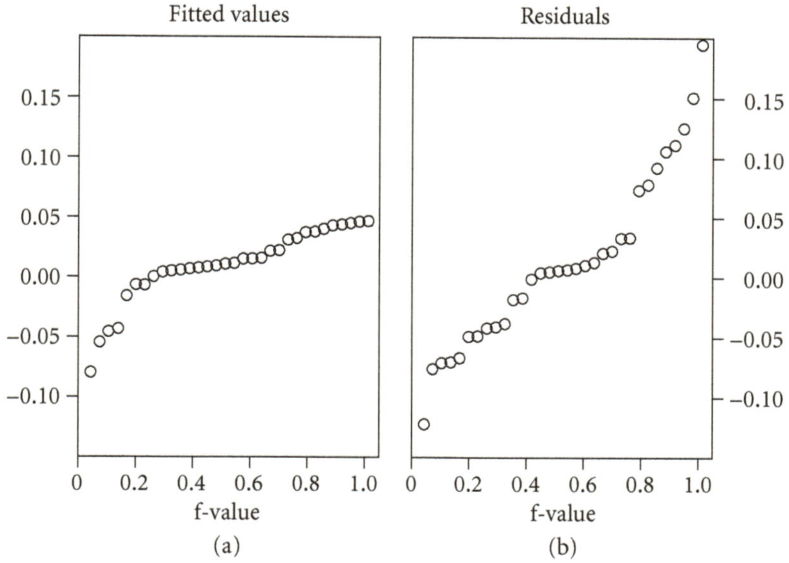

Figure 11.2 This residual-fitted (r-f) spread plot compares the spreads of the residuals and the fitted values (minus their means) for the loess fit of the profit share to output per worker in the cross section.

Overall, it does not seem systematically to change much over large developmental distances, thus extending Kaldor's stylized fact of constant income shares beyond the advanced countries to which he applied it. This was revealed by Gollin (2002), who points out that the apparent decline in the profit share in the naive data may be measurement error. His conventional, or neoclassical, interpretation treats this as evidence for the marginal productivity theory of distribution under technology well approximated by the Cobb-Douglas production function.

11.1.4 Viability: A First Pass

We can subject the conventional interpretation to an empirical test by measuring the viability threshold parameter for each country, using full-period values for technical change, and comparing the results to the country's average profit share. The marginalist interpretation requires an equality or at least close correspondence, since the viability parameter is analogous to the output elasticity of capital in the Cobb-Douglas function. It is clear from

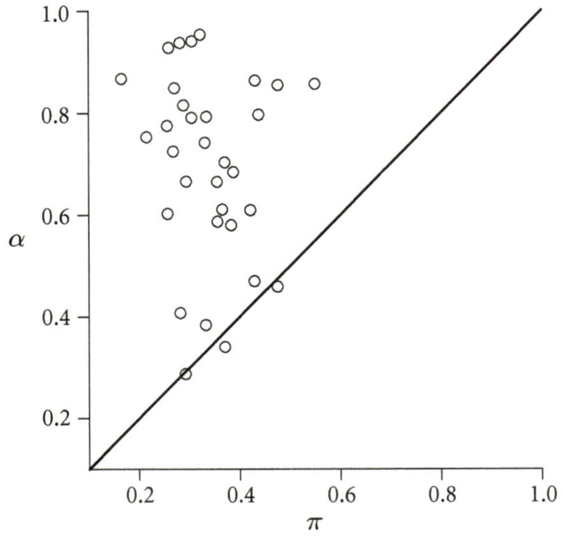

Figure 11.3 The viability threshold parameter has been plotted (o) against the profit share for the subsample with biased technical change. The solid line is a 45-degree reference line of equality. The data are period averages from 1963 to 1998.

Figure 11.3 that the viability parameter exceeds the profit share in almost all the cases; it lies well above the 45-degree reference line of equality in the figure.

There are three observations that lie right along the reference line, in conformity with marginalist theory. These are, from lowest to highest π value, Costa Rica, Jordan, and Paraguay. There are also three observations in a cluster near the reference line. These are Switzerland, New Zealand, and El Salvador. We will have an opportunity to explore these cases in more detail below when we examine the time-series properties of the distribution point by country.

This test imposes few restrictions on the accumulation process. The implicit assumption is that each country operates in a unique technological environment, having a specific value of its technical change parameters. For example, we know that technical knowledge may not be a freely available public good and that the transfer of technology requires effort, appropriate institutions, and other factors that are country-specific.

But as a test of the marginalist theory, this comparison is ultimately inconclusive because, as Chapter 10 points out, the measurement of productivity makes no allowance for "total factor productivity." We can overcome this limitation by studying the cross-sectional data.

11.2 The Wage-Profit Curves

If technology transfer operates with a simple lag, we might view each observation in the full-period cross section as a stage of economic development. The cross section can then be interpreted as a reflection of the common or average development process, and we pursue this line of attack in the next section. This viewpoint ignores the diversity in development that has been highlighted by Veblen (1915) and Gerschenkron (1962). We can incorporate this diversity to some extent, without throwing away information from comparisons, by pooling the time-series data. In either case, the theory in the previous chapter suggests that the behavior of the distribution point (v, w) along the integral wage-profit curve constitutes an appropriate object of analysis.

11.2.1 Cross-Sectional Data

We proceed by first letting the data speak for themselves using the loess technique before imposing a linear form on the wage-profit curve.

Nonparametric Estimates

Like a road cut through geological strata, the cross section of period averages in the sample with biased technical change shown in Figure 11.4 makes visible the different stages in the process of economic development and capital accumulation. An economy undergoing Marx-biased technical change will leave behind a statistical record of the fossil production function. Each technical change will be associated with a different wage-profit curve, and biased technical change expresses itself in the gradual increase in the slope of this progression of curves. We observe only one point on each curve, but these points over time (or across countries at different stages of development) should lie on the trajectory or the integral wage-profit curve.

With respect to evaluating marginalist theory, this approach avoids the ambiguity of the simple comparison in the previous section. A standard

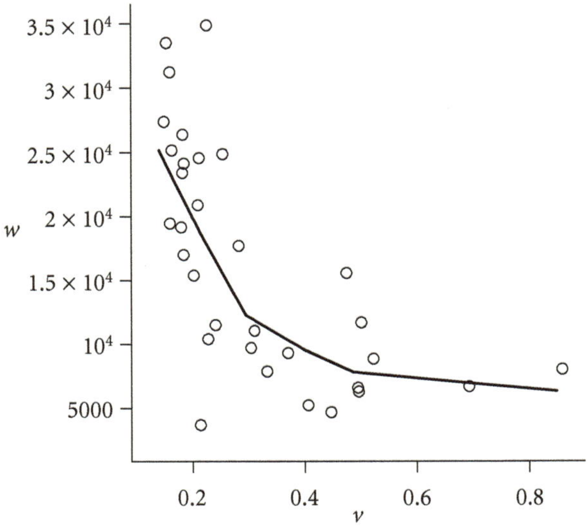

Figure 11.4 The real product wage rate is shown plotted (∘) against the gross profit rate with loess fit (solid line). The smoothing parameter is 0.92 and the degree of local polynomials is 1. Data are period averages for 1963 to 1998 from the subsample with biased technical change.

neoclassical interpretation of Figure 11.4 is that technology is a public good (Mankiw 1995), all countries share the same aggregate technology, and therefore the wage-profit points are all taken from the same underlying aggregate production function, albeit in its dual form as the "factor price frontier" or efficiency frontier consisting of the envelope formed by all the wage-profit curves, each representing a unique technique of production. Since each country shares the same technology, there is no question of controlling for total factor productivity.

The loess fit shown in Figure 11.4 uses locally linear fitting. It brings out a well-defined nonlinearity in the underlying wage-profit surface. This surface can be interpreted as the integral wage-profit curve of the distribution point, such as in Figure 10.3 or 10.4. The underlying theory in the previous chapter suggests a logarithmic transformation of the variables. Recall that the integral curve takes the form

$$\log w = \mathcal{B} - \frac{\alpha}{1-\alpha} \log v$$

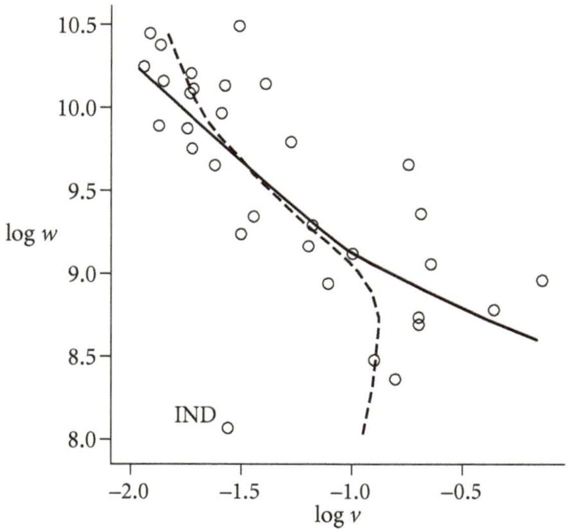

Figure 11.5 The log product wage is shown plotted against the log profit rate. The solid line shows the robust loess fit for the wage as a function of the profit rate; the smoothing parameter is 1 and the degree of local polynomials is 1. Loess fit is nonparametric; the linear form has not been imposed on the data. The dashed line shows the robust loess fit for the profit rate as a function of the wage; the smoothing parameter is 0.6 and the degree of local polynomials is 1. The observation for India is labeled.

under the assumption of constant exponential rates of technical change.

Even without the guidance of economic theory, conscientious application of Cleveland's visualization techniques suggests a logarithmic transformation of the wage-profit data. Figure 11.5 shows the same data in (natural) log form along with two robust loess fittings. Robust loess uses an additional layer of weighting on the local regressions to reduce the influence of outliers that might obscure underlying structure. The weights are chosen using a bisquare weight function that discounts the influence of large outliers (Cleveland 1993). This technique for weighting can also be used to improve least-squares parametric estimates, and we employ it below for that purpose.

Because the integral wage-profit curve is not in factor-response form, there is no particular reason to estimate the (log) wage as a function of the profit rate, or the profit rate as a function of the wage. We are interested in the structure that links them. The solid line in Figure 11.5 is the robust loess fit for the former function. Remarkably, a linear (i.e., Cobb-Douglas) relationship emerges unprompted. There is no sign of a vertical segment that might indicate a stage of development with a rising profit share that offsets declining capital productivity.

On the other hand, the robust loess estimate of the profit rate as a function of the wage (dashed line) does exhibit this vertical segment. This estimate was achieved through iteration and judgment. First, the loess fit that minimized the AIC was obtained; the smoothing parameter was 0.45. Second, this estimate and its residual-location (r-l) plot were examined visually and judged to display a surplus of fit. The vertical segment in Figure 11.5 was in fact positively sloped, a pattern that does not seem supported by the data. In response, the smoothing parameter was increased to 0.6 (additional smoothing resulted in a lack of fit). It became clear from the r-l plot that one outlier, India (labeled on the figure), was responsible for the vertical segment. Leaving India out of the sample then resulted in a robust loess fit (not shown) for the profit rate as a function of the wage that is linear and slightly steeper than the fit for the wage as a function of the profit rate. There is only so much that bisquare can do with outliers.

Checking the source of the data confirmed that India may represent a truly suspicious observation. Gollin, who compiled the India data, writes in his worksheets that "India's employee compensation line includes part of net operating surplus of unincorporated enterprises which cannot be separated from labor income of own-account." This information that the profit share in India is probably understated helps justify discounting the nonlinearity in order to exploit the power of regression analysis. The linear form of the loess estimates endorses the use of parametric techniques[9] that will permit point-estimates of the viability threshold parameter.

Parametric Estimates

Ordinary least squares (OLS) estimates of the two alternative specifications of the integral wage-profit curves are presented in Table 11.2. These two regressions establish upper and lower boundaries on the underlying slope of the integral curves that form the basis for estimates of the viability threshold

9. With the exception of the prominent outlier, the residuals from these estimates were not noticeably distorted by leptokurtosis. A normal distribution of the error terms is a standard assumption for ordinary least squares.

Table 11.2 Estimates of viability parameter, cross-sectional data

Dependent Variable	Independent Variable	Coefficient (standard deviation)	($n = 32$) 95% Confidence Interval Absolute Values	$\hat{\alpha}$	$\bar{R}^2$
			OLS		
log w	log v	−0.9266 (0.1742)	0.5708–1.2824	0.4809	0.468
log w	log v/w	−0.5832 (0.0376)	0.5062–0.6601	0.5832	0.885
log v	log w	−0.5237 (0.0984)	0.3226–0.7248	0.6562	0.468
			Bisquare		
log w	log v	−0.9793 (0.1478)	0.6895–1.2690	0.4947	0.541
log w	log v/w	−0.5625 (0.0324)	0.4990–0.6260	0.5625	0.800
log v	log w	−0.6125 (0.0883)	0.4394–0.7856	0.6201	0.487
			OLS (w/o India)		
log w	log v	−0.9852 (0.1352)	0.7086–1.2618	0.4962	0.634
log w	log v/w	−0.5560 (0.0302)	0.4941–0.6179	0.5560	0.918
log v	log w	−0.6562 (0.0901)	0.4720–0.8405	0.6037	0.634

parameter. A single point-estimate is provided by rearranging the integral curve as follows:

$$\log w = \mathcal{B}' - \alpha(\log v - \log w)$$

where $\mathcal{B}' = \mathcal{B}(1 - \alpha)$. The results of this estimation are shown in the middle rows of each panel.

From the OLS estimates, the threshold parameter appears to lie in an interval between one-half and two-thirds. In fact, the 95 percent confidence interval for the point-estimate of α places it in the interval 0.51–0.66.

The second panel shows the estimates using bisquare weights to discount the influence of outliers. This results in slightly more precise coefficient estimates, and narrows the 95 percent interval to 0.50–0.63. The bisquare procedure also permits an objective test that identifies outliers.[10] Reassuringly, only one observation passed the test and it was India. The third panel simply removes India and runs OLS estimates. The effects are similar to the bisquare correction.

Recalling from Table 11.1 that the subsample profit share mean was 0.33 and standard deviation was 0.08, it is clear that we have obtained a statistically important difference between the viability threshold parameter and the profit share. The profit share would have to be well over two standard deviations larger to reach the lowest boundary of the 95 percent confidence interval. Economists looking for confirmation of the marginalist prediction will find little comfort in this result.

11.2.2 Pooled Data

We can relax the requirements imposed in the previous section by pooling the data and analyzing a panel of time-series cross-sectional observations. Because of differences in time coverage, some of the profit share data does not correspond to the cross-sectional sample. In each case, a judgment was made to use the profit share measure that provides the most time coverage subject to the prioritization described above (see Section 11.1.1).

Time-series data introduce a new complication. The profit rate and share are cyclically sensitive. The profit rate, for example, directly reflects the degree of capacity utilization (see Chapter 2). This introduces noise, and potentially spurious correlations. In particular, it could bias the slope estimate of the wage-profit curve and the estimate of the viability parameter, most likely downward. In a recession, the profit rate and the wage rate move toward the origin, obscuring their inverse relationship along the wage-profit curve.

Table 11.3 repeats the estimate of the integral wage-profit curve in the pooled data. The first panel shows OLS estimates. The range of estimates for the viability parameter is somewhat more compact and the point estimates are more precise than in the cross section. The bisquare estimates in the

10. An outlier is identified when its standardized robust residual exceeds a predetermined cutoff, conventionally set to 3.

Table 11.3 Estimates of viability parameter, pooled data

		($n = 776$)			
Dependent Variable	Independent Variable	Coefficient (standard deviation)	95% Confidence Interval Absolute Values	$\hat{\alpha}$	$\bar{R}^2$ (F-value)
		OLS			
log w	log v	−0.9452 (0.0307)	0.8849–1.0055	0.4809	0.549
log w	log v/w	−0.5690 (0.0068)	0.5556–0.5823	0.5690	0.900
log v	log w	−0.5823 (0.0189)	0.5452–0.6194	0.6319	0.549
		Bisquare			
log w	log v	−0.9658 (0.0303)	0.9064–1.0252	0.4913	0.521
log w	log v/w	−0.5567 (0.0067)	0.5567–0.5798	0.5567	0.802
log v	log w	−0.5954 (0.0188)	0.5586–0.6322	0.6268	0.490
		Fixed Effects			
log w	log v	−0.6295 (0.0276)	0.5754–0.6835	0.3863	0.925 (120.70)
log w	log v/w	−0.4940 (0.0085)	0.4773–0.5106	0.4940	0.976 (79.26)
log v	log w	−0.6646 (0.0287)	0.6083–0.7208	0.6007	0.874 (61.74)

second panel are comparable. This confirms our previous finding that there is a statistically important difference between the profit share and viability threshold parameter. There is surprisingly little difference between these estimates and their cross-sectional counterparts.

The final panel of Table 11.3 includes country fixed effects. These estimates pass the F-test rejecting no fixed effects by a comfortable margin at the 0.01 level.[11] The fixed effect models lower the estimates for the threshold

11. In fact, almost all the country dummies were individually significant. The dummy for India was routinely twice as large in absolute magnitude as its next largest rival.

parameter, in some cases substantially. Without some control for capacity utilization, it is hard to judge whether this represents a move toward greater precision or whether the fixed effect model simply brings out the cyclical bias described above. The central value for the threshold parameter estimate now lies just below one-half, rather than just above. This is closer to the one-third value of the profit share, but there is still too much daylight between them to accept the predictions of the marginalist interpretation of the Cobb-Douglas fossil production function.[12]

11.2.3 Country Studies

A final exercise examines the behavior of the distribution point on a country-by-country basis. Countries that are severely constrained by labor supplies should show signs of a vertical trajectory or, if their profit share has achieved equality with the viability threshold parameter, movement along the integral curve of the switchpoints. Countries that conform to the endogenous growth model should move along the integral wage-profit curve. Countries that do not experience very stable technical change (e.g., departures from exponential growth) or that otherwise deviate from the assumptions of the model will obviously not display any particular profile.

A regression in the time-series data from each country of the log profit rate on the log wage rate could detect the vertical trajectory predicted by the exogenous growth model, as well as the negatively sloped integral wage-profit curve. Table 11.4 reports the span of the time series by country and the results of an OLS regression, showing the slope coefficient and its p-value in a regression of the log profit rate on the log wage. The preponderance (25 out of 32) of countries show a negative slope, and most of these (20) are statistically significant (i.e., nonzero) at or below the 5 percent level. None of the positive coefficients are significant, but some are fairly large. Of the nonsignificant estimates, several are candidates for zero values (small estimate with large p-value). Hong Kong and Singapore are good illustrations. We cannot rule out the possibility that these are examples of labor-constrained growth.

12. For comparison, the 95 percent confidence interval for the profit share as measured in the original cross section of countries with biased technical change is 0.2998–0.3571. This is a more meaningful statistic than the interval calculated in the pooled data, where we would be awarding weights arbitrarily to countries based on data coverage.

Table 11.4 Wage-profit paths by country

Country	Years	Coefficient	P-value
Australia	1963–1995	0.0418	0.8242
Austria	1963–1996	−0.5419	0.0000
Belgium	1963–1997	−0.3241	0.0113
Botswana	1973–1995	0.1479	0.5035
Canada	1980–1992	−0.8506	0.0381
Switzerland	1963–1995	−1.3071	0.0000
Colombia	1963–1992	−0.4912	0.0000
Costa Rica	1963-1993	−0.9936	0.0076
Denmark	1966–1995	0.4067	0.0649
Egypt	1963–1979	−0.1151	0.8149
Spain	1970–1996	−0.2370	0.1686
France	1970–1990	0.3126	0.1856
United Kingdom	1963–1996	−0.1250	0.3315
Greece	1964–1995	−0.7895	0.0000
Hong Kong	1980–1996	−0.0682	0.2069
India	1970–1980	0.8435	0.4200
Jordan	1967–1995	−0.4505	0.0021
Japan	1963–1995	−0.6514	0.0000
Korea	1966–1996	−0.5957	0.0000
Sri Lanka	1963–1996	−0.6517	0.0000
Morocco	1969–1980	−1.0105	0.0003
Malaysia	1968–1983	−0.5388	0.0429
New Zealand	1970–1995	−1.5420	0.0000
Panama	1984–1994	−1.2597	0.0634
Philippines	1980–1997	−0.7812	0.0079
Portugal	1970–1995	−0.3322	0.3988
Paraguay	1964–1995	−0.9780	0.0000
Singapore	1988–1997	0.1461	0.0701
El Salvador	1990–1993	0.4580	0.7867
Trinidad and Tobago	1966–1994	−1.0967	0.0000
Turkey	1970–1996	−0.9570	0.0000
United States	1963–1995	−0.5178	0.0000

We observed earlier that six countries were candidates for exogenous growth along the integral curve of the switchpoints, based on Figure 11.3. The three strongest candidates, Costa Rica, Jordan, and Paraguay, all have significant, negative slope estimates. Of the remaining three, only Switzerland shows signs of moving along this path. These might be cases of labor-constrained growth. In this event, they provide examples of the syncretic convergence between the fossil and neoclassical models that occurs when a labor-constrained system achieves equality between the viability parameter and the profit share.

But these isolated cases should not be allowed to obscure the most significant finding here: a pattern consistent with endogenous or capital-constrained growth appears to predominate in these data. Most of the observations describe countries moving along an integral wage-profit curve with a viability threshold parameter well above the profit share.

The actual profiles of the distribution point over time are presented in Figure 11.6. In order to squeeze in all 32 countries and convey a strong visual impression, the figures are stripped of coordinate values; the units are log v and log w (rather than levels). The beginning and ending dates can be found in Table 11.4; most of the trajectories run from southeast to northwest. Finally, the observations have been joined by a line in chronological order, and the individual data points are suppressed (in most cases they can be inferred from the kinks).

There are several nice examples of well-behaved integral wage-profit curves, such as Japan, Korea, or the United States. There are also several examples of cases that grossly violate the assumptions of the model, perhaps the result of technological or distributional shocks. For example, Denmark shows signs of experiencing an outward shift in its wage-profit curve during the later period.

The six candidates for exogenous growth along the integral wage-profit curve do not all present such a clear picture. Costa Rica appears to experience a sharp shift in its trajectory. Jordan, Paraguay, and Switzerland are closer to the prototype; New Zealand looks messy; and El Salvador offers too few observations to make any judgment.

Finally, the countries that are candidates for labor-constrained growth away from the integral wage-profit curve do present a vertical profile. Hong Kong and Singapore are good examples, judging both from the visual impression of the figure and from casual empiricism invoking geography and recent economic history.

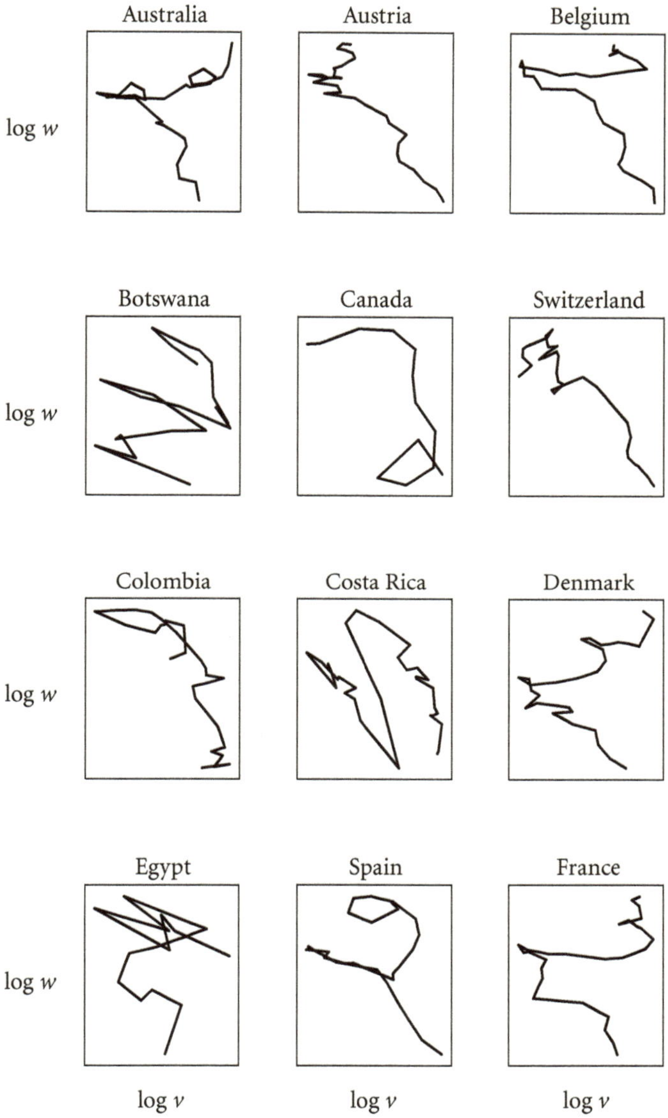

Figure 11.6 Log wage-profit profiles

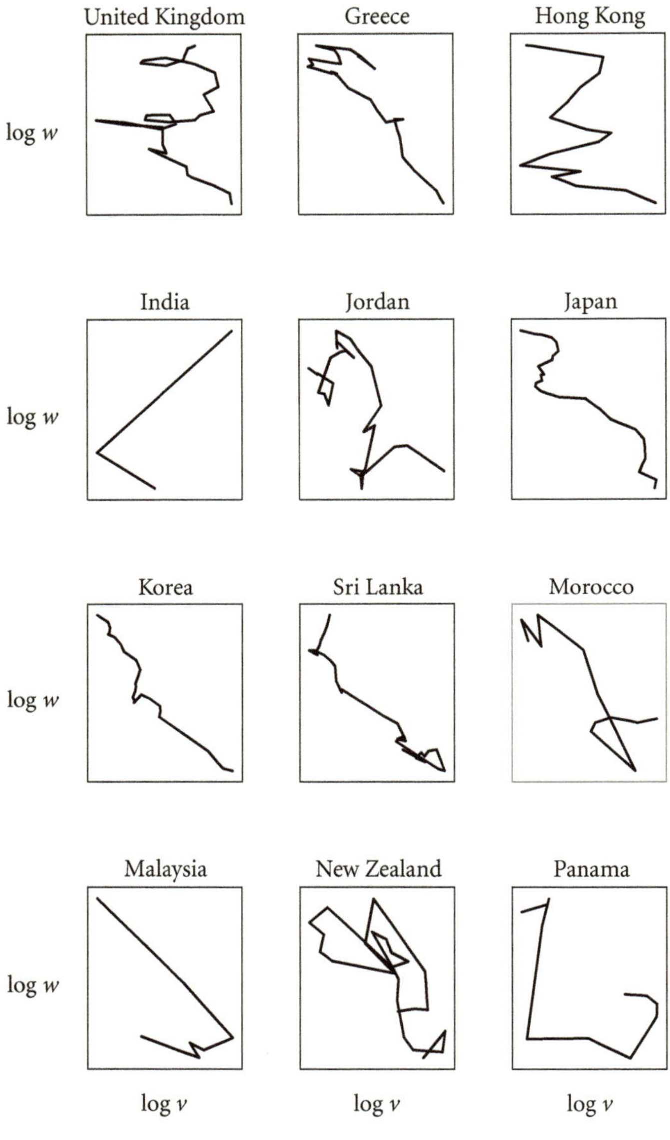

Figure 11.6 *(continued)*

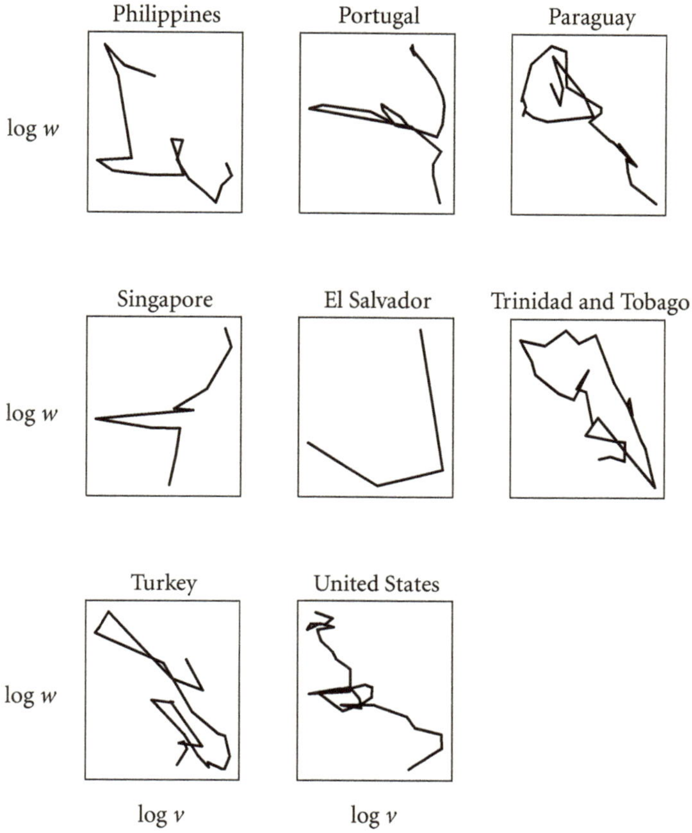

Figure 11.6 *(continued)*

11.3 Conclusion

Chapters 10 and 11 endeavor to substantiate a claim upon which the core of the book rests—that the choice of technique, not being closely regulated by distribution, does not play a central role in mediating the relationships between the structure of accumulation and such critical growth determinants as fiscal policy, saving rates, or population growth. While there are a few cases in which one could make the argument that technical choice has apparently been sensitive to the real wage in the data presented in this chapter, the preponderance of evidence supports the view that technical change offers capitalist firms new methods of production that dominate the old methods at the existing wage. Under these conditions, a theoretical model that abstracts from technical change or technical choice is unlikely to mislead.

Like many other researchers, we have found that the Cobb-Douglas production function fits the data surprisingly well. But we have also provided a creation myth that explains, if that is not too strong a word, why it takes this mathematical form. Significantly, the key parameters do not conform to the predictions of the neoclassical marginal productivity theory of income distribution.[13]

One by-product of this investigation has been to shed some light (but not a search light) on the constraints over economic growth. If labor constraints are binding, a country experiencing Marx-biased technical change should exhibit one of two characteristics: either a rising profit share, or a profit share that achieves equality with the viability threshold parameter. Only in a handful of cases do we find this pattern. Growth seems to be capital-constrained in most cases that we have examined, although this conclusion needs to be tempered because it depends on interpreting the observations through a particular model. This ambiguity in the historical and statistical record endorses the agnosticism expressed through our insistence on working out the classical models of growth under both labor- and capital-constrained conditions.

13. One obvious objection to the estimates in this chapter is that we have ignored the role of education, or "human capital," and that including it would restore the marginalist theory, as Mankiw et al. (1992) were able to do. As Helpman (2004, ch. 4) makes clear, even among mainstream economists, this restoration remains controversial. Marquetti (2007) has estimated the production function in the EPWT using somewhat different methods than are pursued here and has found that incorporating educational skills does not eliminate the discrepancy between the apparent output elasticity of capital and the profit share.

— IV —

Summary

— 12 —

Fiscal Policy Reconsidered

> The concept of the nation as rentier points the way out . . . .
>
> JOAN ROBINSON (1967)

The objective of this book is to explore the implications of several versions of the Kaldor-Pasinetti model of economic growth and, of course, to communicate the results to as wide an audience of economists as possible. Through the Cambridge theorem, the classical growth models elaborated here provide some insight into the main effects of public debt and pension systems on the class structure of capital accumulation. The Cambridge theorem establishes in its most general form that the relationship between the rate of accumulation and the rate of profit is mediated by the saving behavior of capitalist agents, independent of worker or government saving. This theorem highlights the privileged position occupied by capitalist agents at the commanding heights of the structure of accumulation, both in the capital-constrained (endogenous) and labor-constrained (exogenous) growth models surveyed here.

The capitalist agents in these models are meant to personify the characteristic property relationship of capitalist society, the concentration of wealth ownership. Under nineteenth-century conditions, it might have been reasonable to identify the capitalist agent with some prototypical personality, as in Marx's "Mr. Moneybags," but in the modern corporate economy, such a one-to-one mapping rings hollow. The multiple personalities of the modern capitalist agent, reflecting the division of labor among financial, managerial, and supervisory responsibilities, are spread out across sectors of the economy and within the hierarchical structure of complex business enterprises. The behavioral characteristic that translates into an economic model of growth is the compulsion to accumulate. This compulsion is modeled here using the tools of modern neoclassical rational choice theory, both because that facilitates communication with conventionally trained economists and because it imposes some intellectual discipline. Much will be lost in translation, but the traditional belief held by classical economists, as far back as Ricardo, that capitalists tend to save and invest a large portion of their profits is not inconsistent with conventional theory.

12.1 The Burden of Public Debt

The Cambridge theorem reveals that the high rate of accumulation of the capitalist agents puts them in a position to exert controlling influence over the expansion of the whole system, even when workers are contributing to accumulation through their life-cycle saving and the government is obstructing accumulation through fiscal deficits. In the capital-constrained model, the long-run growth rate is fully determined by the capitalist saving equation (the Cambridge equation). Government saving or dissaving can affect the level and the distribution of capital wealth, but not its growth rate. An exception to this rule occurs when capitalist agents are myopic with respect to public debt, so that they violate Ricardian equivalence. In this case, changes in the debt burden are reflected in changes in the growth rate, although a modified form of the Cambridge theorem, in which the after-tax rate of profit replaces the before-tax rate, remains valid. The specific burden on workers arises from the need to levy taxes to service public debt, which must eventually be done to satisfy the government's intertemporal budget constraint. These taxes reduce the lifetime wealth of workers, restrict their ability to save, and diminish their ownership share in the capital stock. Because capitalists regard the part of the public debt financed by taxes on workers as net wealth, debt has crowding-out effects and is not neutral.

In the labor-constrained version of the two-class model, where crowding-out is ruled out by assumption, the debt burden expresses itself exclusively in a lower lifetime wealth for workers and a smaller ownership share of capital.

The implication of these results is that there are long-run costs to workers that need to be taken into consideration in evaluating fiscal policies. But this hardly rules out stabilization policy using stimulative fiscal deficits whose immediate benefits may well exceed these long-run costs. In fact, the back-of-the-envelope calibrations of the effect of increasing the debt–GDP ratio performed here do not suggest that the effects on the distribution of wealth are very dramatic. Yet the existence of these effects deserves more attention from citizens, policy makers, and economists who, it is argued here, have been excessively attached to the productivity narrative that originates in the neoclassical growth model's treatment of crowding-out.

12.2 Pensions and the Nation as Rentier

The two-class setup provides similar insights into the macroeconomic effects of an idealized public pension system. In this case, the system is supported by payroll taxes, so that the accumulation of capitalist wealth is not affected. But using a simple life-cycle model with workers saving toward a fixed retirement date, as is done here, prejudices the results toward the conclusion that unfunded pension benefits tend to reduce social saving. It is well known that more nuanced models do not yield such an unambiguous answer because, for example, workers may be inclined to save more in order to take advantage of the earlier retirement afforded by their pension benefit. Nonetheless, since a consensus view is that the saving effects are negative, and since critics of existing pension systems often rely on this view, it makes some sense to concede the point in constructing an *a fortiori* case for progressive reform of the system. The two-class model suggests that the critics may have exaggerated the importance of any negative saving effect because they have underestimated or ignored the extent to which capitalist saving dominates national saving. The Cambridge theorem teaches us that the public pension system may affect the level and distribution of the capital stock, but not its long-run growth rate. And if growth is strictly constrained by labor resources, an unfunded pension system does not even alter the level of capital, although it will reduce the workers' ownership share.

The two-class model also points the way toward progressive reform of the public pension system by revealing the potentially salubrious effects of prefunding on growth and distribution. Prefunding establishes "the nation as rentier," to use Joan Robinson's felicitous aphorism, used to open this chapter. The benefits of prefunding are particularly dramatic in the capital-constrained setting because the required fiscal surpluses temporarily raise the rate of capital accumulation (which, of course, must eventually return to its long-run value according to the Cambridge theorem), resulting in broad prefunding. At the end of the policy reform, workers will be able to own a larger share of capital because the pension reserve fund subsidizes the pension benefit, reducing payroll taxes and increasing the representative worker's lifetime wealth. Of course, if the policy reform is achieved by surplus payroll taxes, as in most proposals for prefunding, this will merely reflect a wealth transfer between generations of workers. But if the policy reform is achieved by means of progressive taxes on capitalist wealth, it will deliver benefits to workers in all generations. By transferring some wealth from capitalist agents to the control of accountable public authorities, this policy reform will at least potentially democratize the structure of accumulation.

If labor constraints on growth are binding, of course, the temporary burst of growth described here is ruled out by assumption; only narrow prefunding can be achieved. But the long-run benefits for workers remain. The subsidy created by the nation as rentier reduces their payroll tax, increases their lifetime wealth, and allows them to own a larger share of the national capital. The increase in the money's worth of the public pension system ought to strengthen it politically by erecting a defense against a perennial complaint of its critics. (The complaint that unfunded social insurance carries a below-market rate of return, of course, ignores the program's insurance functions, as we have also done for purposes of simplification only, but it does seem to resonate.)

Surprisingly, in the labor-constrained model, there appears to be no particular advantage, from the workers' perspective, to using a tax on capitalist wealth to provide the seed money for prefunding. A payroll tax turns out to have general equilibrium effects on income distribution that make it work just as well. This is a good example of a modeling result that needs to be filtered through common sense. But it does raise the issue of how important in practice labor constraints may be on growth, and at least some of the evidence presented above questions whether they are generally binding.

Our analysis of the nation as rentier in the context of a public pension system should not be interpreted too narrowly. The basic principle extends to a range of programs. For example, the Medicare Trust Fund, which in 2005 held just under $283 billion in assets as compared with over $1,858 billion in the Social Security Trust Fund, might be another candidate for implementing such a program in the United States. The analytical foundations developed here provide compelling support for the general idea of using public reserve funds as a vehicle for redistributing wealth in the interests of social justice and economic democracy.

Moreover, while the nation as rentier may strike some readers as bordering on socialism, it would be premature to judge the existence of substantial public ownership of privately issued financial liabilities (bonds and equities) as incompatible with entrepreneurial capitalism. In fact, the public sector (mainly through state and local retirement funds) already owns a substantial share (almost 11 percent in 2006) of the corporate equities held in the United States. And the financial architecture needed to implement ownership without control by public authorities has been adumbrated in the policy discussions surrounding the disposition of the Clinton surpluses.[1]

One thing prefunding cannot be expected to do is somehow prepare us for the demographic shock associated with lower fertility and improvements in life expectancy. The heterodox (classical-Keynesian) approach to economic growth raises the question of how serious this shock will be. The heterodox tradition envisions a capital accumulation process that cunningly escapes constraints imposed by labor supply through changes in institutions, behavior, or technology. And even if we accept the conventional wisdom that the developed economies are entering an era of unprecedented slow growth and labor shortages, the two-class model gives us some reason to hope that this will actually result in net gains for workers through higher wages that will more than compensate for the increased burden of a public pension system.

12.3 The Production Function

The neoclassical production function provides the theoretical foundation for thinking of prefunding as a way to transfer real resources to the future (or of public debt as a way to transfer them from the future to the present). The classical tradition insists that this abstraction is misleading, and that it is more helpful to think of capital as an ensemble of social, property, and technological relationships rather than as a resource that can be transferred

1. Most proposals for introducing equity ownership into the U.S. Social Security Trust Fund draw on the federal government's experiences with the Thrift Saving Plan (TSP) that it operates for its own employees. The TSP portfolio is invested in index funds that are managed by private financial service firms under contract. Congressional Budget Office (2001, 51–53) provides a summary of the debates over public ownership of financial wealth.

through time. In this book we have assumed, as is fairly standard in classical growth theory, that technical conditions evolve independently from distribution. That decision brings into sharp relief the effects of parameter changes on the structure of accumulation, sometimes, as in our consideration of an optimal pension in a pure life-cycle setting, with substantive implications.

Because neoclassical growth theorists have rejected this fixed coefficient formalism from an early date, we have taken some care to present a reasoned preemptive defense. Rather than recycling old criticisms of the aggregate production function, we fashion an alternative explanation for the empirical success of the Cobb-Douglas production function that leaves room for the postulate of technological independence. Even among the founders of the neoclassical growth model, notably Samuelson and Solow, the production function has never been regarded as a rigorously defensible concept, and their successors, such as Temple (2006), have continued to treat this abstraction as a "parable" or heuristic device. Our purpose in elaborating the fossil production function is simply to demonstrate that an alternative parable can be constructed and empirically implemented, and that it arguably captures what Joan Robinson (1953) called the "common sense" of the production function.

12.4 A Final Admonition

The generally favorable approach toward fiscal surpluses that emerges from the growth models developed here has not been well represented among heterodox economists in the classical and Keynesian tradition. In fact, the policy of prefunding social security is often associated with free market economists of more conservative persuasion, such as Martin Feldstein. This underrepresentation probably reflects the dominance of demand-constrained growth theory among heterodox economists. The purpose of elaborating a model of aggregate demand at the outset of the book is to illustrate (not to prove) the judgment that capitalist economies function along Keynes-Kalecki lines in the short run but that their long-run growth path exhibits both classical and Keynesian features. Again, the Cambridge theorem provides some insight here, for the steady state growth rate obeys the Cambridge equation (the saving function of capitalists) and does not display the famous paradoxes of thrift or cost. However, the levels of capital, output, and employment depend on the cumulative history of demand

and supply shocks owing to path dependencies that are suppressed in conventional trend-stationary macroeconomic models. Monetary policy is one potential source of demand shock. The premise on which the rest of the book depends is that monetary policy is capable of shepherding demand so that a fiscal surplus (or any increase in national saving) need not deliver a permanently deflationary blow. Without some such foundational support, it is hard to defend the extensive use of a long-run growth model that embraces Say's law by treating investment and saving as indistinguishable.

Having begun with some warnings about the limitations of economic models, it is appropriate to end with another qualifying observation. The models in this book are only designed to provide an initial analytical framework for attacking the problem of fiscal policy from a heterodox perspective. The sensitivity of the results to specific assumptions about preferences, tax policy, debt management, labor supply, and technology deserves the scrutiny of future researchers. The heterodox research program offers economists intellectual challenges of undeniable political significance.

References

Armstrong, P., Glyn, A., and Harrison, J. 1991. *Capitalism since 1945*. Cambridge, MA: Basil Blackwell.

Atkinson, A. B. 1971. The distribution of wealth and the individual life-cycle. *Oxford Economic Papers* 23(2): 239–254.

Atkinson, A. B. 1981. *The Economics of Inequality*. New York: Viking Press.

Auerbach, A., Hagemann, R., Kotlikoff, L. J., and Nicoletti, G. 1989. *The Economics of Aging Populations: The Case of Four 0ECD Economies*. Paris: Organization for Economic Cooperation and Development. Working paper no. 62.

Baker, D., and Weisbrot, M. 1999. *Social Security: The Phony Crisis*. Chicago: University of Chicago Press.

Baker, D., DeLong, J. B., and Krugman, P. R. 2005. Asset returns and economic growth. *Brookings Papers on Economic Activity* no. 1, 289–330.

Baldani, J. P., and Michl, T. R. 1987. A balanced budget multiplier for interest payments. *Journal of Post Keynesian Economics* 9(3): 424–439.

Baran, P., and Sweezy, P. M. 1966. *Monopoly Capital: An Essay on the American Economic and Social Order*. New York: Monthly Review Press.

Baranzini, M. 1991. *A Theory of Wealth Distribution and Accumulation*. Oxford: Oxford University Press.

Barro, R. J. 1974. Are government bonds net wealth? *Journal of Political Economy* 81(6): 1095–1117.

Bellman, R. E. 1957. *Dynamic Programming*. Princeton: Princeton University Press.

Berlin, I. 1953. *The Hedgehog and the Fox: An Essay on Tolstoy's View of History*. New York: Simon and Schuster.

Berman, E., Bound, J., and Machin, S. 1998. Implications of skill-biased technological change: International evidence. *Quarterly Journal of Economics* 113(4): 1245–1279.

Bernanke, B. S., and Gürkaynak, R. S. 2001. Is growth exogenous? Taking Mankiw, Romer, and Weil seriously. In B. S. Bernanke and K. Rogoff, eds., *NBER Macroeconomics Annual*, 11–57. Cambridge, MA: MIT Press.

Blackburn, R. 2002. *Banking on Death or Investing in Life: The History and Future of Pensions*. New York: Verso Books.

Bleaney, M. F. 1976. *Underconsumption Theories: A History and Critical Analysis*. London: Lawrence and Wishart.

Blecker, R. A. 2002. Distribution, demand and growth in neo-Kaleckian macromodels. In M. Setterfield, ed., *The Economics of Demand-Led Growth: Challenging the Supply-Side Vision of the Long Run*, 129–152. Cheltenham, MA: Edward Elgar.

Blinder, A. S. 1988. Life cycle saving vs. intergenerational transfers: Comments. In D. Kessler and A. Masson, eds., *Modelling the Accumulation and Distribution of Wealth*, 68–76. Oxford: Clarendon Press.

Bohn, H. H. 1995. The sustainability of budget deficits in a stochastic economy. *Journal of Money, Credit, and Banking* 27(1): 257–271.

Bohn, H. H. 1999. The behavior of U.S. public debt and deficits. *Quarterly Journal of Economics* (113)3: 949–963.

Bohn, H. H. 2004. *The Sustainability of Fiscal Policy in the United States*. University of California, Santa Barbara. Photocopy.

Borjas, G. J. 1994. The economics of immigration. *Journal of Economic Literature* (32)4: 1667–1717.

Borjas, G. J. 2003. The labor demand curve is downward sloping: Reexamining the impact of immigration on the labor market. *Quarterly Journal of Economics* (118)4: 1335–1374.

Brenner, R. 2002. *The Boom and the Bubble: The US in the World Economy*. New York: Verso Books.

Buiter, W. H. 1990. *Principles of Budgetary and Financial Policy*. Cambridge, MA: MIT Press.

Buiter, W. H. 2002. The fiscal theory of the price level: A critique. *Economic Journal* 112(481): 459–480.

Card, D. 2006. *Is the New Immigration Really So Bad?* Working paper no. 11547. Cambridge, MA: National Bureau of Economic Research.

Carroll, C. D. 2000. Why do the rich save so much? In J. Slemrod, ed., *Does Atlas Shrug? The Economic Consequences of Taxing the Rich*, 465–484. Cambridge, MA: Harvard University Press.

Carter, S. 2007. Real Wage Productivity Elasticity across Advanced Economies, 1963–1996. *Journal of Post Keynesian Economics* (29)4: 573–600.

Cesaratto, S. 2005. *Pension Reform and Economic Theory: A Non-Orthodox Analysis*. Northampton, MA: Edward Elgar.

Cesaratto, S., Serrano, F., and Stirati, A. 2003. Technical change, effective demand and employment. *Review of Political Economy* 15(1): 33–52.

Chiang, A. C. 1974. *Fundamental Methods of Mathematical Economics*. 2nd ed. New York: McGraw-Hill Book Co.

Chow, G. C. 1997. *Dynamic Economics: Optimization by the Lagrange Method*. New York: Oxford University Press.

Clarida, R., Gali, J., and Gertler, M. 1999. The science of monetary policy: A New Keynesian perspective. *Journal of Economic Literature* (37)4: 1661–1707.

Cleveland, W. S. 1993. *Visualizing Data*. Summit, NJ: Hobart Press.

Cobb, C. W., and Douglas, P. H. 1928. A theory of production. *American Economic Review* (18)1: 139–165.

Cochrane, J. H. 1999. A frictionless view of U.S. inflation. In S. Fischer, ed,. *NBER Macroeconomics Annual*, vol. 13. Cambridge, MA: MIT Press.

Cohen, A., and Harcourt, G. 2003. Retrospectives: Whatever happened to the Cambridge capital theory controversy? *Journal of Economic Perspectives* (17)1: 199–214.

Congressional Budget Office. 1998. *Social Security and Private Saving: A Review of the Empirical Evidence*. Washington, D.C.: Government Printing Office. CBO Memorandum.

Congressional Budget Office. 2001. *Social Security: A Primer*. Washington, D.C.: Government Printing Office.

Congressional Budget Office. 2006a. *The Budget and Economic Outlook: Fiscal Years 2007 to 2016*. Washington, D.C.: Government Printing Office.

Congressional Budget Office. 2006b. *Historical Effective Federal Tax Rates: 1979–2004*. Washington, D.C.: Government Printing Office. CBO Memorandum.

Council of Economic Advisors. 2006. *Economic Report of the President*. Washington, D.C.: Government Printing Office.

Dalziel, P. 1991. A generalization and simplification of the Cambridge Theorem with budget deficits. *Cambridge Journal of Economics* (15)3: 287–300.

David, M., and Menchik, P. L. 1985. The effect of social security on lifetime wealth accumulation and bequests. *Economica* (52)28: 421–434.

Davies, J. B., and Shorrocks, A. F. 2000. The distribution of wealth. In A. B. Atkinson and F. Bourguignon, eds., *Handbook of Income Distribution*, 1: 605–675. Amsterdam: Elsevier Science.

de la Croix, D., and Michel, P. 2002. *A Theory of Economic Growth: Dynamics and Policy in Overlapping Generations*. Cambridge: Cambridge University Press.

de Sismondi, J. C. L. S. [1819] 1991. *New Principles of Political Economy: Of Wealth In Its Relation to Population*. Richard Hyse, transl. and ed. New Brunswick, NJ: Transactions Publishers.

DeLong, J. B. 2003. A history of bequests in the United States. In A. H. Munnell and A. Sundén, eds., *Death and Dollars: The Role of Gifts and Bequests in America*, 33–52. Washington, D.C.: Brookings Institution Press.

Denicolo, V., and Matteuzzi, M. 1990. Public debt and the Pasinetti paradox. *Cambridge Journal of Economics* (14)3: 339–344.

Diamond, P. A. 1965. National debt in a neoclassical growth model. *American Economic Review* (55)5: 1126–1150.

Diamond, P. A., and Orszag, P. R. 2004. *Saving Social Security: A Balanced Approach.* Washington, D.C.: Brookings Institution Press.

Domar, E. D. 1944. The "burden of the debt" and the national income. *American Economic Review* (34)4: 798–827.

Duménil, G., and Lévy, D. 1995. A stochastic model of technical change: An application to the US economy, 1869–1989. *Metroeconomica* (46)3: 213–245.

Duménil, G., and Lévy, D. 1999. Being Keynesian in the short term and classical in the long term: The traverse to classical long-term equilibrium. *The Manchester School* (67)6: 648–716.

Duménil, G., and Lévy, D. 2004. *Capital Resurgent: Roots of the Neoliberal Revolution*. Cambridge, MA: Harvard University Press.

Duménil, G., Glick, M., and Lévy, D. 1993. The rise of the rate of profit during World War II. *Review of Economics and Statistics* (75)2: 315–320.

Dutt, A. K. 1990. *Growth, Distribution, and Uneven Development*. New York: Cambridge University Press.

Dutt, A. K. 1997. Equilibrium, path dependence and hysteresis in post-Keynesian models. In P. Arestis and M. Sawyer, eds., *Essays in Honour of G. C. Harcourt: Markets, Unemployment and Economic Policy* 2: 238–253. London: Routledge.

Dutt, A. K. 2006. Aggregate demand, aggregate supply and economic growth. *International Review of Applied Economics* (20)3: 319–336.

Dutt, A. K., and Ros, J. 2007. Aggregate demand shocks and economic growth. *Structural Change and Economic Dynamics* (18)1: 75–99.

Dynan, K. E., Skinner, J., and Zeldes, S. P. 2004. Do the rich save more? *Journal of Political Economy* (112)2: 397–444.

Eisner, R. 1986. *How Real Is the Federal Deficit?* New York: Free Press.

Elaydi, S. 2005. *An Introduction to Difference Equations*. New York: Springer.

Eltis, W. 2000. *The Classical Theory of Economic Growth*, 2nd ed. Houndmills, UK: Palgrave.

Epstein, G. A., and Schor, J. B., eds. 1990. *Macropolicy in the Rise and Fall of the Golden Age*. Oxford: Oxford University Press.

Evans, J. 1998. *The History and Practice of Ancient Astronomy*. New York: Oxford University Press.

Feldstein, M. S. 1974. Social security, induced retirement, and aggregate capital accumulation. *Journal of Political Economy*. (82)5: 905–926.

Feldstein, M. S. 1976. On the theory of tax reform. *National Tax Journal* (29)2: 123–130.

Feldstein, M. S. 1996. Social security and saving: New time series evidence, *National Tax Journal* (49)2: 151–164.

Felipe, J. 2001. Why do aggregate production functions work? *International Review of Applied Economics* (14)2: 187–209.

Felipe, J., and McCombie, J. S. 2005. Why Are Some Countries Richer Than Others? A Skeptical View of Mankiw–Romer–Weil's Test of the Neoclassical Growth Model. *Metroeconomica* (56)3: 360–392.

Finley, M. I. 1981. *The Economy and Society in Ancient Greece.* New York: Viking Press.

Fischer, S. 1997. Comment. In R. Pollin, ed., *The Macroeconomics of Saving, Finance, and Investment*, 161–164. Ann Arbor: University of Michigan Press.

Foley, D. K. 2003. Endogenous technical change with externalities in a classical growth model. *Journal of Economic Behavior and Organization* (52)2: 167–189.

Foley, D. K. 2006. *Adam's Fallacy*. Cambridge, MA: Harvard University Press.

Foley, D. K., and Michl, T. R. 1999. *Growth and Distribution.* Cambridge, MA: Harvard University Press.

Friedman, B. M. 1988. *A Day of Reckoning: The Consequences of American Economic Policy under Reagan and After*. New York: Random House.

Galbraith, J. K. 1958. *The Affluent Society*. Boston: Houghton Mifflin.

Galbraith, J. K. 2005. *Breaking Out of the Deficit Trap: The Case against the Fiscal Hawks*. Public Policy Brief no. 81. Annandale-on-Hudson, NY: Jerome Levy Economics Institute.

Gale, W. G., and Orszag, P. R. 2004. Budget deficits, national saving, and interest rates. *Brookings Papers on Economic Activity* (2): 101–187.

Gale, W. G., and Potter, S. 2003. The impact of gifts and bequests on aggregate saving and capital accumulation. In A. H. Munnell and A. Sundén, eds., *Death and Dollars: The Role of Gifts and Bequests in America*, 319–335. Washington, D.C.: Brookings Institution Press.

Gale, W. G., and Scholz, J. K. 1994. Intergenerational transfers and the accumulation of wealth. *Journal of Economic Perspectives* 8(4): 145–160.

Gandolfo, G. 1997. *Economic Dynamics: Study Edition*. Berlin: Springer-Verlag.

Gerschenkron, A. 1962. *Economic Backwardness in Historical Perspective*. Cambridge, MA: Harvard University Press.

Ghilarducci, T. 1992. *Labor's Capital: The Economics and Politics of Private Pensions*. Cambridge, MA: MIT Press.

Gollin, D. 2002. Getting income shares right. *Journal of Political Economy* (110)2: 458–474.

Goodwin, R. M. 1967. A growth cycle. In C. H. Feinstein, ed., *Socialism, Capitalism and Growth*, 54–58, Cambridge: Cambridge University Press.

Gordon, D. M. 1997. Must we save our way out of stagnation? The investment-savings relationship revisited. In R. Pollin, ed., *The Macroeconomics of Saving, Finance, and Investment*, 95–160. Ann Arbor: University of Michigan Press.

Gullason, E. T., Kolluri, B. R., and Panik, M. J. 1993. Social security and household wealth accumulation: Refined microeconometric evidence. *Review of Economics and Statistics* (75)3: 548–551.

Hamilton, J. D., and Flavin, M. A. 1986. On the limitations of government borrowing: A framework for empirical testing. *American Economic Review* (76)4: 808–819.

Harcourt, G. C. 1972. *Some Cambridge Controversies in the Theory of Capital*. Cambridge: Cambridge University Press.

Harris, D. J. 1978. *Capital Accumulation and Income Distribution*. Stanford, CA: Stanford University Press.

Harrod, R. 1939. An essay in dynamic theory. *Economic Journal* 49(103): 14–33.

Helpman, E. 2004. *The Mystery of Economic Growth*. Cambridge, MA: Harvard University Press.

Hesse, M. B. 1966. *Models and Analogies in Science*. Notre Dame, IN: University of Notre Dame Press.

Hurvich, C., Simonoff, J. S., and Tsai, C. L. 1998. Smoothing parameter selection in nonparametric regression using an improved Akaike information criterion. *Journal of the Royal Statistical Society B* 60: 271–293.

International Monetary Fund. 2007. *World Economic Outlook: Spillovers and Cycles in the Global Economy*. Washington, D.C.: International Monetary Fund.

Kaldor, N. 1956. Alternative theories of distribution. *Review of Economic Studies* (23)2: 83–100.

Kaldor, N. 1957. A model of economic growth. *Economic Journal* 68(268): 591–624.

Kaldor, N. 1965. Capital accumulation and economic growth. In F. A. Lutz and D. C. Hague, eds., *The Theory of Capital*, 177–222. London: Macmillan.

Kaldor, N. 1966. *Causes of the Slow Rate of Economic Growth in the UK*. Cambridge: Cambridge University Press.

Kaldor, N. 1996. *Causes of Growth and Stagnation in the World Economy*. Cambridge: Cambridge University Press.

Kalecki, M. 1968. Trend and business cycle reconsidered. *Economic Journal* 78(310): 263–276.

Kalecki, M. 1971. *Selected Essays on the Dynamics of the Capitalist Economy*. Cambridge: Cambridge University Press.

Kenway, P. 1980. Marx, Keynes and the possibility of crisis. *Cambridge Journal of Economics* (4)1: 23–36.

Kessler, D., and Masson, A., eds. 1988. *Modelling the Accumulation and Distribution of Wealth*. Oxford: Clarendon Press.

Keynes, J. M. 1920. *The Economic Consequences of the Peace*. New York: Harcourt, Brace, and Howe.

Kopczuk, W., and Saez, E. 2004. Top wealth shares in the United States 1916–2000: Evidence from estate tax returns. *National Tax Journal* (52)2: 445–487.

Kotlikoff, L. J. 2003. Comment. In A. H. Munnell and A. Sundén, eds., *Death and Dollars: The Role of Gifts and Bequests in America*, 339–344. Washington, D.C.: Brookings Institution Press.

Kotlikoff, L. J., Smetters, K., and Walliser, J. 2001. *Finding a Way Out of America's Demographic Dilemma*. Working paper no. 8258. Cambridge, MA: National Bureau of Economic Research.

Kotlikoff, L. J., and Summers, L. H. 1981. The role of intergenerational transfers in aggregate capital accumulation. *Journal of Political Economy* (89)4: 706–732.

Krueger, A. B., and Pischke, J. S. 1992. The effect of social security on labor supply: A cohort analysis of the notch generation. *Journal of Labor Economics* (10)4: 412–437.

Kurz, H. D. 1990. *Capital, Distribution and Effective Demand: Studies in the "Classical" Approach to Economic Theory*. Cambridge: Polity Press.

Kurz, H. D. 1994. Growth and distribution. *Review of Political Economy* (6)4: 393–420.

Kurz, H. D., and Salvadori, N. 1995. *Theory of Production: A Long-Period Analysis*. Cambridge: Cambridge University Press.

Lavoie, M. 1995. The Kaleckian model of growth and distribution and its neo-Ricardian and neo-Marxian critiques. *Cambridge Journal of Economics* (19)6: 798–818.

Lavoie, M., Rodíguez, G., and Seccareccia, M. 2004. Similitudes and discrepancies in post-Keynesian and Marxist theories of investment: A theoretical and empirical investigation. *International Review of Applied Economics* (18)2: 127–149.

Lazonick, W. 1990. *Competitive Advantage on the Shop Floor*. Cambridge, MA: Harvard University Press.

Leimer, D. R. 1994. *Cohort-Specific Measures of Lifetime New Social Security Transfers*. ORS Working paper no. 59. Washington, D.C.: Social Security Administration Office of Research and Statistics.

Lerner, A. P. 1959a. Consumption-loan interest and money. *Journal of Political Economy* (67)5: 512–518.

Lerner, A. P. 1959b. Consumption-loan interest and money: Reply. *Journal of Political Economy* (67)5: 523–525.

Lewis, W. A. 1954. Economic development with unlimited supplies of labor. *Manchester School of Economics and Social Studies* 22: 139–191.

Ljungqvist, L., and Sargent, T. J. 2000. *Recursive Macroeconomic Theory*. Cambridge, MA: MIT Press.

Lucas, R. E. Jr. 2002. *Lectures on Economic Growth*. Cambridge, MA: Harvard University Press.

Maddison, A. 1995. *Monitoring the World Economy: 1820–1992*. Paris: Organization for Economic Cooperation and Development.

Mankiw, N. G. 1995. The growth of nations. *Brookings Papers on Economic Activity* (1): 275–326.

Mankiw, N. G., Romer, D., and Weil, D. N. 1992. A contribution to the empirics of economic growth. *Quarterly Journal of Economics* (107)2: 407–437.

Marglin, S. A. 1984. *Growth, Distribution, and Prices*. Cambridge, MA: Harvard University Press.

Marglin, S. A. 1997. Comment. In R. Pollin, ed., *The Macroeconomics of Saving, Finance, and Investment*, 231–242. Ann Arbor: University of Michigan Press.

Marquetti, A. A. 2007. A cross-country nonparametric estimation of the returns to factors of production and the elasticity of scale. *Nova Economia* (17)1: 95–126.

Marx, K. 1968. *Theories of Surplus Value*, vol. 2. Moscow: Progress Publishers.

Marx, K. [1867] 1977. *Capital: A Critique of Political Economy*, vol. 1, New York: Vintage Books.

Michl, T. R. 1999. Biased technical change and the aggregate production function. *International Review of Applied Economics* 13(2): 193–206.

Michl, T. R. 2002. The fossil production function in a vintage model. *Australian Economic Papers* (41)1: 53–68.

Michl, T. R. 2006a. Capitalists, workers, and the burden of debt. *Review of Political Economy* (18)4: 449–467.

Michl, T. R. 2006b. Comments on Cesaratto's "Transition to fully funded pension schemes: A non-orthodox criticism." *Cambridge Journal of Economics* (30)6: 981–984.

Michl, T. R. 2007. Capitalists, workers, and social security. *Metroeconomica* (58)2: 244–268.

Michl, T. R. 2008. Tinbergen rules the Taylor rule. *Eastern Economic Journal* 34(3): 293–309.

Michl, T. R., and Foley D. K. 2003. A classical alternative to the neoclassical growth model. In G. Argyrous, M. Forstater, and G. Mongiovi, eds., *Growth, Distribution, and Effective Demand: Essays in Honor of Edward J. Nell*. Armonk, NY: M.E. Sharpe.

Michl, T. R., and Foley, D. K. 2004. Social security in a classical growth model. *Cambridge Journal of Economics* (28)1: 1–20.

Michl, T. R., and Foley, D. K. 2007. Crossing Hubbert's peak: Portfolio effects in a growth model with exhaustible resources. *Structural Change and Economic Dynamics* (18)2: 212–230.

Michl, T. R., and Georges, C. 1996. Debt and taxes in a Marxian growth model. *Review of Radical Political Economics* (28)3: 50–56.

Modigliani, F. 1988. The role of intergenerational transfers and life cycle saving in the accumulation of wealth. *Journal of Economic Perspectives* (2)2: 15–40.

Munnell, A. H. 1974. The impact of social security on personal savings. *National Tax Journal* (27)4: 553–567.

New York Times, correspondents of. 2005. *Class Matters*. New York: Times Books.

Okishio, N. 1961. Technical changes and the rate of profit. *Kobe University Economic Review* 7: 86–99.

Orszag, P. R., and Stiglitz, J. E. 2001. Rethinking pension reform: Ten myths about social security systems. In R. Holzmann and J. E. Stiglitz, eds., *New Ideas about Old Age Security: Toward Sustainable Pension Systems in the Twenty-first Century*, 16–56. Washington, D.C.: World Bank.

Palley, T. I. 1996a. Growth theory in a Keynesian mode: Some Keynesian foundations for new endogenous growth theory. *Journal of Post Keynesian Economics* (19)1: 113–136.

Palley, T. I. 1996b. *Post Keynesian Economics: Debt, Distribution, and the Macro Economy.* New York: St. Martin's Press.

Palley, T. I. 2000. *Stabilizing Finance: The Case for Asset-Based Reserve Requirements*. Report in the Financial Markets and Society Series. Philomont, VA: Financial Markets Center.

Pasinetti, L. L. 1962. Rate of profit and income distribution in relation to the rate of economic growth. *Review of Economic Studies* 29(4): 267–279.

Pasinetti, L. L. 1974. *Growth and Income Distribution: Essays in Economic Theory*. Cambridge: Cambridge University Press.

Pasinetti, L. L. 1989. Ricardian debt/taxation equivalence in the Kaldor theory of profits and income distribution. *Cambridge Journal of Economics* (13)1: 25–36.

Piketty, T., and Saez, E. 2003. Income inequality in the United States, 1913–1998. *Quarterly Journal of Economics* 118(1): 1–39.

Pollin, R. 1993. Public credit allocation through the Federal Reserve: Why it is needed; how it should be done. In G. Dymski, G. Epstein, and R. Pollin. eds., *Transforming the U.S. Financial System*, 95–160. Armonk, NY: M.E. Sharpe.

Pollin, R., ed. 1997. *The Macroeconomics of Saving, Finance, and Investment*. Ann Arbor: University of Michigan.

Robinson, J. 1942. *An Essay on Marxian Economics*. London: St. Martin's Press.

Robinson, J. 1953. The production function and the theory of capital. *Review of Economic Studies* 51: 81–106.

Robinson, J. 1962. *Essays in the Theory of Economic Growth*. New York: St. Martin's Press.

Robinson, J. 1967. *Economics: An Awkward Corner*. New York: Random House.

Roemer, J. E. 1988. *Free To Lose: An Introduction to Marxist Economic Philosophy*. Cambridge, MA: Harvard University Press.

Romer, D. 1996. *Advanced Macroeconomics*. New York: McGraw-Hill.

Romer, P. M. 1987. Crazy explanations for the productivity slowdown. In S. Fischer, ed., *NBER Macroeconomics Annual*. Cambridge, MA: MIT Press.

Romer, P. M. 1994. The origins of endogenous growth. *Journal of Economic Perspectives* (8)1: 3–22.

Ruggles, N., and Ruggles, R. 1992. Household and enterprise saving and capital formation in the United States. *Review of Income and Wealth* (38)2: 119–163.

Samuelson, P. A. 1958. An exact consumption-loan model of interest with or without the social contrivance of money. *Journal of Political Economy* 66(6): 467–482.

Samuelson, P. A. 1959. Consumption-loan interest and money: Reply. *Journal of Political Economy* (67)5: 518–522.

Samuelson, P. A. 1962. Parable and realism in capital theory: The surrogate production function. *Review of Economic Studies* 29: 193–206.

Samuelson, P. A. 1966. A summing up. *Quarterly Journal of Economics* (80)4: 568–583.

Samuelson, P. A. 1967. Social security. *Newsweek* (February 12): 119–163.

Samuelson, P. A. 1975a. Optimum growth rate for population. *International Economic Review* 16(3): 531–538.

Samuelson, P. A. 1975b. Optimum social security in a life-cycle growth model. *International Economic Review* (16)3: 539–544.

Samuelson, P. A., and Modigliani, F. 1966. The Pasinetti paradox in neoclassical and more general models. *Review of Economic Studies* 33: 269–301.

Schieber, S. J., and Shoven, J. B. 1999. *The Real Deal: The History and Future of Social Security*. New Haven, CT: Yale University Press.

Sedgley, N., and Elmslie, B. 2004. The conventional wage share vs. full employment: Implications for the development of growth theory. *Cambridge Journal of Economics* (28)6: 875–888.

Setterfield, M. 2002. Introduction: A dissenter's view of the development of growth theory and the importance of demand-led growth. In M. Setterfield, ed., *The Economics of Demand-Led Growth: Challenging the Supply-Side Vision of the Long Run*, 1–18. Northampton, MA: Edward Elgar.

Shaikh, A. 1974. Laws of production and laws of algebra: The humbug production function. *Review of Economics and Statistics* (56)1: 115–120.

Shaikh, A. 1978. An introduction to the history of crisis theories. In Crisis Reader Editorial Collective, ed., *U.S. Capitalism in Crisis*, 219–240. New York: Union for Radical Political Economics.

Shaikh, A. 1989. Accumulation, finance, and effective demand in Marx, Keynes, and Kalecki. In W. Semmler, ed., *Financial Dynamics and Business Cycles*, 65–86. Armonk, NY: M.E. Sharpe.

Shaikh, A. 1991. Wandering around the warranted path: Dynamic nonlinear solutions to the Harrodian knife-edge. In E. J. Nell and W. Semmler, eds., *Nicholas Kaldor and Mainstream Economics: Confrontation or Convergence?* 320–334. New York: St. Martin's Press.

Shaikh, A. 1992. A dynamic approach to the theory of effective demand. In D. Papadimitriou, ed., *Profits, Deficits, and Instability*, 271–294. London: Macmillan.

Shields, M. 1990. Socialism for the rich. *The Washington Post* (April 16): A15.

Skott, P. 1989. *Conflict and Effective Demand in Economic Growth*. Cambridge: Cambridge University Press.

Smith, A. 1976. *The Theory of Moral Sentiments*. Oxford: Clarendon Press.

Solow, R. M. 1956. A contribution to the theory of economic growth. *Quarterly Journal of Economics* (70)1: 65–94.

Solow, R. M. 1957. Technical change and the aggregate production function. *Review of Economics and Statistics* (39)3: 312–320.

Solow, R. M. 1966. Review of *Capital and Growth*. *American Economic Review* (56)5: 1257–1260.

Solow, R. M. 1994. Perspectives on growth theory. *Journal of Economic Perspectives* (8)1: 23–44.

Solow, R. M. 2000. *Growth Theory: An Exposition*. New York: Oxford University Press.

Solow, R. M. 2005. Reflections on growth theory. In P. Aghion and S. N. Durlauf, eds., *Handbook of Economic Growth*, 1A: 3–10. Amsterdam: Elsevier Science.

Sraffa, P. 1960. *Production of Commodities by Means of Commodities: Prelude to a Critique of Economic Theory*. Cambridge: Cambridge University Press.

Steindl, J. [1976] 1952. *Maturity and Stagnation in American Capitalism.* New York: Monthly Review Press.

Stern, N. 2007. *The Economics of Climate Change: The Stern Review.* Cambridge: Cambridge University Press.

Stewart, I. 1989. *Does God Play Dice?: The Mathematics of Chaos.* Cambridge, MA: Blackwell Publishers.

Stokey, N. L., and Lucas, R. E., Jr. 1989. *Recursive Methods in Economic Dynamics.* Cambridge: MA: Harvard University Press.

Summers, R., and Heston, A. 1991. The Penn World Table (Mark 5): An expanded set of international comparisons. *Quarterly Journal of Economics* (106)2: 327–368.

Swan, T. W. 1956. Economic growth and capital accumulation. *Economic Record* (32)63: 334–361.

Sweezy, P. M. 1942. *The Theory of Capitalist Development: Principles of Marxian Political Economy.* New York: Monthly Review Press.

Taylor, L. 2004. *Reconstructing Macroeconomics: Structuralist Proposals and Critiques of the Mainstream.* Cambridge, MA: Harvard University Press.

Teixeira, J. R., Sugahara, R. N., and Baranzini, M. 2002. On micro-foundations for the Kaldor-Pasinetti growth model with taxation on bequest. *Brazilian Journal of Business Economics* (2)1: 9–24.

Temple, J. 2006. Aggregate production functions and growth economics. *International Review of Applied Economics* (20)3: 301–317.

Thirlwall, A. P. 2002. *The Nature of Economic Growth.* Cheltenham, UK: Edward Elgar.

Veblen, T. 1915. *Imperial Germany and the Industrial Revolution.* New York: Macmillan.

Weitzman, M. L. 2003. *Income, Wealth, and the Maximum Principle.* Cambridge, MA: Harvard University Press.

Wilcox, D. W. 1989. The sustainability of budget deficits: Implications of the present-value borrowing constraint. *Journal of Money, Credit, and Banking* (21)3: 291–306.

Wolff, E. N. 1981. The accumulaton of household wealth over the life cycle: A microdata analysis. *Review of Income and Wealth* (27)2: 75–96.

Wolff, E. N. 2003. The impact of gifts and bequests on the distribution of wealth. In A. H. Munnell and A. Sundén, eds., *Death and Dollars: The Role of Gifts and Bequests in America*, 345–377. Washington, D.C.: Brookings Institution Press.

You, J. I., and Dutt, A. K. 1996. Government debt, income distribution and growth. *Cambridge Journal of Economics* (20)3: 335–351.

Author Index

Subject Index

www.ingramcontent.com/pod-product-compliance
Ingram Content Group UK Ltd.
Pitfield, Milton Keynes, MK11 3LW, UK
UKHW041421290926
475585UK00013B/30/J